Praise for *Building the Bridge As You Walk On It*

"Prepare yourself for a journey into intellectual, emotional, and spiritual integrity—a journey that will span the remaining course of one's life."
—Allen C. Bluedorn, author, *The Human Organization of Time*

"Bob Quinn makes exquisite use of real-life experiences in such a way that his book is engaging as well as profound. It speaks to me directly."
—Ricardo B. Levy, founder and chairman of the board, Catalytica Energy Systems, Inc.

"This book is not about superheroes, but about how each one of us has the power to create positive change—if only we are willing to see and step into our own capabilities."
—Sim B. Sitkin, director, Fuqua-Coach K Center on Leadership and Ethics, Duke University

"For someone who has struggled for twenty-five years with change, personally and professionally—as an internal change agent, external consultant, and academic—*Building the Bridge As You Walk On It* provides a profound integration of the self/other/organizational contexts and a timely reminder that all change is self-change."
—Mike McGrath, vice president of consulting services, Executive Development Associates

"I picked up *Building the Bridge* on a gray, rainy California morning thinking I would peruse a few pages before a nap. I laid the manuscript down only when the last page had been turned many hours later. No nap! Instead a bright awakening to insight and wisdom regarding leadership that Robert Quinn lucidly structures through stories carefully paired with precise conceptualization."
—André L. Delbecq, Thomas J. and Kathleen L. McCarthy University Professor, Leavey School of Business, Santa Clara University

"Quinn details the practices to follow in the journey towards the fundamental state of leadership. Leaders of corporations, governments, nonprofits, community action, families, academic departments—all find resonance with this book!"
—Laurie N. DiPadova-Stocks, founding director, Scripps Howard Center for Civic Engagement, Northern Kentucky University

"This book provides a guide for change that leaders at all levels of the organization can understand and use. More important, it will help them become people who really like themselves. Because they live and act from principle, they will not have to worry about the craziness of organizations and life."
  —Lloyd Baird, director, the Leadership Institute, Boston University

"With more and more people reading this book, the notion of resistance to change may gradually fade. Quinn's attractive concept of positive deviancy is not only an antidote to resistance but a way of thinking and acting that embraces change."
  —W. Warner Burke, Edward Lee Thorndike Professor
    of Psychology and Education, Teachers College,
    Columbia University

"Effective leadership is crucial for successful organizational change, but the person as leader is often ignored in discussions of change. This wonderful book places the person of the leader front and center. It invites, encourages, and inspires its readers to find in themselves the leadership of which they are capable."
  —Jean M. Bartunek, professor of organization studies,
    Boston College

"This book highlighted for me that leadership is an endogenous development, not an exogenous event. The most effective leaders are those whose who remain coachable themselves, and focus on developing themselves."
  —Bert Whitehead, author, *Facing Financial Dysfunction: Why
    Smart People Do Stupid Things With Money*

"If you or your family or your organization are in pain, and you want the pain to stop but it won't, read this moving, action-oriented book."
  —Bill Torbert, author, *Action Inquiry: The Secret of Timely and
    Transforming Leadership*

"Robert Quinn's book is fascinating, I wish its valuable insights had been available to me when I led a major bank. It is so easy to glide along in your comfort zone. I was particularly taken by the quote 'real leadership is about moving forward in faith, and doing so requires both head and heart.'"
  —Jack Hoag, director, First Hawaiian Bank and BancWest Corp.

Robert E. Quinn

Building the Bridge As You Walk On It

A Guide for Leading Change

JOSSEY-BASS
A Wiley Imprint
www.josseybass.com

Published by Jossey-Bass
A Wiley Imprint
989 Market Street, San Francisco, CA 94103-1741   www.josseybass.com

Jossey-Bass books and products are available through most bookstores. To contact Jossey-Bass
directly call our Customer Care Department within the U.S. at 800-956-7739, outside the U.S.
at 317-572-3986, or fax 317-572-4002.

Jossey-Bass also publishes its books in a variety of electronic formats. Some content that
appears in print may not be available in electronic books.

Library of Congress Cataloging-in-Publication Data

Quinn, Robert E., 1948-
  Building the bridge as you walk on it : a guide for leading change /
by Robert E. Quinn.—1st ed.
    p. cm.
Includes bibliographical references and index.
  ISBN 0-7879-7112-X (alk. paper)
  1. Leadership. 2. Executive ability. 3. Organizational change. I. Title.
  HD57.7.W56 2004
  658.4′092—dc22   2003027454

Printed in the United States of America
FIRST EDITION
HB Printing   10 9 8 7 6 5 4 3 2

⟋⟋⟍ Contents

~~~ Preface

A book emerges as an author attempts to meet the challenges of life. This book takes root in many contextual patterns but two are of particular note. The first concerns my experiences at the University of Michigan.

During the past few years at the Michigan Business School, I have been involved in a movement. My colleagues Kim Cameron, Jane Dutton, and Gretchen Spreitzer and I have been facilitating the emergence of a new field that we call positive organizational scholarship. This field brings together scholars who focus their research on that which is unusually positive in organizational life. They seek to understand not ordinary patterns of organizing but patterns of positive deviance, that is, behavior at the far right of the normal curve. It is behavior of extraordinary positive impact.

The Positive Organizational Scholarship group meets regularly to discuss key questions, and we participate in research presentations and in larger conferences. Recently we finished the first book on the topic (Cameron, Dutton, and Quinn, 2003). We have also organized a research center. In all of this activity, we have been focused on the question, What gives rise to extraordinary patterns of positive organizing? The question consumes my interest.

During this time, another contextual pattern was also unfolding. For thirty years, I have maintained one foot in the world of research and one foot in the world of action. During this time, I have been trying to both study and create more positive patterns of organizing, and as I have done so, it has become clear that some notions are more important than others.

One key notion is the fact that entropy—the dissipation of energy, slow death—operates on both the human ego and the organizational culture. Individuals and organizations are continually pulled toward entropy. This happens while individuals and organizations deny that their decisions are taking them individually and collectively toward slow death. Denial takes place because people are terrified of remedy. The remedy is to make deep change. No one ever wants to make deep change because that means letting go of control. This book is about how real people find the courage to make deep change.

This book is the third in a trilogy on the process of helping individuals and organizations to make deep change. The first book was *Deep Change: Discovering the Leader Within* (1996). The second book was *Change the World: How Ordinary People Can Accomplish Extraordinary Results* (2000). When I published *Deep Change,* the book started slowly and then took off. It very gradually became one of the publisher's all-time best-sellers. This meant that *Deep Change* was a word-of-mouth book: people read it and then recommended it to others. Some of the readers wrote to me. They liked the book because it helped them in engaging in the very difficult process of making personal and organizational change. They told me how they used the concepts to navigate a personal crisis or to lead the transformation of their organization. These were usually potent episodes. The publication of *Change the World* in 2000 stimulated still more readers to share their reactions.

In 2002, the publisher asked me to update and revise *Deep Change.* I agreed and began the revision project. Then a surprise occurred: the revision became an entirely new book. The new book emerged because I ended up listening to some very special people. I contacted the people who had written me those original letters, and I asked them to write a full account of what happened when they used *Deep Change* to make deep change. They shared cases ranging from very personal transformations to the transformation of major organizations. Every case was intimate, candid, rich, inspiring, and instructive.

Each person spoke of significant outcomes. One example comes from a man you will meet later. For four years, he worked at the head of his organization and thought of himself as a leader. Then he experienced a crisis that led him to make a deep personal change. Afterward he wrote of the impact on his organization: "I have a critical mass of individuals from both the staff and board who are willing to look at our challenges in a new way and work on solutions together. At our meetings, new energy is present. What previously seemed unimaginable now seems to happen with ease. I sometimes wonder why it seems so easy, why we now have such a positive culture."

He wonders why his organization that was once quite ordinary is now extraordinary. Then he goes on to answer his own question. The answer defies what is written in almost all textbooks on management and leadership. It defies common understanding and practice. It is a promising answer in that it suggests that every one of us has the capacity to transform our organizations into more positive, productive communities like his. Yet it is a painful answer that almost no one wants to hear. That is why it is not in the books on management and leadership. Painful answers have no market. The man states: "I know it all happened because I confronted my own insecurity, selfishness, and lack of courage."

In that seemingly illogical and impossible sentence is the essence of this book. From the many people who read and applied *Deep Change,* we learned many lessons, but this one is most central. We can transform our organizations by transforming ourselves. This is one of the central answers to the question asked among my colleagues: What gives rise to patterns of positive organizing?

A NEW APPROACH TO LEADERSHIP

This book provides an approach to leadership that is derived from the reports of people like the man I referred to. The central argument is that most of us, no matter how high or low our position, spend most of our time in the normal life state. In this state, we tend to be comfort centered, externally driven, self-focused, and internally closed. Yet it is possible for anyone, no matter how high or low their position, to enter the extraordinary state which I call the fundamental state of leadership. In this state, we become results centered, internally directed, other-focused, and externally open.

When we enter the fundamental state of leadership, we become a distortion to the social system in which we reside. We are a new signal to which others must respond. In this sense, we become creators of a new order. We become a stimulant of positive organizing or the emergence of a more productive community. The man who thought he was a leader captures the phenomenon. He entered the fundamental state of leadership, and his organization changed. It was at that point that he became a leader indeed.

His personal transformation gave rise to positive organizing, to a more productive community. He suddenly had a critical mass of people who saw things in a new way. They were more willing to join together and produce innovative initiatives. They were more energized. Seemingly impossible accomplishments began to happen in an effortless way. Leading suddenly became easy. That effortless accomplishment was born of agonizing change. In this book, you will learn how to enter the fundamental state of leadership.

ABOUT THIS BOOK

This book presents a radical, inductive, and applied theory of leadership. *Radical* means returning to the root or foundations of a thing. The foundation of leadership is not thinking, behavior, competencies, techniques, or position. The foundation of leadership is who we are— our identity or foundational state. When people alter their interior world, they also alter their exterior world. As we come to understand this fundamental framework, our understanding of leadership is radically altered.

Inductive means we build the theory not from abstract numbers but from the actual observation of people who are transforming. These are not normal people living in the middle of the normal curve. These are people who are temporarily at the far right end of the curve. These are positive deviants. A theory derived from such observation will not be a normal theory of leadership but a unique theory that does not derive from the identification of normal patterns.

Applied means we are focusing on the how. We are providing an approach that tells people what they can do if they want to radically alter and improve the groups within which they reside.

The book is divided into three parts. Part One introduces the stories of some of the people who read *Deep Change* and then made deep change themselves. The stories are intimate, compelling, and transformational. To read them is to be inspired. Across the stories, we see important patterns. The stories help us to come to an alternative view of leadership. I thank these incredible people for their marvelous contributions.

In Part Two, we journey even further from the realm of normal leadership thinking and move to a more dynamic and complex view of leadership. In doing so, we explore eight unusual concepts that are presented as practices that can help us enter the fundamental state of leadership. To illustrate the eight disciplines, I have drawn cases from *Change the World: How Ordinary People Can Achieve Extraordinary Results* and *Letters to Garrett: Stories of Change Power and Possibility*. In this sense, this book contains the best of three books.

In Part Three, we turn from the emphasis on changing ourselves to how we can best learn to help others change. We approach the question from the point of view of helping others that we associate with entering the fundamental state of leadership. We then approach the question from the point of view of education and training. How do we teach people in a classroom to enter the fundamental state of leadership?

At the end of each chapter are a variety of tools, including sets of questions that can be used for reflection or discussion, designed to help readers make progress. It is my hope that they will help readers to construct a radically more positive world.

ACKNOWLEDGMENTS

Many people have helped along the way with this book. John Bergez has been extraordinary as a developmental editor, and Kathe Sweeney has been a most supportive editor. Pauline Farmer has worked tirelessly on the manuscript. Many colleagues, students, and family members have contributed opinions. Horst Abraham, Susan Ashford, Kim Cameron, Jeff DeGraff, Jane Dutton, Bill Leigh, Ryan Quinn, Shauri Quinn, Shawn Quinn, Gretchen Spreitzer, Anjan Thakor, Karl Weick, and many others have made contributions that have shaped my thinking. I am particularly grateful to those wonderful people who have made deep change and then had the courage to share their own stories. Those stories are gifts to help each of us more frequently enter the fundamental state of leadership.

Ann Arbor, Michigan　　　　　　　　　　　　　　　Robert E. Quinn
February 2004

Dedicated to Kim Cameron, Jane Dutton, and Gretchen Spreitzer. Thank you for spending so much time in the fundamental state of leadership. You have thus made it possible for me to live in the flourishing of a productive community.

PART ONE

An Invitation to the Fundamental State of Leadership

"What lies behind us and what lies before us are tiny matters compared to what lies within us."
—RALPH WALDO EMERSON

In 1996, I published a book entitled *Deep Change: Discovering the Leader Within*. The premise of the book was that anyone can be a leader of change, but to do so requires the transformation of self. Some readers shared their reactions and described how the book helped them in their own journeys into deep change. They usually also described the profound impact those journeys had on their own lives, the lives of the people around them, and the systems and organizations of which they were a part.

In reading their stories, I began to notice some shared characteristics. Analyzing these characteristics led me to develop new model of leadership. I began to think of leadership not as behaviors and techniques but as a state of being. Leadership is first about what we are. I call the new model the fundamental state of leadership.

Seeing leadership in this new fashion also helped me to conceptualize practices that can help people more frequently enter the fundamental state of leadership. These practices, in turn, led to radically new proposals for how we can develop leadership in ourselves and others. These three notions—what the fundamental state of leadership is, the practices that can help us enter that state, and the implications for leadership development—are, respectively, the subjects of the three parts of this book.

As the book unfolds, the fundamental state of leadership will take on increasingly precise meaning. We begin, however, where my own journey began—with the stories of people who have had the courage to embrace deep change. Each of these stories illustrates a facet of the fundamental state of leadership and its impact. Read these stories attentively and receptively. Each of them is about someone who has entered the creative state. Each is a story that illustrates the truth of Emerson's statement: "What lies behind us and what lies before us are tiny matters compared to what lies within us."

Building the Bridge
As You Walk On It

*"I decided to acknowledge my fears and close off my
exits. Suddenly, my workplace became a place filled
with people doing their best to either avoid deeper
dilemmas or face them and grow. The previous
importance of titles and roles began to melt away
before my eyes. . . . My own change of perspective
led me to see a new organization without having
changed anyone but myself."*

—JEREMY FISH

How do we create extraordinarily positive organizations? This is the central question that integrates the research of my colleagues at the Center for Positive Organizational Scholarship.

The organizations we study tend to excel in two areas. They do very well at accomplishing their central, instrumental task, like making quality products, educating people, or providing health care. And they also excel in a second domain. The people who work in them tend to flourish. They are deeply connected to the objective, and they are deeply committed to one another. As a result, the organization can do things that other organizations cannot do.

I usually refer to such organizations as *productive communities.* They are not only highly productive but highly nurturing places. They are places where people live by the highest of human values, extending themselves for the instrumental purpose and for one another.

Recently my colleagues and I visited such an organization. We went with the director of nursing at a large hospital to visit one of her outstanding units. As always happens when we visit these kinds of settings, we were inspired by deeply committed human beings performing well beyond normal expectations.

We asked some questions about their culture of success, and they spent a half-hour describing the innovative practices that had developed in the units. These practices were unique and very impressive. It would have been tempting to believe that they were the explanation. Eventually the director of nursing shook her head. She said, "Don't be fooled by these practices. They are important, but they are a consequence, not the cause."

The other people in the room nodded. They all knew what she was talking about. One of them began to speak of the woman who had run this wonderful unit for over a decade. They spoke of her in reverent tones. We posed probing questions, asking them to describe specific incidents. Some of the respondents spoke in tears as they shared the ways this woman had changed their organization and their lives.

Afterward the director told us that of her sixty managers, she has five or six like the woman we just heard about. No matter where she assigns them, they build units that achieve extraordinary performance.

One of my colleagues asked, "What do they do?" There was a long silence. Finally the director said, "That is the wrong question. It is not what they do, because each one of them is unique in how they pull it off. It is not about what they do; it is about who they are."

> *"It is not what they do, because each one of them is unique in how they pull it off. It is not about what they do; it is about who they are."*

In that last sentence is a key to positive organizing and productive community. Management and leadership books are naturally preoccupied with the search for behaviors, tools, techniques, and practices that can be exported and imitated elsewhere. It may be that they are telling us about the wrong thing. Organizational excellence tends not to be a function of imitation. It tends to be a function of origination. It begins with one person—the one in ten who has the capacity to create productive community. In this hospital, five or six out of sixty supervisors fit this category. If we examine one hundred plant managers or one thousand CEOs, we tend to find the same pattern. The majority are normal. And a few are extraordinary in that they know how to enter a creative personal state that gives rise to a creative collective state. I call that personal state the *fundamental state of leadership.* The collective state is productive community, which emerges as someone in the fundamental state of leadership attracts others into the process I refer to as "building the bridge as you walk on it."

THE ORIGINS OF THIS BOOK

As I noted in the introduction to Part One, this book originated in the messages I received from readers of my book *Deep Change.* The people who wrote to me usually told me how they had used the book's concepts to navigate a personal crisis or lead the transformation of their organization. Later, I contacted them and asked them to write a full account of what had happened. They shared cases ranging from very personal transformations to the transformation of major organizations. As I read those cases, I began to have new insights about the process of deep change. Eventually I began to formulate a new concept: the fundamental state of leadership.

In this book, you will meet some of these people. You will discover what the fundamental state of leadership is and what practices are likely to help you enter it. As preparation and background, let's do a quick review of the notion of deep change.

THE BACKGROUND

An anchor on a ship is a device attached by a rope or cable that is cast overboard. The anchor digs into the bottom and holds the ship in place. The anchor is thus a useful tool that keeps the ship from aimless drifting.

In a dynamic world, the tools that we usually see as assets can turn into liabilities. I remember, for example, watching a movie about a ship caught in a sudden storm. As the storm grew in ferocity, the sailors realized that they had to cut away the anchor. They chopped madly at the rope so they could avoid being swamped. Their only hope was to ride out the storm on the tumultuous sea. They needed to be free from what was normally a useful source of stability. Their lives depended on it.

Over time, it is natural for both individuals and for organizations to develop anchors. Individuals, for example, develop a system of beliefs about how they can best cope in a world of scarce resources. This system becomes a personal identity. We sometimes refer to this anchor as an ego. Organizations also develop systems of belief about identity and coping. We refer to this anchor as the organizational culture. The individual ego and the organizational culture are normally valuable sources of stability.

Yet like ships, individuals and organizations are often confronted by storms. As individuals, we may need to cope with physical illness, the death of a loved one, divorce, abusive treatment, burnout, job loss, or other life demands. In organizations, we may need to cope with recession, new competitors, regulatory changes, evolving customer preferences, and many other such challenges.

These storms are usually preceded by dark clouds and other signals of danger. While the signals often call for a transformation, or what I call deep change, we tend to resist. When our old habits of thought and action seem to be ever less effective in the face of the change, we are slow to abandon them in favor of learning our way into a transformed state. To cut away our anchors and move forward into the storm of real-time learning is no easy decision.

In fact, rather than accepting the need for deep change, most of us practice denial. We rationalize away the signals that call us to courage and growth. We work very hard to preserve our current ego or culture. To give them up is to give up control. Normally we work hard to avoid the surrender of control. Instead, we strive to stay in our zone of comfort and control. Given the choice between deep change or slow death, we tend to choose slow death.

Yet nature tends to have its way with us. The path to slow death still ends at death. For individuals, it can be the death of the ego or the body. For corporations, it can be the death of a particular set of assets or the overall enterprise. As we progress down the path of denial, our agony grows. The growing pain tends to force us to do what we do not want to do. We make deep change.

When we make deep change, we enter the fundamental state of leadership. This central concept will be developed and defined over the next several chapters. Here we meet some people who have learned to make deep change. Their stories provide a first look at what it means to enter the fundamental state of leadership. From these stories, we can also specify the objectives of this book.

OBJECTIVE ONE: HELPING PEOPLE WHO ARE ASSIGNED TO LEAD CHANGE

Jeremy Fish is a physician and an executive who was in charge of a transformation at a regional medical center in California. He found this task most challenging. In fact, he describes his feelings as the "emotions of a patient facing cancer." As he moved forward in the transformational process, he felt a combination of fear, hope, and dread.

Most managers charged with leading a transformation have such feelings. As they move forward, they become increasingly aware of the political dangers. They begin to feel more and more insecure. While trying to convey confidence, they find themselves contemplating escape strategies that will minimize the political damage to their careers. As they do this, they deny that they are doing it. Integrity decays, and insecurity grows. While verbally they continue to call for the commitment of others, they implicitly, but clearly, communicate their hypocrisy. In response, people espouse commitment while actually withholding commitment. Frustration, distrust, and conflict expand. The leader becomes even more insecure and intensifies the effort, which makes everything worse. The vicious cycle then continues to expand, sucking the leader and the project into the vortex of failure, the very thing the leader feared in the first place.

Jeremy reports reading *Deep Change* and how he came to recognize his self-deception. In his words, "My fear of being fired, ridiculed, or marginalized at work was impairing my ability to lead. I also saw how my 'exit strategy' of leaving if things got uncomfortable rather than face my fears and discomfort was impairing my ability to commit fully to leadership."

Jeremy was an executive, yet he was no different than most first-line employees. It is normal for all people in organizations, from the janitor to the CEO, to live in fear. It is normal for people in organizations to say one thing while believing another. This means that hypocrisy is normal. The recognition of his hypocrisy led Jeremy to make a decision that was not normal. Since the decision was exceptional, the results were exceptional as well. He reports:

I decided to acknowledge my fears and close off my exits. Suddenly, my workplace became a place filled with people doing their best to either avoid deeper dilemmas or face them and grow. The previous importance of titles and roles began to melt away before my eyes. Feared organizational figures became less menacing. . . . My own change of perspective led me to see a new organization without having changed anyone but myself. I brought my new perspective to my role.

Although Jeremy made a fundamental commitment, he still did not know exactly how to get where he wanted to go. In a transformation, we never do. Nor did it put him in control of the process of transformation. During a transformation, we cannot be in control. So what good was the commitment? The commitment moved Jeremy to a new state, or way of being: the fundamental state of leadership. In this state, we see ourselves differently, more positively. We therefore see others differently, more positively. What were once constraining problems are suddenly seen as rich opportunities. When we enter the fundamental state of leadership, we tap new sources of power and, as the next case shows, attract others to join us on the transformational journey.

In this illustration, we find the first objective of this book: to help people who are in charge of change efforts to enter the fundamental state of leadership. As we will see, when this happens, a unique set of behaviors, tools, and techniques will naturally arise to facilitate the emergence of a more productive community.

OBJECTIVE TWO: PROVIDING A NEW LANGUAGE FOR PEOPLE WHO ARE ALREADY ENGAGED IN TRANSFORMATION

Mike Alvis is a retired military officer who now works as a consultant. He spent much of his time with General Eric Shinseki, former chief of staff of the army. Shinseki's vision for the transformation of the army was one of the most ambitious undertakings of any chief of staff since General George Marshall. The vision called for a dramatic shift to a lighter and faster army.

The concept was simple, but the amount of change involved was staggering. Although Shinseki had a vision, he did not have a map telling him how to negotiate his way through all the required changes. No visionary ever does. When we commit to a vision to do something that has never been done before, there is no way to know how to get there. We simply have to build the bridge as we walk on it. I sometimes refer to this process as "walking naked into the land of uncertainty" or "learning how to walk through hell effectively."

When we commit to a vision to do something that has never been done before, there is no way to know how to get there. We simply have to build the bridge as we walk on it.

The early years of army transformation were very difficult. Shinseki did what he had to do. He pushed on, taking one step at a time. Shinseki's role became punishing. He experienced many dark nights of the soul. With each big, symbolic move, he came under intense criticism. He was privately criticized by those on the inside and publicly attacked by the media. What was particularly remarkable about Shinseki is that he never displayed any ego needs. Unlike Jeremy, who was initially afraid of what might happen to him, Shinseki was fearless. He was not concerned about looking good. And although his critics questioned the wisdom of his every move, they never questioned his motive. It was clear that he was doing what he thought was best for the army. So he just kept doing what he thought was right, absorbed the pain, and pushed on.

Mike Alvis had an inside view of each move that Shinseki made. Watching the chief of staff had a major impact on Mike. His own level of commitment began to deepen. As this happened, Mike, like Jeremy, began to see his world differently and to relate to people in a new way. He stopped seeing the resisters as "the enemy." He says, "I started to meet people where they were." And as he started to see them differently, he began to work with them differently.

Mike shares another interesting point about the transformation of the army. Outsiders assume the army changes when a commander gives an order. As with all other organizations, when the army culture is threatened, people resist. In fact, it is often the people at very high levels who become the invisible resisters. As result, an organizational transformation never follows a clean, top-down process. It is, instead, a social movement in which commitment spreads.

In this case, commitment spread from the chief of staff to people like Mike and then to larger and larger groups, including some of the people who were initially very resistant. Eventually the army transformation reached the point of "irreversible momentum." The process was still unfolding when Shinseki finished his term of office in 2003. It will continue to unfold for decades into the future.

While most people responsible for a transformation are like Jeremy Fish, a very few are like Eric Shinseki. They set aside their natural concern for their own self-preservation. They choose to put their own welfare second to the good of the vision. As they do so, they become increasingly passionate about the vision. Then they make a terrible discovery.

Since they are taking the organization where no one has been before, no one can know how to get there. No one has the necessary expertise. Furthermore, without the normal assumptions of equilibrium and expertise, the traditional principles of good management no longer work. Since there is no safe path, no way to be in control, they are forced to move forward one blind step at a time. They are forced to build the bridge as they walk on it. They then experience exponential learning about self, others, and the organization.

Yet when people ask such leaders to explain what is happening, they usually struggle. Like the exceptional people in the outstanding nursing units, they point to creative practices that have emerged. The leaders themselves struggle to explain what they have done. Because we lead transformation does not mean we can explain transformation. Normal models are not useful. The necessary language is not readily available. A second objective of this book therefore is to provide a new language, one that turns our attention not to behaviors and techniques but to who we are. It provides a language to talk about and change who we are.

OBJECTIVE THREE: HELPING INDIVIDUALS TO TRANSFORM THEMSELVES AND OTHERS

We often confuse leadership with position. Another of the lessons provided by those who have experienced deep change is that any of us has the power to transform the organizations and systems of which we are a part. Meet Roman Walley.

Roman Walley is a middle manager in a global oil company. He indicates that he has always had an inclination not to make waves. Roman then tells of experiencing some formidable trigger events in his life. They included the death of two loved ones. Afterward, he indicates, "I felt as if I was moving through life as a spectator. I was watching a play that I didn't like, but I had no power to change the script."

At this point, Roman was becoming attentive to signals that something needed to change, but he did not yet know what that something might be. Then he attended a workshop in which he was challenged to examine the principles of deep change and how he was living his life. He found himself wanting. He concluded that his life was too externally driven and that *he* had to change. In particular, he had always been reticent to ask hard questions of those in authority. Now he felt that for the good of the company, he had to begin doing exactly that. He says he determined to put "my integrity and self-respect first." For the first time, he began to confront senior people on important corporate issues.

Instead of getting fired, as we might expect, Roman began to flourish. He says that senior managers began to see him in a new way. They began to invite him to consult on more complex, strategic issues. Roman goes on to describe a group of middle managers who were simply going through the motions on a key assignment. Roman boldly challenged the group, telling them they were acting like victims and that they had the choice to pursue a more creative path. Again there was a surprise: instead of rebelling, the people changed. Roman, a man who had been afraid to make waves, seemed to gain power. This once passive middle-level professional ended up leading deep change up, down, and across the system. He challenged people, and they responded.

Roman was not a senior executive in charge of a transformational process. He was a middle-level professional whose influence stemmed from his own process of self-change.

Our usual ways of thinking and talking about leadership do not account for stories like those of Jeremy Fish, General Shinseki, Mike Alvis, and Roman Walley. Nor do they account for the stories of the other people we will meet in this book—people who leave behind normal ways of being and enter the fundamental state of leadership.

No one remains in the fundamental state of leadership continuously, but it is possible to learn how to enter it more and more frequently. To do so requires a commitment to deep change and a willingness to embrace uncertainty—to build the bridge as we walk on it. Understanding that leadership is a temporary, dynamic state brings us to a radical redefinition of how we think about, enact, and develop leadership.

We come to discover that most of the time, most of us—including CEOs, presidents, and prime ministers—are not in the fundamental state of leadership. By the same token, we discover that any of us can be a leader who attracts others to join us in the process of deep change. We find that there are practices or disciplines that can help us enter the fundamental state of leadership more frequently. Finally, we discover that we must rethink how we develop leadership in ourselves and in others.

The rest of this book develops these themes. In the next chapter, we continue our journey by exploring more deeply what it means to say that leadership is a state.

PREPARATION FOR ENTERING THE FUNDAMENTAL STATE OF LEADERSHIP

Choose a quiet time when you can reflect on the meaning this chapter has for you. Strive to be as honest as you can.

Questions for Reflection

1. What did the director of nursing mean when she indicated that to understand the managers who tend to build productive communities, we must focus not on their behaviors and techniques but on who they are? What are the implications of this statement?

2. What are the positive and negative functions of the ego and the organizational culture? How do we normally deal with the negative functions?

3. Why is it natural for people and organizations to deny the signals for deep change? Think of an example, and indicate what you learned from it.

4. Why are individuals and organizations eventually driven to deep change? Think of an example, and indicate what you learned from it.

5. Do you agree that fear and hypocrisy are normal in organizations? Why might this be true? If it is true, what are the implications for change leaders?

6. In what form of hypocrisy was Jeremy Fish involved? What was the impact of that hypocrisy on the people he was leading?

7. After choosing to "close off his exits," Jeremy reports some surprising consequences. How do you explain these consequences? Have you ever made a decision that altered how you saw the people and things around you? What happened?

8. What meaning do the following phrases have for you: "building the bridge as we walk on it," "walking naked into the land of uncertainty," and "learning how to walk through hell effectively"?

9. Why was it possible for Roman to successfully challenge his superiors? Why does this so seldom happen? Why do you think the middle managers responded to him?

Self-Improvement

1. Drawing on the stories you have read about people who either resist or embrace uncertainty and deep change, write a paragraph describing yourself as you are today.

2. Write a paragraph describing ways in which you would like to change in order to be someone who can lead transformation.

Sharing Insights

If in responding to the questions above, you have an important insight or a meaningful story that you would like to share, visit www.deepchange.com and look for the links to submit stories for possible posting on the Deep Change Web site. You may thus help many people. If you would like to review such insights and stories, go to the same Web site.

CHAPTER TWO

The Fundamental State of Leadership

"I have a critical mass of individuals from both the staff and board who are willing to look at our challenges in a new way and work on solutions together. At our meetings new energy is present. What previously seemed unimaginable now seems to happen with ease. I sometimes wonder why it seems so easy, why we now have such a positive culture."
—ROBERT YAMAMOTO

In Chapter One, you met several people who live through the process of transformation. Here we will meet another.

For four years Robert Yamamoto had served as the executive director of the Los Angeles Junior Chamber of Commerce. He had always felt good about his accomplishments in the job. Then a new board president met with him and told him that he lacked the leadership capacity necessary to move the organization forward. It would be necessary for Robert to be replaced.

As you might imagine, the meeting with the board president was a shock for Robert. Before reading on, stop and think for a moment about how you would have reacted to this jolting news. What would you have felt? What would you have done?

ROBERT'S STORY

The shock Robert experienced was the beginning of a personal odyssey of discovery and deep change. It began with a great deal of soul searching. As Robert moved into the valley of personal exploration, he experienced significant pain. Listen as he tells the story:

> During the next few months, I encountered a period of deep introspection. I began to distrust my environment and staff and to question my own management skills and leadership ability. During this dark time, I was also told that the members of my own executive committee shared this perspective. I felt that the board had lost confidence in my ability, so I resigned my position. As I did, I became very afraid for myself and my family. I began to fantasize about ways to somehow keep my job (do it better, faster). I also started to search for a new job. I engaged recruiters, and I turned to my network of friends. It was all very difficult.
>
> In the meantime, I went to what I thought was my last board meeting. The subject of my resignation came up to the *surprise* of most board members, and interestingly enough, some of the executive committee members. A board member then confronted the president, shared letters of support from stakeholders and my staff, and my role in the organization was reconsidered.

What a happy turn of events! At this point, it would have been natural for Robert to feel vindicated and to lay the blame for an unpleasant experience on others. His introspection might have ended. Instead, his journey was only beginning. He was about to make a deep commitment and take on an entirely new perspective:

> After that board meeting, I did a lot of soul searching. I paid more attention to what I was doing. I began to notice my tendency to gravitate toward routine tasks. I began to see it as a trap. I knew I needed to change.
>
> I was a member of the board of another organization, and a short time later I was at a strategic planning retreat. At the retreat, something happened to me. I stopped thinking like a manager. I began to think more strategically. I began to commit to achieve larger outcomes. I suddenly decided to really lead my organization. It is as if a

new person emerged. The decision was not about me. I needed to do it for the good of the organization.

Shortly after, I had lunch with the board president. I described new plans. I said, "This is what I must do; this is what the organization must do. If the board doesn't like it, I will leave the organization with no regrets." In the language of *Deep Change,* I was suddenly "walking naked through the land of uncertainty."

To my surprise, she was completely supportive. It was as if a large weight was lifted. I began to see things from multiple perspectives and not just from my own lens. Learning (not in the traditional sense, but from a holistic sense) became exponential. I saw things with greater clarity and understanding. While before I needed to have a clear understanding of the goal and steps to get there, now I trusted my ability to arrive at the destination and learn from the unscripted journey.

Most people, including those in the highest administrative positions, tend to think like managers. There is a universal tendency to call high-level administrators "leaders" simply because they are in positions of authority. Most administrators, however, are like Robert was. They live in the normal state. As long as they are in this state, they are managers. They think and act like managers. The management role tends to be a role of reactive problem solving, of preserving the hierarchical status quo and minimizing personal risk. Managers tend to avoid leading others into new, unexplored territory. To do so is to become a leader.

Robert made a fundamental decision, and he was no longer following the management mentality. He was beginning to build the bridge as he walked on it. The results were profound:

I believe there are many degrees of transformational change. Certainly, there are moments in one's life that force decision making, but with newfound courage and trust because these experiences have a way of building on each other, I find myself in a state of constant change. I have begun a journey that has no end.

In my new condition, I was able to see what had been happening previously. Many people surrounding me were on self-interested journeys. The organization had no unifying goal. The operating strategy was to simply respond to the personal agendas of strong personalities. Roles had been defined through practice and tradition. People often blamed others because they themselves felt insecure and lacked leadership. When I changed, all these things also began to change.

Currently I see myself as a change agent. The board has accepted my leadership. I have a critical mass of individuals from both the staff and board who are willing to look at our challenges in a new way and work on solutions together. At our meetings, new energy is present. What previously seemed unimaginable now seems to happen with ease. I sometimes wonder why it seems so easy, why we now have such a positive culture. Yet I know it all happened because I confronted my own insecurity, selfishness, and lack of courage.

Real leadership is about moving forward in faith, and it requires both head and heart. The word *courage* comes from the French word *corage,* which means head and heart. Without courage, we tend to live in our heads and leave behind our hearts. We do not need to be heroes, like the firefighters running into the World Trade Center, to exercise courage. We can do it every day in quiet ways. Each of us has unique gifts; we are as different as snowflakes, but to realize and use these gifts, we have to use our courage and move forward with a commitment to true service.

"Certainly, there are moments in one's life that force decision making, but with newfound courage and trust because these experiences have a way of building on each other, I find myself in a state of constant change. I have begun a journey that has no end."

Here Robert answers the question he asked in the quotation that begins this chapter. He knows why his people now engage in positive organizing, why he has a productive community, a positive culture. Since most of us want to live in such organizations, most of us should be deeply interested in his answer. Yet his answer is actually one that few of us are comfortable hearing: "Yet I know it all happened because I confronted my own insecurity, selfishness, and lack of courage."

This answer is profoundly important. Robert did not come up with the painless quick fix that everyone searches for and that management books regularly promise. He came up with a painful quick fix. Robert chose to change himself. He chose to enter the fundamental state of leadership.

The fundamental state of leadership is the central topic of this book. We can understand it best by contrasting it with our usual way of being, or the normal state. The normal state is what we see others occupying most of the time. It is also the state in which we find ourselves most of the time.

THE NORMAL STATE

According to the second law of thermodynamics, all systems tend toward entropy. Entropy is a measure of disorder or a measure of the energy in a system that is not available for productive work. In essence, all closed systems tend to break down. The principle applies not only to physical systems but also to individuals and organizations.

People and organizations tend to progress and then plateau. At first, the plateau provides time for consolidation and recovery. Later, it becomes a zone of comfort. In our comfort zone, we know how to be in control. We know how to manage. We know how to do the things we need to do. They become routine. And as long as nothing changes, we can be successful.

The problem is that the universe is an ever-changing system. From the external world, we receive signals suggesting the need for change—the need to grow beyond our routines and move to a higher level of personal complexity. We all tend to deny these signals. Usually it is not until we are jolted that we are willing to make a significant alteration in who we are and how we do things.

Until he was jolted by a surprising external message, Robert saw himself as a successful executive. Much later, he would come to realize that he had been living in a zone of comfort. His tendency was to gravitate toward the routine tasks, the tasks he knew how to do. He was not aware of all the critical things that were going on around him. He was certainly not leading his organization.

Notice the description of the organization that he could provide only later. The people around him were on self-interested journeys, the organization had no unifying goal, and the operating strategy was to respond to the personal agendas of strong personalities. Roles were defined by tradition, blame was rampant, and people were insecure and projecting their insecurities on others.

This description is not unique. It reflects the normal organizational condition. In a close examination of a Fortune 500 company or the local school district, this is what we tend to find. Self-interested exchange and the lack of excellence are so common that we expect and accept them. We cannot see that everyone is colluding in avoiding the pursuit of excellence. In fact, we usually prefer not to see this fact because to do so would bring increased personal accountability.

Robert's description of himself is also not unique. He was in the normal state. He did not yet perceive a need to make deep personal change.

The failure to change is a process of closing down, of ceasing to respond to the changing signals from the world around us. As we become increasingly closed, we lose energy and hope. We experience negative emotions such as fear, insecurity, doubt, and denial that lead us to shut out the signals being sent by evolving external realties. We thus become increasingly disconnected and lose still more energy. We become trapped in a vicious cycle. In the meantime, we deny that we are losing vitality. We work to stay in our zone of comfort. But in our comfort zone, we can only imitate that which has been done in the past. We cannot integrate the unique self with the emerging realties of the present.

In organizations, the same dynamics come into play. We all spend most of our time unconsciously colluding in our own diminishment and the diminishment of the organization. We collectively lose hope, turn to self-interest, and experience increasing conflict. The organization becomes more disconnected and loses more energy. At both individual and organizational levels, we tend to choose slow death over deep change.

This slow death is the consequence of remaining in the normal state. To be in the normal state is to be externally driven, internally closed, self-focused, and comfort centered (see Figure 2.1).

It is normal to be comfort centered. Each of us yearns to live in a predictable culture. As we do so, we develop an ego that helps us survive in that culture. When our culture is stable, we tend to live in a reasonable zone of comfort. We know what we need to know. If there are signals for a need for change, we may have to face uncertainty and learn new things. This is perceived as a threat to our ego and tends to give rise to negative emotions. The need for change is a problem to be solved. We react. We seek to maintain the current equilibrium. It is a normal thing to do.

It is also normal to be externally directed. Implicitly we know that we must survive in a system of social exchange. We belong to a group. In that group, we must acquire social and physical resources. It is

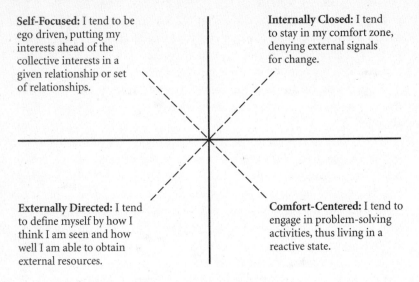

Self-Focused: I tend to be ego driven, putting my interests ahead of the collective interests in a given relationship or set of relationships.

Internally Closed: I tend to stay in my comfort zone, denying external signals for change.

Externally Directed: I tend to define myself by how I think I am seen and how well I am able to obtain external resources.

Comfort-Centered: I tend to engage in problem-solving activities, thus living in a reactive state.

Figure 2.1. The Normal State

therefore important to know how we are being perceived. Since we cannot know for sure, we have to make judgments about what we think people are thinking about us. This process helps to determine our self-image. Normally we are very influenced by what we think certain others are thinking about us. We go to great lengths to respond to what we think they are thinking. As we do, we become more externally driven. It is a normal thing to do.

It is also normal to be focused on our own needs. There is a natural tendency to be self-centered and self-conscious. As this happens, it is difficult to be fully present with other people. As we drift away from authentic contact with the moment, we become less directly connected to what is happening. We also become less directly connected to the people in our network. Although we want the external approval of the people in the network, we do not obtain it. We feel increasingly lonely and, given the need for affiliation, tend to become even more self-focused and more externally driven. It is a normal thing to do.

It is also normal to be internally closed. As we seek to preserve our ego and our culture, as we strive to impress others, as we become increasingly self-conscious, we also tend to feel increasingly less secure. We thus call on our defense mechanisms to shut out any signals calling for change. This further increases our sense of insecurity. When we most need to be externally open is the moment when we most tend to be internally closed. It is the normal thing to do.

The alternative to remaining in the normal state is deep change. The deep change process, however, is always terrifying because it means letting go of control. We avoid this and continue in our efforts to preserve our current organizational equilibrium and our current ego. We espouse a desire to create new results while in fact our primary desire is to stay in our zone of comfort. In Chapter One, we observed three people in the normal state. As an executive who had been assigned the responsibility to lead change, Jeremy claimed that he wanted to achieve a transformational set of outcomes, yet his first concern was self-preservation. Mike, who was working to assist in the transformation of the army, was giving only his body and mind to the task. Roman, who lived in fear of making waves, was being shaped by those fears. He was externally rather than internally directed.

At the outset of his story, Robert also was externally driven, responding to the agendas of strong personalities. He was more self-focused than he cared to admit, not truly committed to the good of the organization. He was comfort centered, unclear about what the organization really was and where it really needed to go. He also tended, like all of us, to be internally closed to any of the first three claims. In short, he was living, as we all live most of the time, in the normal state.

THE FUNDAMENTAL STATE OF LEADERSHIP

To remain in the normal state, refusing to change while the universe changes around us, is ultimately to choose slow death. To enter the fundamental state of leadership is to reverse the process by making deep change. The fundamental state of leadership is a temporary psychological condition. When we are in this state, we become more purpose-centered, internally driven, other-focused, and externally open (see Figure 2.2).

In the fundamental state of leadership, we become less comfort centered and more purpose-centered. We stop asking, What do I want? Since what we want is to be comfortable, this question keeps us in the reactive state. Instead we ask, What result do I want to create? (Fritz, 1989). An honest answer to this question tends to create an image or vision that may attract us outside our comfort zone and into the uncertain

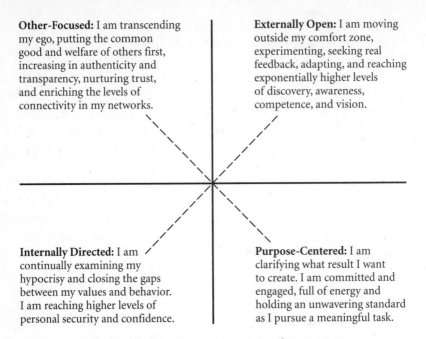

Other-Focused: I am transcending my ego, putting the common good and welfare of others first, increasing in authenticity and transparency, nurturing trust, and enriching the levels of connectivity in my networks.

Externally Open: I am moving outside my comfort zone, experimenting, seeking real feedback, adapting, and reaching exponentially higher levels of discovery, awareness, competence, and vision.

Internally Directed: I am continually examining my hypocrisy and closing the gaps between my values and behavior. I am reaching higher levels of personal security and confidence.

Purpose-Centered: I am clarifying what result I want to create. I am committed and engaged, full of energy and holding an unwavering standard as I pursue a meaningful task.

Figure 2.2. The Fundamental State of Leadership

journey that is the creative state. As we begin to pursue purpose in the face of uncertainty, we gain hope and energy. As we move toward purpose, we experience meaning and become filled with more positive emotions. Yet becoming truly purpose-centered is an extraordinary thing to do.

In the fundamental state of leadership, we also become less externally directed and more internally directed. As we move toward purpose, we feel better about ourselves. We begin to transcend our own hypocrisy, closing the gap between who we think we are and who we think we should be. In this process of victory over self, we feel more integrity, and we feel more whole. Our values and behavior are becoming more congruent. Our internal and external realities are becoming more aligned. Yet becoming more internally directed is an extraordinary thing to do.

In the fundamental state of leadership, we also become less self-focused and more other-focused. As our sense of achievement and integrity increases, we feel more secure, less selfish, more willing to put the common good ahead of the preservation of self. As we feel better about ourselves, we are more capable of being genuinely concerned for others. We often become more transparent and authentic. Our relationships increase in meaning, trust, and caring. Yet becoming other-focused is an extraordinary thing to do.

In the fundamental state of leadership, we become less internally closed and more externally open. When we meet our needs for increased achievement, integrity, and affiliation, we increase in our confidence that we can learn our way forward in an uncertain and changing world. When we have such adaptive confidence, we become genuinely open to all forms of feedback. We are better able to embrace the truth of the dynamic world. When we do this, we learn and adapt. We then further grow in awareness, competence, and vision. Yet becoming externally open is an extraordinary thing to do.

When we are in the fundamental state of leadership, we are very different than when we are in the normal state. We begin to attract new flows of energy. We overcome entropy and slow death. We become more fully alive. Furthermore, we begin to attract others to the fundamental state of leadership. Like Robert, we become extraordinary, and our organization changes. It becomes a system of positive organizing, a more productive community with increased energy, commitment, and capability.

Jeremy, Mike, and Roman all entered the fundamental state of leadership. Jeremy, for example, stopped worrying about his need for an exit strategy. He decided to face his fears and move forward. He says that decision was the most empowering one of his life. He was committed to a result, internally directed, other-focused, and externally open. Mike became increasingly drawn by the moral power of General Shinseki and found himself embracing the transformation at a deeper level. As he became more purpose-centered, he began to see people differently. He began to accept them "where they were." He understood how much support it would take to attract them to an externally open state so they too could facilitate the transformation of the army.

Many of the personal stories in this book illustrate this basic point: what we see around us depends on our own state of being. When we make deep change and enter the fundamental state of leadership, we see a different world. We also behave differently. The world then reacts differently.

Robert describes the process in some depth. The jolt of being told that he was "not good enough" leads him to examine his own behavior more closely. For the first time, he recognizes his tendency to gravitate toward the routine. In the midst of this self-reflection, he has an experience that allows him to see an organization from a more strategic view, and he suddenly stops thinking like a manager. He commits himself to making a difference, to leading his organization. As soon as he does, "a new person" seems to emerge. Significantly, he notes that his motive has changed. He is suddenly working for the "good of the organization." He is no longer reactive.

If, prior to this moment, we had given Robert feedback that he was not working for the good of the organization, he would have been deeply offended and would have provided many claims to the contrary. I know this because I have watched it in case after case. We are all like Robert in that we let the good of the system slip away, and we are incredibly good at self-deception. In short, we are hypocrites. The normal state is a state of hypocrisy. In it, we deny the emergence of the slow death phenomenon while we ourselves move toward slow death.

Here is a surprising point: recognizing our hypocrisy is a source of power. When we become willing to monitor our hypocrisy, we discover that intense personal shame drives us to close our integrity gaps. Accepting the truth about our hypocrisy helps us to transform ourselves and others.

Others are transformed because our courage and integrity replace our cowardice and hypocrisy. Our new self becomes a catalyst of collective change. Consider what happens when Robert tells the board president that he is going to execute his new plans or leave with "no regrets." Interestingly, the woman who wanted to fire him now expresses support. We will see similar effects throughout the stories of personal transformation in this book. When we make deep change, the people around us respond to us differently. When we change ourselves, we change how people see us and how they respond to us. When we change ourselves, we change the world. This is the legacy of people who operate in the fundamental state of leadership.

> *When we change ourselves, we change how people*
> *see us and how they respond to us. When we change*
> *ourselves, we change the world. This is the legacy of*
> *people who operate in the fundamental state of*
> *leadership.*

With his new commitment and vision, Robert is no longer in a reactive and self-deceptive state. He is more internally directed, living in greater alignment with his higher values. He is more purpose-centered, no longer responding to the agendas of strong personalities but taking his organization where it needs to go so it can create the outcomes it needed to create. In the process, he is more other-focused. He is no longer working to stay in his comfort zone and preserve his ego; instead, he is working for the "good of the organization." Finally, he is more externally open. He is now on an unscripted journey, and he is learning and developing at an exponential rate. As you will see, all these consequences are typical of people who enter the fundamental state of leadership.

BECOMING ALIGNED WITH THE DYNAMIC UNIVERSE

When we clarify what result we want to create and commit to move forward without knowledge or control, as did Robert and the others, we enter a state of elevated attention and exponential learning. One reason this happens is that we now stop espousing the need for accurate feedback while really wanting to avoid it, and we begin to insist on it. In the fundamental state of leadership, we care more deeply about what we are trying to accomplish than we do about the preservation of our ego. We are desperate for any information that will allow us to move forward more effectively. We seek feedback on our successes and our failures. As result, like Jeremy Fish, we come to dramatic new insights about ourselves and about the organization. When we release our fears and embrace the common good, "titles and roles begin to melt away." Like Jeremy, we come to "see a new organization without having changed anyone but myself."

Robert describes entering a period of exponential learning. Before his personal change, he could not see the problematic organizational or personal dynamics as clearly as he could see them later. After his change, many hidden things became clear about his organization and about himself. He began to see things with greater clarity and understanding. He had increased integrity and increased complexity. He was therefore more like the dynamic and complex universe in which he lives. Robert states, "While before I would need to have a clear understanding of the goal and steps to get there, I trusted my ability to arrive at the destination and learn from the unscripted journey."

When we embark on the unscripted journey, we become, in Gandhi's phrase, the change we want to see in the world. We are a creative and adaptive system that is in dynamic connection with a constantly changing universe. We attract energy and expand in awareness, learning at an exponential rate. At such times, we know what result we want to create, and we are moving toward it, even if we do not know how to get there. In this state of increased integrity, courage, and energy, we are leading in the most powerful way possible. We have a purpose or message, and we are living symbols of the purpose. Moreover, we attract others to enter the fundamental state of leadership, to join us in building the bridge as we walk on it. A new social movement emerges. In the chapters to come, we will see numerous examples of these dynamics at work.

PREPARATION FOR ENTERING THE FUNDAMENTAL STATE OF LEADERSHIP

Choose a quiet time when you can reflect on the meaning this chapter has for you. Strive to be as honest as you can.

Questions for Reflection

1. Robert had been the head of his organization for four years and had done a very credible job. Why does he say that he finally decided to "really lead" his organization? What does this mean? Do you know authority figures in organizations who do not really lead? Who are they? How do you feel about them? What are the implications for your current efforts as a leader?

2. Robert also indicates that the decision caused him to engage in "exponential learning." Why do you suppose this is so? When does a person experience exponential learning?

3. "Self-interested exchange and the lack of excellence are so common that we cannot see them. In fact we usually prefer not to because to do so brings accountability." What does this statement mean to you?

4. Think of an example from your own experience that illustrates this statement: "We all spend most of our time un-

consciously colluding in our own diminishment and the diminishment of the organization."

5. What is your response to the idea that "the normal state is a state of hypocrisy"? Can you identify a specific way in which you live in the state of hypocrisy, espousing a need for change while trying to remain in your comfort zone?

6. Have you experienced the power of recognizing your own hypocrisy and closing one of your integrity gaps? What happened?

7. Consider each of the four characteristics of the fundamental state of leadership. How would your life be different today if you increased in each of these characteristics?

Self-Improvement

1. Drawing on the descriptions of the normal state and the fundamental state of leadership, write a paragraph describing yourself as you are today.

2. Write a paragraph describing ways in which you would like to change.

Sharing Insights

If in responding to the questions above, you have an important insight or a meaningful story that you would like to share, visit www.deepchange.com and look for the links to submit stories for possible posting on the Deep Change Web site. You may thus help many people. If you would like to review such insights and stories, go to the same Web site.

CHAPTER THREE

Entering the Fundamental State of Leadership

"In a moment of profound awareness, I had taken personal responsibility for my own sense of well-being, and I had changed in that instant on a deep, fundamental level. The shift in me completely changed the way I regarded myself and profoundly changed the way he [my husband] interacted with me forever."

—GAIL PARKER

We have read of Jeremy Fish, Mike Alvis, Roman Walley, and Robert Yamamoto. Although they did not have the language to express themselves in the specific terms of this book, each one chose to move from the normal state to the fundamental state of leadership. Each one reports that this deep change altered how he saw the world and how he then behaved. And we have glimpsed how their personal transformation began to transform others.

Another common theme in these stories is a moment of courageous commitment to a new way of being. This act of commitment is key to entering the fundamental state of leadership. Listen as Gail Parker describes an extraordinary moment of transformation.

GAIL'S STORY

Gail is a practicing psychologist who sometimes works with me on one of my courses in executive education. In that course, we have regular breakouts run by professional facilitators. Gail is one of those facilitators.

The course is designed to be an experience in authentic communication. The first two hours are spent preparing people to tell three stories that communicate the essence of who they are. Participants in the first session of a course see this as a most challenging assignment. When the participants go to the first breakout session, the facilitators are asked to begin the process by modeling the necessary authenticity, telling three stories that are particularly honest. Gail tells what happened to her:

> On the first day of class, we were asked to break up into small groups and tell our own stories of an important event in our lives that had shaped us in some particular way. My job as group facilitator was to share my story first to demonstrate the process. I had purposefully not planned a story in advance and shared one (which I do not remember now) that was personal in nature, but I was aware as I told the story that it was a safe one for me to tell.
>
> We were instructed to do three rounds of storytelling and to just observe what occurred in each round. Not surprisingly, with each round of storytelling, we became more intimate in our revelations. With that intimacy came feelings of vulnerability. Our defenses were coming down.
>
> When the class reconvened for the afternoon session, to illustrate a point, Quinn shared a story about a professionally successful woman who, in spite of having been in an abusive marriage, left the relationship and learned from that situation to be very discerning in her choice of whom to date, eventually remarrying and enjoying a successful relationship. From this story, the class discussion shifted to how personal transformation might affect an abusive partner. The question was asked, "If you transform yourself, can you change an abusive relationship either personally or organizationally into a loving and respectful one?" In keeping with my commitment to be open and authentic, without planning to, I spontaneously intervened, telling the following story.

My first husband was a verbally, emotionally, and physically abusive man, and I was the object of his abuse. I experienced his abuse as coming out of nowhere. I had grown to fear him and was as careful as I knew how to be not to trigger his rages—walking on eggshells all of the time. We were a young married couple and shared a car. Both of us worked. It was my habit to pick him up from work in the evening. On one occasion, I made a decision to remain at work to complete an interview I was conducting. I had no way of reaching him to let him know I would be about fifteen minutes late. When I arrived to pick him up, he was not there. My heart sank, knowing that instead of waiting for me, he had taken the bus home in a driving rainstorm.

I knew he would be furious. When I arrived home, he was waiting for me inside the foyer of our apartment with a leather belt in his hand. When I walked through the door, he began screaming obscenities at me and beating me with the belt. As usual, I was totally unprepared for the assault and unable or unwilling to defend myself. As usual, I felt victimized.

Aside from the extremity of the attack, there was something different this time. I am not really certain how long the attack continued, but at some point during it, something inside me literally clicked. Time slowed down, almost coming to a stop, and I remember hearing a voice inside me say as clearly as if there had been someone in the room talking to me, "You know he's crazy, but you must be crazy too for putting up with this." In that moment of realization, I was transformed from the victim of an abusive husband to a woman who had choices, and I knew, even though I was not yet ready emotionally or financially, that I would leave the relationship.

I never said a word to him or lifted a finger to defend myself, but the most amazing thing happened. Immediately following, or maybe simultaneously to my thought and my decision to leave, he stopped hitting me and screaming at me, dropped the belt, and walked away. We never spoke of the incident, and he never raised his voice to me or lifted a finger to harm me in any way after that. It was as if he somehow sensed that he would never be able to treat me that way again.

In a moment of profound awareness, I had taken personal responsibility for my own sense of well-being, and I had changed in that instant on a deep, fundamental level. The shift in me completely changed the way I regarded myself and profoundly changed the way he interacted with me forever. Within months I had enrolled in graduate school, moved out of our apartment, and filed for divorce. I had changed the world by changing myself.

THE IMPACT OF ENTERING
THE FUNDAMENTAL STATE
OF LEADERSHIP

Gail's story of her moment of decision was breathtaking. At first glance, the story may seem to have little to do with leadership or organizations. Yet in working with executives from the lowest to the highest levels, I find that they often resist facing the deep change that clearly needs to be made. In resisting, they take on a victim mentality. They have ready and well-polished explanations as to why their situation is overwhelming and why they cannot make the necessary change. They communicate that they feel trapped. There is nothing they can do. Whether they do all this in a posture of helplessness or in a very macho posture, they remain in the role of victim. They are in a trap. They can only lose.

At the time of the incident she describes, Gail also appeared to be trapped. She was in an extreme situation over which she seemed to have no control, no power. She could only submit herself. Then there was a profound moment, and Gail made a decision. Although she was not an executive, although she had no position or followers, she entered the fundamental state of leadership. She chose a result to pursue, and she became more internally directed. She took responsibility for herself. In that moment, she changed at a fundamental level. The decision altered how she regarded herself.

Her commitment to change also changed how others related to her. Note the amazing impact. At the moment she decided to change, the man stopped screaming, dropped the belt, and walked away. Gail never said a word. Yet he stopped—and he never again abused her in any fashion. How do we explain this extraordinary effect?

I like to think that inside each of us are two unconscious systems: one broadcasts implicit messages and one receives implicit messages. At all times, we communicate who we are. When we enter the fundamental state of leadership, the message is changed. Without words, we communicate that we have become more purpose-centered, internally directed, externally open, and other-focused. Like Mike Alvis responding to Eric Shinseki, others respond to the change in us.

Here I think of Thoreau's words in *Civil Disobedience:* "Action from principle, the perception and the performance of right, changes things and relations; it is essentially revolutionary, and does not consist wholly with any thing that was. It not only divides states and churches, it divides families; aye, it divides the individual, separating the diabolical in him from the divine" (1993, p. 7).

I love the words "does not consist wholly with any thing that was." Why is it that "action from principle, the perception and performance of right," represents radical change? Choosing to live from principle—to create the future—separates, divides, and changes relationships. When we claim our integrity, when we exercise the courage to enter the fundamental state of leadership, we leave all existing patterns of social exchange. We leave the middle of the curve. We become truly unique. We become creative actors who bring about something radically new.

> *Choosing to live from principle—to create the*
> *future—separates, divides, and changes relationships.*
> *When we claim our integrity, when we exercise the*
> *courage to enter the fundamental state of leadership,*
> *we leave all existing patterns of social exchange. We*
> *leave the middle of the curve. We become truly*
> *unique.*

Gail moved to this fundamental place. At the moment she made the decision to leave, she destroyed the dysfunctional bond with her husband. She refused any longer to accept the old culture or the old ego. Both were killing her. Instead, she chose to reinvent the normal self, the self that she believed was of no value and was worthy of abuse. She was choosing to claim her unique self, the self of highest potential. She was choosing to engage in the "performance of right." This is always a revolutionary act. Why? "It does not consist wholly with any thing that was." Such a decision is a decision to split with the past, to give up the reactive stance and move into the creative stance. When we, in the words of Gandhi, become the change we want to see in the world. In choosing to move toward a new and a better self, we become more virtuous. We see more virtue. We attract people toward greater virtue. We become a catalyst of change. When we choose to be who we really are, we move to the edge of the future, which is the most powerful and creative form of the present.

Thoreau believed that action from principle gives rise to new organization. Why? In choosing to enact our best self, we change for the better, and people must react to us. In creating a better and more complex self, we destroy some of the existing social arrangements. Csikszentmihalyi (1997) links this kind of action to the definition of virtue. He recognizes that all systems are pulled toward entropy or lower levels of organization. Good, he argues, is a form of action that works against entropy. It is a kind of action that preserves order but prevents rigidity. It is creative, future-oriented action that takes into account the needs of the most evolved systems, or those larger systems of which we are a part. It takes into account the common good and the well-being of others. It is action from principle, and it leads to the evolution of human consciousness. Such action tends to give rise to new levels of organization. To engage in such action is very difficult work, and the ability to do so, he argues, is the essence of virtue. With this thought in mind, note what happened next to Gail.

THE REST OF THE STORY

Recently Gail stopped me in a cafeteria to tell me the rest of the story. It turns out that her moment of sharing the incident with her husband sparked another transformation. She begins by referring to the original decision to leave the abusive marriage:

> This incident happened thirty years ago, and prior to my participation as a cofacilitator in the course "Change the World," I had never shared that story with anyone—not my parents, my current husband, or any of my closest friends. I had buried the memory of that incident, and along with it the feelings of humiliation and shame I felt.
>
> As I finished sharing the story, before I could feel regret or embarrassment about what I had shared with students and my colleagues in a very public forum, Quinn said the most amazing thing. He said, "That is an incredibly powerful story. Thank you for sharing it."
>
> An incredibly powerful story? Not the story of a pathetic victim of abuse who had put up with it for two years? Not a shameful story that should have remained a lifelong secret? I had "walked naked into the land of uncertainty," sharing a story that I had always regarded as a sign of weakness in me. In the telling, I watched the story transform

into a story of courage and strength. In telling the story, which was itself an act of courage, my perspective shifted, and I saw for the first time my courage and strength in that situation.

It has been almost one year since I participated in that class, and I would say the fundamental change in me is my willingness to lovingly and wholeheartedly embrace those parts of me that I have regarded as flawed, which somehow miraculously and paradoxically, through sharing and being affirmed for sharing, transforms those flaws and weaknesses into strengths.

This shift in perspective has changed how I see and relate to the world. Clearly my clients have benefited from this shift, as I am much better able to help them embrace their weaknesses and flaws, which paradoxically transforms them into strengths. My family and friends also benefit as I am much less guarded and defensive, more willing to be open and vulnerable, and have a greater sense of self-esteem, all of which allows for greater intimacy and closeness.

So the upshot of what occurred for me is a pathway opened to transforming what I had internalized as a shameful experience to be kept secret into a story of courage and strength that I can now use to instruct others and to be a more compassionate, open, and loving person. It also released me from a long-held but deeply buried belief that I am not "good enough," which has opened many internal doors that were formerly locked away, freeing me to be more fully myself and therefore much more effective in all that I do.

THE BONDING POWER
OF THE UNIQUE SELF

In the second part of Gail's story, we learn more about how entering the fundamental state of leadership alters our view of ourselves and our relations with others. Gail felt humiliation and shame about her abusive relationship, and for thirty years, she had held the story inside. This is normal behavior. A few minutes before she shared her story, she had failed in her attempt to expose herself by telling truly authentic stories. A few moments later, seeking to help others understand a critical point about self-change, she exercised the courage to tell her most terrible story, the one about which she was most ashamed. Her telling led to a redefinition of the entire event. For the first time, she saw the greatness in her supposedly dark past.

There is an important lesson in what happened to Gail when she shared her experience with others. The exercise of telling honest stories about oneself with which I begin my course is based on a simple principle: that which you or I think is unique about ourselves we hide. In ordinary discourse, in the normal state, we share our common self, our superficial self.

Yet what is unique about us is what has the greatest potential for bonding us. When we share our uniqueness, we discover the commonality in greatness that defines everyone. That simple exercise usually transforms the participants and opens the way for personal and group transformation.

> *Yet what is unique about us is what has the greatest potential for bonding us. When we share our uniqueness, we discover the commonality in greatness that defines everyone.*

In exercising the courage to tell her story, Gail discovered that the willingness to recognize and share her unique self was a transformational act that helped her to let go of the secret fear that she was not "good enough." As a result, she could live more fully and was better able to help others redefine their negative images of themselves. Since she became more internally directed and more other focused, she has been able to be more purpose-centered and more externally open. She has entered the fundamental state of leadership, and she now radiates a new self. Others feel it and are likely to respond.

Once Gail opened up her locked doors, they became easier to open again and again. This is also a common experience. If we spend enough time in the fundamental state of leadership, if we are centered on purpose and other-focused, we become much less reticent to tell the stories that others would be terrified to reveal. And when we tell our stories, we attract others to the fundamental state of leadership. As we get in touch with and share our best self, as we become more virtuous, we create a more virtuous world. This notion was understood by both Thoreau and Csikszentmihalyi. It was also understood by William Blake.

BECOMING WHAT YOU BEHOLD AND BEHOLDING WHAT YOU BECOME

The great visionary poet and artist William Blake, whose career spanned the mid-eighteenth to early nineteenth century, was deeply concerned with the idea of transformation. Blake was a revolutionary in the sense that he believed society needed not just reform but profound change. What distinguishes Blake from many other social critics of his time—recall that this was the period of the American and French revolutions—is the depth of his psychological insight. He did not believe that political action alone would bring about radical change. Revolutions have a way of reestablishing the tyranny they were intended to overthrow (an interesting double meaning of the word *revolution,* which also means a turning of the wheel). Instead, the revolution had to come first of all in people's thinking and being. Truly meaningful change would happen only when people awoke to the infinite potential that was inside them.

In Blake's mythical language, the world we usually inhabit—what I have described as the world of the normal state—is "fallen." Blake's fallen world is our normal state. It is the world of self-concern, routine, conformity, and hypocrisy. We know it is fallen because of the gap between this world of limited possibilities and the one we desire. Our longing for a more virtuous world is a sign that a better world is possible.

Most of us, however, see the fallen world as a given, as something to accept and conform to, much as Gail once tacitly accepted her husband's abuse. When we are in that state of passive acceptance, when we stay in our normal world or zone of comfort, our view of ourselves diminishes. According to Blake, that is because our relationship to the world around us is reciprocal: the reality we perceive and the view we have of ourselves go together and feed back on each other.

Blake had an interesting phrase to describe this relationship: "They became what they beheld" (Blake, 1965, p. 175). When we accept the world as it is (that is, when we are in the normal state), we deny our innate ability to see something better, and hence our ability to *be* something better. We become what we behold. Whereas other revolutionary thinkers might rail against tyrants or unjust systems of laws, Blake penetrated more deeply. The chains that bind us are "mind-forg'd manacles." When we accept the social order as "reality," as something that cannot change, then we are complicit in our own enslavement. By the same token, the better world we seek is within us, if only we change our vision:

> In your own Bosom you bear your Heaven
> And Earth & all you behold; tho' it appears Without,
>   it is Within [Blake, 1965, p. 223].

We see an example of this in Gail's story. As long as Gail saw her first husband as an abuser whom she could not resist, she saw herself as a helpless victim. This self-perception was the analogue to what she perceived as the real world. But when Gail made the decisive commitment to transform herself from a victim into an active, powerful agent, the world changed with her. It turned out that her husband's abuse was not a fact that could never change. The "fact" disappeared along with her old view of herself. In a sense, what she beheld came to be. If there was no victim, then there was no abuser with the power to hurt her.

When Blake tried to describe this kind of profound shift in our way of being, he had to resort to apocalyptic imagery. That is because a fundamental shift in ourselves brings about a reciprocal change in the world around us. The old "reality" is consumed, and a new one takes its place, one of limitless possibilities that reflect our new state. Error, Blake said, "is Burnt up the Moment Men cease to behold it" (Blake, 1965, p. 555).

These are not just metaphorical truths. When Gail's husband ceased abusing her as a result of her decisive commitment to change her state, that was a real change in the world. As you proceed through this book, you will see numerous other examples of how the world around us alters when we have the courage to enter the fundamental state of leadership.

PREPARATION FOR ENTERING THE FUNDAMENTAL STATE OF LEADERSHIP

Choose a quiet time when you can reflect on the meaning this chapter has for you. Strive to be as honest as you can.

Questions for Reflection

1. The first half of Gail's story is the story of an abused woman who makes a decision to leave her husband. What links does this story have in your mind to the leadership of organizations?

2. How do you explain why Gail's husband stopped beating her and never again approached her in a negative way?

3. Even small acts can be revolutionary in making a radical break with the past. Can you think of an example from your own experience that illustrates how "action from principle, the perception and performance of right, does not consist wholly with anything that was"?

4. In the second half of her story, Gail suggests that she had been long held prisoner by the belief that she was not "good enough." Have you ever been held prisoner by this same belief? Have you let go of that belief? If so, what happened? If not, does Gail's story encourage you to try something different?

5. What is most uniquely good about you? How often do you share that uniqueness with others? What fears keep you from doing it more often? How might sharing what is uniquely good about you help someone else?

6. What meaning does the saying, "They became what they beheld," have for you? Can you think of a time when you radically changed your view of a particular person or a part of your world? In what way were you different as a result? In what way was "reality" different?

7. Identify a time in your life when you were in the victim role. What happened? Did you choose to leave it? What was the result? What does your story have to do with entering the fundamental state of leadership?

Self-Improvement

1. Drawing on the account in this chapter of what it means to enter the fundamental state of leadership, write a paragraph describing yourself as you are today.

2. Write a paragraph describing ways in which you would like to change.

Sharing Insights

If in responding to the questions above, you have an important insight or a meaningful story that you would like to share, visit www.deepchange.com and look for the links to submit stories for possible posting on the Deep Change Web site. You may thus help many people. If you would like to review such insights and stories, go to the same Web site.

CHAPTER FOUR

Personal Revitalization

"I had been at a critical fork in my personal road. I made decisions I did not think it was possible for me to make. Making them changed my life. I rediscovered my sense of purpose. Doing so refueled my life and relationships."

—MARK SILVERBERG

The cases presented so far suggest the profound shift involved in entering the fundamental state of leadership and some of the effects of such deep change on the individual and the world he or she inhabits. Inasmuch as the fundamental state of leadership is the antithesis of our normal, comfort-seeking state, people tend to think of this way of being as a very intense condition. Transcending our own egos, entering uncertainty, being open and seeking increased awareness, challenging our own hypocrisy, being purpose-centered—it all sounds very intense and difficult to sustain.

This way of being is indeed intense. When we enter the fundamental state of leadership, we are operating at a peak level. We tend to get fatigued, and we often then return to the normal state. It is difficult to stay in the fundamental state of leadership. Yet being in this state can be quite renewing. In fact, it is staying in the normal state that leads to a loss of energy and ultimately to slow death. This is the paradox of the normal state: in clinging to comfort and safety, we lose precisely what we seek to preserve.

When we commit to leaving our zone of comfort and seeking deep change, we experience a renewal that is not limited to one segment of our lives. Entering the fundamental state of leadership at work often revitalizes relationships at home, and entering the fundamental state of leadership at home often revitalizes relationships at work. Meet Mark Silverberg and Roger Newton.

GETTING REVITALIZED

Mark Silverberg is the president of a company in Cleveland. After years of putting all he had into the organization, he was burning out. At age fifty, he felt his life was badly out of balance and losing meaning fast. Eventually he decided to take ten days off for a personal sabbatical. As he made this decision, a friend recommended that he read *Deep Change*. Mark writes:

> I wasn't reading the book. I was devouring it. I was underlining and highlighting, and I was following my wife around the house, excitedly reading her sections that hit me the hardest. I have no doubt this book changed my life. The book challenged me to clarify my value system. What was my purpose?
>
> I had to evaluate my actions. What did my behavior tell me about my values in action? I examined the gaps between what I was saying and what I was doing. I did not like the result of that analysis. My behaviors were inconsistent with what I really wanted to accomplish.
>
> I began by focusing on my family life. I rethought how I experienced being in a family. I began to look at my marriage of twenty-plus years in a very different light. My wife and I had begun to grow apart, and I had been content to blame her, my work schedule, our daughter's teenager status, or whatever. I redefined how I wanted to live with my family. As a result, I now spend more quality time with them. I reduced my hypocrisy, and I feel enriched and happier.
>
> I also had issues at work. While I am president of our small company, I was acting like a frantic manager, running myself and others ragged, jumping from crisis to crisis. I began to rethink my behavior at work. I formerly thought that a good decision-making process involved my making the right decision and talking others into agreeing with my solution. I let go of that, opened up the decision-making

process in a very different way, and found a well of interest, intelligence, and excitement among our staff. I had no idea that those assets were available to me.

Finally, I examined my own basic needs. For years, I had thirsted to return to photography, an activity I have loved since I was eight years old. I had also lost touch with a community of activists working for peace in the Middle East. I thought I no longer had time for either passion. I decided to make time. The decision reinvigorated me. In making that decision, I was responding to an inner voice—one I had been ignoring for a long time. The results were dramatic. I came alive. I moved to a new level of happiness and fulfillment.

I had been at a critical fork in my personal road. I made decisions I did not think it was possible for me to make. Making them changed my life. I rediscovered my sense of purpose. Doing so refueled my life and relationships.

Mark had a problem: he was working too hard. The fact that he was working hard as the president of a company does not mean that he was in the fundamental state of leadership. He was far from it. This very busy company president was in the normal state. He was dying a slow death.

THE MYTH OF THE RUTHLESS HERO

It may seem strange to say that in working too hard, Mark was "comfort-centered" and "self-focused." Was he not sacrificing himself and his own comfort for the good of the company? Isn't that what leaders are supposed to do?

That is how things often look to us when we are in the normal state. We admire leaders who are "driven," who seem to "sacrifice" themselves by neglecting their lives outside the job. In reality, however, people who do this are often externally driven and internally closed. They are comfort-centered in the sense that it is easier to work harder than to risk deep personal change and recover their integrity. If they were fully honest with themselves, they would acknowledge that their "sacrifice" is, in reality, an attempt to preserve their ego, the existing self, the identity they have created. If they were truly focused on the good of the organization, they would see the damage they are doing by draining themselves and the people around them.

Here I think of the image of the "ruthless hero" (Csikszentmihalyi, 1997). Csikszentmihalyi offers a wonderful illustration of the frustrations of the ruthless hero. He also illustrates how a small shift in perception can often alter the obsessive pattern and bring that which was initially unobtainable:

> Keith is one example of many managers I have met who have spent a decade or more desperately trying to impress their superiors in order to get promoted. He worked seventy hours and more a week even when he knew it was not necessary, neglecting his family and his own personal growth in the process. To increase his competitive advantage, Keith hoarded all the credit he could for his accomplishments, even if it meant making colleagues and subordinates look bad. But despite all his efforts, he kept being passed over for important promotions. Finally Keith resigned himself to having reached the ceiling of his career, and decided to find his rewards elsewhere. He spent more time with the family, took up a hobby, became involved in community activities. Because he was no longer struggling so hard, his behavior on the job became more relaxed, less selfish, more objective. In fact, he began to act more like a leader whose personal agenda takes second place to the well-being of the company. Now the general manager was finally impressed. This is the kind of person we need at the helm. Keith was promoted soon after he had let go of his ambition. His case is by no means rare: To be trusted in a position of leadership, it helps to advance other people's goals as well as one's own [Csikszentmihalyi, 1997, pp. 113–114].

As long as Keith pursued the role of ruthless hero, he was trapped in a power struggle. The world treated him as he treated the world. It was impossible to move up that ladder of power because this system, which he had helped to create, did not treat him fairly. From his perspective, he believed that he sacrificed all for the system, and yet the system did not reward him. It was not until he gave up in frustration that there was hope. Once he let go, once he became other-focused, the system began to respond to him differently. Keith was now cocreating a new world, where individual efforts, including his own, were appreciated. When he changed, the world changed.

There are armies of people like Keith. Some get into very high positions. They tell me they are leaders and are doing all they can do. They may be expending all their energy, but that does not mean they are doing all they can do. They may have high (often negative) impact on those around them. Yet this does not mean they are in the fundamental state of leadership.

Mark Silverberg was president of his company, but he became a leader when he began listening to his inner voice, facing his hypocrisy, and then making decisions he had not thought possible. He committed to more time with his family and to more time with his personal interests. This sounds like a recipe for failure, but it was just the opposite. He was reinvigorated at work as well as at home, not because he was "taking time off" but because he was choosing a more authentic way of being. It is our hypocrisy and self-focus that drains us. When we become purpose-centered, internally directed, other-focused, and externally open, we discover energy we didn't know we had.

> It is our hypocrisy and self-focus that drains us.
> When we become purpose-centered, internally
> directed, other-focused, and externally open, we
> discover energy we didn't know we had.

What happened to Mark is what I have seen happen to many other people. In today's corporate settings, there is enormous pressure to put in more time. The pressure comes from a culture of mindlessness and fear. The cultural assumption is that time is money, and the more time we can get from our people, the better off the organization is. So people get completely out of balance; they become "ruthless heroes" or burned-out victims, and corporate performance still fails to improve.

In such situations, I have seen many people come to the same conclusion as Mark. Their terrifying decision is not to do some difficult task at work. Their decision is to work less and to put in more time in other areas of their lives. For them, this is the deep change to which their inner voice invites them. When they exercise the courage to respond, they enter the fundamental state of leadership because they are no longer oblivious to the signals that change is needed. They are no longer closed to themselves, externally directed, and comfort-centered. They often report a paradoxical outcome: their effectiveness as leaders improves. Why? Mark provides the answer: "I formerly thought that a good decision-making process involved my making the right decision and talking others into agreeing with my solution. I let go of that, opened up the decision-making process in a very different way, and found a well of interest, intelligence, and excitement among our staff. I had no idea that those assets were available to me."

Compare this to the claim made by Robert Yamamoto, whom we met in Chapter Two. Robert wondered why he had such a positive culture. You may remember his response to his own question: "Yet I know it all happened because I confronted my own insecurity, selfishness, and lack of courage." When we enter the fundamental state of leadership, we allow change in the people around us. Relationships are altered, and new possibilities and patterns emerge. In claiming our integrity, we discover assets that previously we were quite sure did not exist.

BRINGING NEW VITALITY TO EVERY AREA OF LIFE

Roger Newton was facing a decision somewhat like Mark's. He was a scientist in a large pharmaceutical company. Roger was no ordinary scientist. He led the team that discovered and developed what could become the largest-selling drug of all time. He had managed to improve the lives of millions of people while creating enormous wealth for his company. He seemingly had life by a string. Yet Roger began to have great misgivings about his work situation. He tells the following story:

> I was undergoing a major transition in my professional career, having been part of an unwanted and unpopular organizational restructuring, which left me and others compromised in our capacity to perform our primary job responsibility of discovering and developing new pharmaceuticals to treat cardiovascular disease. As with many other professionals who are passionate about what they do, this change in reporting structure and responsibility was not welcomed. Unfortunately, "the tyranny of competence" had overtaken the organization, leaving many of us to engage in the personal and group debate of accepting the process of slow death or entering into the transformational cycle for deep change.
>
> I had enjoyed a great deal of autonomy in building a strong community of collaborative scientists, whose vibrant teamwork had not only moved forward the frontiers of science in cholesterol research, but also had taken that basic science knowledge and found therapeutic application to treat human disease. After the restructuring, I felt

trapped, betrayed, and completely frustrated by the lack of communication of the leadership of the organization and how they had unilaterally mandated the recent structural changes. It was at that point that I came across a copy of *Deep Change*. The concepts really resonated with me.

The dilemma that confronted me was how to initiate the transformation of the current organization and what, if any, role I should play in this transformation. What were the warning signs that would tell me whether my efforts to initiate change might lead to my having to leave the company entirely and seek other opportunities of employment elsewhere, perhaps even cofounding a start-up?

I came to realize that I had always been an entrepreneur, but was able to flourish in the current hierarchy because of the support from upper management. Now the support was no longer there, and the program that I had helped build was either scattered to other departments or merged into one that was unfocused and without clear leadership. I knew that the opportunity for deep change within the company would take months or even years before there could be a level of trust of management. Did I want to become a sacrificial lamb within the organization to promote change? Did I have the support base to attempt to change an organization that might not want to change? And how much blood, sweat, and tears would I want to dedicate to support certain leaders I could no longer trust?

To make a long story short, with the help of *Deep Change* and many good listeners and advisers, including my fellow cofounders, I decided to leave the secure but now hopeless and stagnating slow death situation in a large pharmaceutical company for a more unsure, exciting, and challenging one of becoming a real entrepreneur. We left our previous jobs in May 1998 and cofounded Esperion Therapeutics, Inc., two months later in July.

> *"Unfortunately, 'the tyranny of competence' had overtaken the organization, leaving many of us to engage in the personal and group debate of accepting the process of slow death or entering into the transformational cycle for deep change."*

Faced with his own deep change–slow death dilemma, Roger chose the risk of change. He refused to ignore the signals that it was time to leave his zone of comfort in a large, secure hierarchy. He opted for the terrifying decision to strike out into the unknown and start his own company. By this act, he entered the fundamental state of leadership.

The rest of Roger's story indicates what can happen when we make this kind of choice:

> The other three cofounders have all read and integrated *Deep Change* into their leadership philosophy. I have distributed the book to all colleagues and used its life's lessons in conducting workshops throughout the organization. As a result, we have built a vision and a corporate culture based on three important values: (1) individual dignity, (2) excellence in science, and (3) vibrant teamwork. Our company's purpose is "to explore, to create and to build." Lastly, our company name, Esperion, embodies *esp*rit de corps (teamwork), *esper*ance (hope) and *ion* (activity or resulting from). Our mission statement reads as follows: "Through vibrant teamwork discover new medicines in the hope of treating cardiovascular and metabolic diseases."
>
> So far, the vision has been viable. The company has just celebrated its fifth anniversary. We have raised $200 million in financing, including venture capital, an initial public offering on the NASDAQ (symbol: ESPR), a private investment in a public equity, and a secondary stock option. We have taken the company to approximately seventy highly valued colleagues and have four product candidates in clinical development to treat patients suffering from acute coronary syndromes and lipid disorders.
>
> Without *Deep Change,* I would never have made the personal changes that have not only allowed me to start a business, but have also improved my relationships with my spouse, children, and friends. I am grateful for the impact that this book has had on my life, and also for the life changes it has facilitated in those treasured colleagues with whom I work every day.

Roger writes of a change that he made in response to a work situation, but notice this striking claim: the change "has also improved my relationships with my spouse, children, and friends." We can make the decision to enter the fundamental state of leadership in any area of life. Recall the example of Gail, whose moment of deep change came in the midst of an abusive relationship. For Roger, the change began with a work decision. But in both cases, making a change in one area affected all the other areas of the individual's life.

In our heads, we tend to maintain a thick boundary between our lives at work and at home. The boundary is an artificial construction. We live one life. If we are in slow death at work, we affect the people we work with, but in our self-focus and despair, we also affect our spouses and our children. By the same token, if we are revitalized and living a vibrant life, we affect not only the people in our organizations but everyone with whom we have a significant relationship.

PREPARATION FOR ENTERING THE FUNDAMENTAL STATE OF LEADERSHIP

Choose a quiet time when you can reflect on the meaning this chapter has for you. Strive to be as honest as you can.

Questions for Reflection

1. At work, what was Mark's original definition of leadership? How common is his orientation? What happened when he let go of his original definition? How might this apply to you?

2. When Mark made the decision to give more time to his family and to causes that engaged him, he became a more effective leader. How do you explain this?

3. "I let go of that, opened up the decision-making process in a very different way, and found a well of interest, intelligence, and excitement among our staff. I had no idea that those assets were available to me." What implications does this statement have for your view of what it means to be a leader?

4. While Mark decided to spend more time outside work, Roger decided to take on the intense task of starting a new company. Yet both men report experiencing improved relationships at both home and work. How do you explain this?

5. How do the decisions that Mark and Roger made illuminate the meaning of being in the fundamental state of leadership?

6. Describe a time when you did something that revitalized you. What might you now learn from that past experience? What did the experience have to do with the fundamental state of leadership?

Self-Improvement

1. Reflect on the meaning of slow death versus personal revitalization. Then write a paragraph describing yourself as you are today.

2. Write a paragraph describing ways in which you would like to change.

Sharing Insights

If in responding to the questions above, you have an important insight or a meaningful story that you would like to share, visit www.deepchange.com and look for the links to submit stories for possible posting on the Deep Change Web site. You may thus help many people. If you would like to review such insights and stories, go to the same Web site.

CHAPTER FIVE

Becoming More Aware and Authentic

"I began to see things from multiple perspectives and not just from my own lens. Learning (not in the traditional sense, but from a holistic sense) became exponential. I saw things with greater clarity and understanding."

—ROBERT YAMAMOTO

One day I was a visiting lecturer in an undergraduate course at Michigan. I began by asking the students to surface their most closely held questions. An especially petite woman who was sitting in the front row raised her hand. She said, "I am about to graduate from the University of Michigan, yet I look like I am twelve years old. How am I going to get anyone, anywhere to listen to what I have to say?"

Everyone laughed, but it was a very friendly kind of laughter. In her own way, she was articulating what everyone asks: How do I establish credibility? How do I get heard? How do I exert influence? Is it possible for me to have an impact, to make a difference? How do I influence the change that is unfolding all around me?

These questions reflect a desire to lead. By now, it should be clear that the fundamental state of leadership has little to do with the formal position we occupy in an organization. Entering that state is an option for all of us, and doing so can empower us to have extraordinary influence. Yet I am convinced that the vast majority of people in the professional world, male and female, old and young, believe they have little or no voice in their organization and, moreover, that it is impossible for them to have a voice. They have tried, and bad things have happened. They are sure that organizations are mechanisms that silence their voice, and they can defend their position by citing endless examples. They therefore choose, as Roman Walley in Chapter One did, to live a professional life in which they do not make waves.

The only problem with their position is the exceptions. Recently one of my associates made an extensive argument about how organizations silence women. She told me, "The only way a woman can be heard is to take on the role of a 'bitch.'" In response, I named a woman we both knew. I indicated that her voice was always heard, and no one saw her as a "bitch." My associate paused and said, "She is different."

My friend was right: the woman I mentioned *is* different. She is a positive deviant, the exception that disproves the rule. And she is not alone. In every organization, there are a few men and women who develop voice. Something prompts these people, some extroverts and some introverts, to spend more time in what I have described as the fundamental state of leadership. They lose their self-focus and are more open to external input. As a result, they come to see things that most other people do not. With expanded awareness comes a desire for a new level of authenticity. They refuse slow death and choose deep change. Almost inevitably, they create new patterns of influence. They develop a new voice.

EXPANDED AWARENESS AND GREATER AUTHENTICITY

Here we meet a young woman, Jennifer, who has much to teach us about expanded awareness, a hunger for authenticity, and the development of new voice. Jennifer writes:

> Two years ago, when I was thirty, I accepted a new position at my company as a change manager. It was a brand-new position reporting to an executive in the organization. I had a read a few books on change management, but I had never been a manager and felt that I was really lacking a lot of the work experience that the job required. Still, I was willing to accept the opportunity.

I spent the first few months in informal interviews with dozens of people at all levels of our organization. During those interviews, I learned a lot about the people I would be working with, as well as the history and challenges of the business. It was exhilarating and mind expanding in a way I'd never experienced.

Already we can see hints of a move toward the fundamental state of leadership. Jennifer is willing to take a risk, and opening herself to external input proves to be "exhilarating and mind expanding." But her change goes much deeper than this:

It was also a time of major transition for me. Becoming a manager led to a shift in perspectives that I had not anticipated. Suddenly, I was seeing the picture of the puzzle from a much higher level, and I was forced to rethink some of my beliefs about business and management. Fortunately, I had a trusted colleague and friend who also had recently taken a position as a manager. We were of like mind on many things and were able to share our frustrations, fears, and successes as we adjusted to our new roles. My biggest challenge was my lack of confidence, specifically, the fear that people would discount anything I had to say because of my youth and inexperience.

During that time, I attended Quinn's Leading Change seminar at the University of Michigan. It turned out to be a pivotal experience for me. The other participants in the class possessed the very things I felt I lacked—experience and clout in their companies. I felt like a kid. But as I always did in those situations, I faked it. And in the end, I realized that I had more experience than I thought. It wasn't the kind of work experience I had been thinking of, but it proved to be equally important. Through the years, I had experienced many transitions and had learned how to be flexible and adapt fairly quickly to most of the changes I faced. This class also allowed for (and encouraged) us to be open and honest with each other and with ourselves. I learned that when I acted from within, people listened, and they listened in spite of my fears.

More important, though, this class introduced a concept that explained so much of my life to me. It was the outline of the transformational person. When I heard this described, I realized that I understood completely what it meant. Even as a child, I had always identified with the stories of transformational change agents and felt attracted to their actions. But until this class, I hadn't really realized that I could be a change agent myself. The Leading Change class helped me see that, and it led me to make some key decisions that have guided me since.

I recognized that I could be a catalyst for change and could see how effective it was when I remained open to new experiences and opinions instead of questioning myself. These things helped me see that I could lead people through the changes we were making and helped me understand how to do that. When I returned to the office after the seminar, I was in many ways a new person. I no longer questioned my authority, and over time, I grew more comfortable with the role I had assumed.

> *"I recognized that I could be a catalyst for change and could see how effective it was when I remained open to new experiences and opinions instead of questioning myself. These things helped me see that I could lead people through the changes we were making and helped me understand how to do that."*

Paradoxically, in losing some of her self-focus, Jennifer began to discover new things about herself. She lost some of her self-consciousness and became more confident. But it would be a mistake to think that once we begin to enter the fundamental state of leadership, all our problems and challenges disappear. To the contrary, we experience many long, dark nights of the soul. The key is how we respond to them—whether by retreating into our zone of comfort or continuing to be open, willing to continue building the bridge as we walk on it. Jennifer continues:

But it wasn't always smooth sailing. Shortly after the class ended, I lost the friendship of the colleague who had helped me so much early on. It was a terrible blow to me, and I found myself in a dark place that I couldn't seem to find my way out of. We still worked together, but the opportunities to share experiences and bounce ideas off each other was gone. It was a situation that I had to accept—I couldn't change it. But I was determined not to see it as a loss. I really believed that there was something good that would come of it, as painful as the experience was. My faith in that idea helped it come to pass.

It can be extremely difficult to remain open and trusting when your trust has been broken, but I found that the more I sought out that openness, the more of it I found. At the beginning, the experience was so overwhelming that I found myself spilling over emotionally, but instead of my driving people away, I found the people around me to be incredibly supportive. Rather than become brittle, I decided that I would continue to trust people instead of shielding myself on the chance that I could be hurt.

My desire to continue my journey of becoming more open fit very well with the work I had ahead of me. To understand the changes that our company would be making and how they would affect people required me to spend a great deal of time with the people who would be affected. I had to earn their trust so that they could feel comfortable sharing their fears and hopes about change. During these meetings, my natural extroversion had an opportunity to really bloom. I learned that one of the driving points in my personality is the desire to make connections with people. Letting this out instead of holding back and being cautious allowed me to share more of myself with people and in turn gave them the space to be more open with me. And as they shared their own stories with me, I came to see the responsibility that is attached to forming connections with people. My patience and sense of compassion reached new levels, and I found that the more open we all became, the more things naturally started to change.

Buffeted by an unhappy experience of loss of trust, Jennifer resisted closing down. Instead, she developed even greater authenticity. Her personal transformation in the work setting then began to influence the other areas of her life:

And it wasn't just in my work that I experienced these shifts. I began to create different relationships with my family. In the past year, I've become closer to both of my parents through sharing the radical transitions that they have been going through in their own lives. My family can be very intense, particularly when experiencing stress, and it can be difficult to be together at those times. This past year was different for me, though, because of the things that I've been learning. For the first time, I found the strength and patience to respond to them, based not on their expectations, but on what I sensed they needed at the time.

Feeling the positive changes occurring in my relationships has spurred me on my journey. And it has helped me seek out the support that I've needed and develop the courage to explore avenues I would never have considered before. I have been reprogramming myself and eliminating the things that were keeping me from fulfilling my own potential. And in doing so, I have become better able to help others discover their own paths. When I think about where I've come from, I can't imagine going back to the place I used to be.

Jennifer's story illustrates the point that making deep change and entering the fundamental state of leadership does not mean that we are continuously in a state of heightened awareness, authenticity, and energy. Nor does it mean that we never again suffer reversals, doubt, or pain. At times, we will revert to the normal state. But as long as we continue to choose the journey, the change can be permanent in the sense that we cannot imagine ever going back to the way we were before.

SEVEN LESSONS IN EXPANDED AWARENESS

Notice how much emphasis Jennifer put on the notion of altered awareness. She started her journey feeling deeply inadequate. Then she reported a number of events that changed her outlook. The first was simply taking on a new role. In becoming a manager, she was forced to see from a higher level and rethink her beliefs. To rethink one's beliefs is to see a new reality. Yet taking a new role was far from the only thing that happened to Jennifer. As Jennifer continued her journey, she reported at least seven elements of changed awareness.

First, she became more aware of the need for support. She found great value in one trusted colleague. As they both moved forward in the process of role change, they were able to share their frustrations, fears, and hopes. There is a great lesson here. Living through transition is lonely. It is very important to find someone who can provide support at an intimate level. Many people are hesitant to look for mentors, coaches, and supporters. It is critical that we do.

Second, Jennifer made a huge discovery: "I had more experience than I thought." She discovered that she had experience outside her work history. Like all of us, she had a past to draw on. She went back and examined other transitions in her life. She reflected on how she had "learned how to be flexible and adapt fairly quickly" in those experiences. Jennifer had a history of practicing something I call *adaptive confidence*. It is the faith to move forward into uncertainty, knowing that continuous clarification of purpose, continuous movement, and openness to feedback will result in the creation of a better state.

She also indicated that she encountered an important concept in the course on Leading Change. She discovered the notion of transformational leadership. She had always been attracted to this image, but now she reported: "I hadn't really realized that I could be a change agent myself."

Jennifer's observation is very important. In the past ten years, I have discussed this very concept in all parts of the globe with people at all levels of organizations. Most react in the same manner. They do not deny the validity of my arguments. Rather, they criticize my lack of relevance. Almost universally, they argue that deep change is for heroes and therefore not applicable to "normal" people such as themselves.

I always meet this objection by having them do what Jennifer describes doing: look at the transitions that have already occurred in their lives. Jennifer's realization that she could attain transformational leadership came from her discovery of adaptive confidence in her own past. This is not exceptional, because we all have historical bank accounts. I spend much time helping people to see what they are sure that they cannot see, that they have already been in the fundamental state of leadership. Most people have already made deep change in some way. When ordinary people like Jennifer get in touch with their own best selves, they are usually astounded. With this insight, they tend to begin to empower themselves. In the end, all heroes are ordinary people who simply have made the courageous decision to give up slow death and enter the fundamental state of leadership.

> *In the end, all heroes are ordinary people who simply*
> *have made the courageous decision to give up slow*
> *death and enter the fundamental state of leadership.*

Third, as a result of her experience with the Leading Change course, Jennifer developed a higher degree of authenticity. She created a climate of open and trusting communication. In such environments, a deeper kind of learning takes place.

Fourth, Jennifer learned that she was not in control. Her role was that of a catalyst. Few people can imagine how to play the role of catalyst in an organizational change process. The temptation is to believe that one has to be in control in order to make change happen. For someone in a position of authority, being a catalyst seems like a weak role in which one simply gives up power. In fact, it is an immensely powerful role in which we recognize the truth that we cannot control transformation, no matter what formal "power" we have. This notion terrifies and paralyzes people in the normal state. In the fundamental state of leadership, we have a different orientation. We learn to live in more trusting relationships and to join with others in building the bridge as we walk on it. When we try to control and force the process, the bridge never seems to move. People go through the motions, but nothing really happens.

Fifth, Jennifer learned how to "walk through hell" effectively. Moving into uncertainty is not a feel-good notion. It often requires dark nights of the soul. Note that one of the first things Jennifer reported was the loss of her precious ally: "It was a terrible blow to me, and I found myself in a dark place that I couldn't seem to find my way out of." Jennifer was in a trap. How did she deal with her challenge? Pay great attention to this claim: "It was a situation that I had to accept—I couldn't change it. But I was determined not to see it as a loss. I really believed that there was something good that would come of it, as painful as the experience was. My faith in that idea helped it come to pass."

Jennifer's faith in the journey she has undertaken allows her to walk through hell effectively. Too often, in similar circumstances, we do one of two things: we become bitter and angry and we lash out, or we withdraw and stop trying. We avoid making waves. In these two conditions, we fail to move, and we fail to learn. In the darkness of uncertainty, the key is to keep moving even though we do not know what to do.

Movement gives rise to learning. Jennifer not only accepted her constraint but redefined it as an opportunity. Although her trust had been broken, she chose to remain open and trusting. The more she did this, the more she altered other people. They met her with trust and openness in return. Even when she "spilled over with emotion," they were still supportive.

Sixth, Jennifer learned to create enriched connections. In doing interviews, she developed a new view of the nature of her organization.

She learned more about people and how they are connected or not connected. She discovered that part of the history that matters. She discovered what the real challenges are. For the first time, she had a larger and deeper view of the system in which she was living. In the process, she became more connected. Later she claimed the people support her. Why do they do it?

By changing herself, Jennifer became the catalyst of change. She drew support because she was radiating support. By entering the fundamental state of leadership, she was altering the nature of the connections in the system. As she discovered the power of connections, she sought to enrich them further: "To understand the changes that our company would be making and how they would impact people required me to spend a great deal of time with the people who would be affected. I had to earn their trust so that they could feel comfortable sharing their fears and hopes about change."

In the normal state, few executives I know are willing to hear the lesson that Jennifer is articulating. They are too busy doing "real work." In fact, they are busy doing what they know how to do. It is the essence of their comfort zone. In trying to lead transformational efforts, they do not want to hear that they must enrich the human connections in the system and that to do so they must spend much time listening, sharing a more authentic self.

Jennifer made important discoveries about authenticity and connection. First, she learned she could do it. Then she discovered that she had a natural desire to make connections. Finally, she discovered how the dynamics of expanding emotional space actually work. When she stopped being cautious and "let out" her own desire to make connections with people and share more of herself, she gave others the "space to be more open with me." She writes, "And as they shared their own stories with me, I came to see the responsibility that is attached to forming connections with people. My patience and sense of compassion reached new levels, and I found that the more open we all became, the more things naturally started to change."

Seventh, Jennifer learned a lesson that we were taught by Mark Silverberg and Roger Newton in Chapter Four. When we enter the fundamental state of leadership, the emerging, more authentic self is a catalyst for change in all areas. Mark made fundamental decisions about his life outside work, and his work life improved. Jennifer, like Roger, made a fundamental decision about her work life, and her family life improved. She reported creating different relationships with her family and growing closer to them.

In summary, Jennifer started out telling us, "My biggest challenge was my lack of confidence, specifically, the fear that people would discount anything I had to say because of my youth and inexperience." Jennifer made a profound discovery, one that most people in organizations never make: "I learned that when I acted from within, people listened, and they listened in spite of my fears."

When people tell me it is impossible to have a voice, that they have tried and failed, I know they have not been where Jennifer is. They have not learned to enter the fundamental state of leadership and communicate from their core. Voice comes as our awareness and authenticity increase.

Yet some people misinterpret what I am saying. They hear about someone like Jennifer or Roman Walley becoming empowered and they say, "That's it! I am going to go back to work and let my boss have it." I tell them I guarantee that they will fail. This confuses them. The fundamental state of leadership is not about being a wild card. It is not about being "authentic" in the sense of unloading our store of pent-up frustrations. It is about being purpose-centered, internally directed, other-focused, and externally open. "Letting the boss have it" is not the answer. Entering the fundamental state of leadership is much more demanding than that. It requires that we change ourselves. When we enter the fundamental state of leadership, we may confront the boss in a more challenging way than we ever imagined, but it will be because we now care for the boss, the organization, and ourselves more than we could have ever imagined. We can let the boss have it because we are angry or because we love the boss. These are two different conditions that give rise to two very different outcomes.

In the stories of the other people we have met in this book so far, we can find echoes of Jennifer's discoveries. Like Jennifer, the other people who have entered the fundamental state of leadership often describe experiencing dramatically increased awareness and greater authenticity, with profound effects on their relationships with others. Gail Parker, for example, claimed:

> This shift in perspective has changed how I see and relate to the world. Clearly my clients have benefited from this shift, as I am much better able to help them embrace their weaknesses and flaws, which paradoxically transforms them into strengths. My family and friends also benefit, as I am much less guarded and defensive, more willing to be open and vulnerable, and have a greater sense of self-esteem, all of which allows for greater intimacy and closeness.

Here Gail personifies the claim of Joseph Campbell when he states that the hero returns from the hero's journey "empowered and empowering to the community" (1949). Robert Yamamoto expresses similar feelings: "I began to see things from multiple perspectives and not just from my own lens. Learning (not in the traditional sense, but from a holistic sense) became exponential. I saw things with greater clarity and understanding."

This statement is important. In the fundamental state of leadership, we see things we cannot normally see because we use lenses that we normally do not use. There is less of the either-or thinking that dominates the normal state and more of the both-and thinking that allows us to transcend old categories and old definitions. Vision of this sort is inseparable from having the courage to claim our true selves. As the poet William Blake wrote, "As a man is, so he sees" (Blake, 1965, p. 677). Awareness and authenticity go hand in hand.

PREPARATION FOR ENTERING THE FUNDAMENTAL STATE OF LEADERSHIP

Choose a quiet time when you can reflect on the meaning this chapter has for you. Strive to be as honest as you can.

Questions for Reflection

1. When Jennifer looked to her own past, she found assets she did not know she had. What were they? What assets exist in your past? How might recognizing those assets help you become more authentic?

2. In considering the notion of transformational leadership, Jennifer writes: "But until this class, I hadn't really realized that I could be a change agent myself." What keeps people from becoming change agents? What holds you back?

3. Why do so many people have difficulty understanding the notion of being a catalyst of change, as opposed to controlling change? Can you think of a time when you witnessed someone being a catalyst of change? What do you learn about your own attempts to be a transformational leader from reflecting on the example?

4. Notice how Jennifer responded when her trust was violated. What do you do when someone violates your trust? Is there a different tack you might take if you are focused on your purpose rather than on yourself?

5. Jennifer observes, "I learned that when I acted from within, people listened, and they listened in spite of my fears." To what extent do you act from within? How might you increase the frequency of times when you do?

6. How much time do you invest in building human connections in your organization? How much do you currently learn by sharing your story with others and listening to their stories?

7. Have you experienced a time when you took the risk of being authentic and discovered that your awareness changed as a result? If so, what can you learn from this experience?

Self-Improvement

1. Reflect on the degree of your authenticity and how it might affect your awareness of the reality around you. Then write a paragraph describing yourself as you are today.

2. Write a paragraph describing ways in which you would like to change.

Sharing Insights

If in responding to the questions above, you have an important insight or a meaningful story that you would like to share, visit www.deepchange.com and look for the links to submit stories for possible posting on the Deep Change Web site. You may thus help many people. If you would like to review such insights and stories, go to the same Web site.

CHAPTER SIX

Transforming Others by Transforming Self

"Were we daring enough to take the 'hero's journey' and become agents for the future? Or were our individual identities so dependent on our existing competencies and skills—and so entwined with the established structure—that change, deep or otherwise, was simply not an option?"

—TOM JONES

The personal journeys of the people we have met vividly illustrate how entering the fundamental state of leadership alters our lives. Their stories have also hinted at how personal transformation leads to organizational change. In this chapter and the next, we pick up this thread and focus on how individual transformation is the key to deep organizational change. In this manner, we will discover a radically different way of thinking about leadership.

To enter the fundamental state of leadership is to reverse the vicious cycle of slow death. Exercising the courage to become more purpose-centered, other-focused, internally directed, and externally open results in increased hope and unleashes a variety of other positive emotions. Research suggests that such positive emotions broaden awareness, expanding thinking, vision, and understanding (Cameron, Dutton, and Quinn, 2003). The interaction of positive emotion and positive thought is a reinforcing upward spiral that is accompanied by expanding energy.

The energy and moral power of people in the fundamental state of leadership tends to be contagious. In our self-transformation, we become a living symbol of change; in the words of Chatterjee (1998), we become "metaphors that bring about metamorphosis" (p. 126). People around us are attracted to empower themselves. This leads to *emergent organizing,* a change in the system that no one "leads" in the traditional sense. Rather, emergent organizing has many leaders.

Emergent organizing is a difficult concept. We are so socialized to the hierarchical experience that even when we experience emergent organizing, we have trouble describing it. Consider an observation from Wheatley and Kellner-Rogers (1996), an observer of leadership, who refers to emergent organization as self-organization (meaning the system is organizing itself):

> We don't have to look beyond ourselves to see self-organization. Each of us has frequent, personal experiences with this process. We see a need. We join with others. We find the necessary information or resources. We respond creatively, quickly. We create a solution that works—but then, how do we describe what we did? Do we dare to describe the true fuzziness, the unexpected turns, the bursts of creative insight? Or do we pretend that we were in control every step of the way? Do we talk about surprises or only about executing plans? Do we brag about our explorations or only our predictions? Our analytic culture drives us to so many cover-ups that it is hard to see the self-organizing capacity in any of us [p. 37].

We see the process of emergent organizing at work in Mike Alvis's experience of organizational transformation in the army, which was described in Chapter One. We assume that the army, of all organizations, could be changed by command. It could not. General Shinseki became a catalyst of change. The general's own courageous transformation attracted and changed people like Mike. Commitment spread in an unpredictable fashion until the process reached a point of irreversible momentum.

This is a key point. Contrary to our assumptions about how leaders create change, deep change at the organizational level is not managed or controlled. It spreads like a contagious disease in a nonlinear fashion. To lead transformation is to become a leader of a social movement.

We attract others to the fundamental state of leadership. They then join us in building the bridge as we walk on it. It was Ralph Nader who once said, "I start with the premise that the function of leadership is to produce more leaders, not more followers." This is an important point for anyone who wants to effectively lead change.

THE RESISTANT ORGANIZATION

The view of change that I have just expressed is antithetical to the logic of the normal state. In the normal state, we design hierarchical controls to preserve equilibrium. Hierarchical controls resist deep change even when the need for change becomes undeniable. When embedded in the normal state, we seek to manage change instead of leading it. The result is slow death.

Because of this built-in resistance to deep change, trying to lead organizational transformation often seems a thankless task, even for people who have had experience. Here we meet Tom Jones, an experienced change leader who finds himself trying to transform an organization that does not want to change:

> As someone who has devoted most of his adult life to building winning organizations through strategic change, I thought I had played a role in every transformation process imaginable. That conceit quickly faded when I was named president of CIGNA's Individual Insurance operation in early 1995.
>
> Individual Insurance was one of CIGNA's flagship divisions, a proud and successful business with a 130-year history of product innovation and profitable earnings growth. At the same time, it was also an organization facing a critical crossroad. The business was growing, but at a pace that trailed industry leaders. Our scale and market presence were problematic. And the focus of the division was out of alignment with both the direction of CIGNA, which was concentrating more and more on workplace benefits, and the expectations and needs of consumers, who were increasingly seeking complete financial solutions rather than individual products and services.
>
> Clearly, the organization needed to change. But resistance was pervasive. After all, why implement new ways of thinking and behaving when the old ways had worked so well for so long? And why journey into the unknown when the tried and true was still delivering steady growth and profitable returns?

This part of Tom's story captures some common elements of transformation. The first is the notion of conceit. I have seen many executives who have successfully led change in the past. They enter a new assignment with great confidence, only to be stymied. One reason for the frustration is that every organization is unique. Another is that experienced change agents really do not understand what it is that made them successful the first time around. Since in the first case they developed unique knowledge, they think that it was the knowledge that made them successful. They believe all they have to do now is apply it.

What we know from past experience is an asset, but what leads to successful transformation is our capacity to learn in real time. While knowledge is useful, learning is essential. What actually made these change agents successful was their decision to enter the fundamental state of leadership. By becoming more purpose-centered, other-focused, internally directed, and externally open, they experienced exponential learning, and they attracted others to participate in the process of transformation. To repeat past successes, they must again enter the fundamental state of leadership. As they move forward into uncertainty, they must experiment and seek accurate feedback. As they do so, they develop a unique theory of how this unique system must change. When success follows, they conclude that they know how to lead change and assume they know how to change the next organization. (For a profound example of this process, see Chapter Nine on authentic engagement.)

Tom's story also illustrates a key aspect of the deep change or slow death dilemma. There were emerging problems in the company. The growth rate was trailing that of the industry leaders, and the division was increasingly out of alignment with the direction of the larger company. Yet the organization was growing. Growth is an indicator of success. Tom's call for change was a call to implement new strategies, processes, and methods—to leave behind the very things that had made the company successful. That meant people were also being called to leave their zone of comfort. They were being asked to build the bridge as they walked on it.

Building the bridge as we walk on it is deeply unsettling because it means learning in real time. It means letting go of the existing self and allowing a new self to emerge. Faced with this challenge, people tend to resist. They cling to what they already know how to do—the things that have brought them success in the past. They tightly grasp any available argument to defend the status quo. With righteous indignation, people in such situations ask questions like the one Tom identifies: "Why journey into the unknown when the tried and true is still delivering steady growth and profitable returns?"

As Mike Alvis discovered, such people are not the enemy. Indeed, they are the secret of our eventual success. They must be met where they are. Over time most people are capable of deep change, but they need help. Tom continues:

> I needed something beyond just my own words and deeds to generate support and enthusiasm for building a new divisional growth strategy. And I needed independent validation for risking the future, especially with members of my senior management team. It was about then that I encountered the book *Deep Change*.
>
> The book seemed to crystallize not only the challenges facing the Individual Insurance operation, but also the choices we needed to make as an organization and as individuals. I shared it with my staff. And slowly, skeptically, each associate in the division began to understand, almost as if a light bulb had been switched on.
>
> After reading and discussing the concepts in the book, members of the organization recognized that Individual Insurance was facing the classic dilemma of deep change versus slow death. They saw that their very success over the years had indeed become an engine for failure. And they acknowledged and identified the many ways the existing divisional structure encouraged and rewarded equilibrium, while denying and repudiating the need for strategic transformation. This new awareness turned into a kind of vision we could build on.
>
> On a personal level, the book challenged each of us—myself included—to test our willingness to change. Were we daring enough to take the "hero's journey" and become agents for the future? Or were our individual identities so dependent on our existing competencies and skills—and so entwined with the established structure—that change, deep or otherwise, was simply not an option?
>
> For some, this self-evaluation led to an "active exit." But for most, it resulted in an understanding that one person can change an entire system and that as a team, we could shape a future as compelling and dynamic as our storied past.
>
> My senior team and I made sure we modeled the behavior—the commitment to change—we expected from others. We rallied support and enthusiasm for a new strategic direction. And over the next year, *Deep Change* became both our guide and inspiration as we crafted our

new strategy . . . encouraged risk taking . . . and became comfortable with the idea of building the bridge as we walked on it.

This story does not conclude in a predictable manner. One would expect an ending in which Individual Insurance fully implemented its new strategy and became an integral part of CIGNA's overall employee benefits value proposition. There is, however, one more twist to the tale. In late 1996, CIGNA sold its Individual Insurance operation to another life insurance company just as the new strategy was beginning to take hold. Was it a shock to the organization? Of course. Was it a paralyzing and disruptive event? No.

The sale of the Individual Insurance division was viewed as part of the organization's ongoing transformation. The importance of change—the value of the journey—had become part of the organization's culture. And this new development was simply the next step in building a winning future. The members of the Individual Insurance team continue to do well and remain committed to seeking and embracing change as fundamental to their long-term success. This is quite a difference from 1995.

ORGANIZATIONAL TRANSFORMATION AS AN EMERGENT PROCESS

To enter the fundamental state of leadership is to invite others into the process of deep change. This is the key to Tom's story. In distributing the book *Deep Change,* Tom was taking a first step. He was providing others with the concepts and language they needed to discuss the meaning of the change the organization needed, and he was inviting them into the process. As a result, his people became aware of the problems in their existing structure and of their own tendency to deny the need for change.

Of particular importance in Tom's story is the fact that this new awareness "turned into a kind of vision we could build on." Notice that there was not a definite vision laid out for them; rather, "a kind of vision *that we could build on*" emerged.

Much has been written about the need for leaders to have a clear vision. Too often it sounds as if the leader's vision is just another mandate from on high. In the transformational process, there is usually a general outcome that is desired, a result to be created. Yet this kind of vision emerges over time. It is a vision of how we become a new community as we pursue the desired result. It can never be announced ahead of time. It is emergent. It is part of building the bridge as we walk on it.

Eventually Tom and the people around him had to get to the crux of the matter. They had to examine their own willingness to change. Although Tom was experienced in corporate transformation, he had to return to the question of self-change. Did he and his people have the courage to walk naked into the land of uncertainty? Were they willing to model the process of entering the fundamental state of leadership?

For some of his top people, the answer was no, and they had to leave. This is also worthy of note. In top management teams, it is common in times of transformation to have strong resisters. Most are capable of turning around. Some are not. Usually these are competent people who are playing a powerful role. The common temptation is to make excuses for such powerful senior people and to move ahead. Indeed, one of the most frequent problems that I observe is the unwillingness of top executives to confront the "tyranny of competence" and remove those who are clearly unwilling to grow into the change process. As Tom notes, "One person can move a system." By the same token, one contrary person at the top can have a devastating effect. Such people seldom speak up and express their opposition. Instead, they consciously or unconsciously sabotage the change process.

While a change leader needs to develop a team that moves with one mind, that team is often not the formal top management group. It is often a network of converts that cuts across formal boundaries. Over time the change spreads to more and more people. Eventually there is a critical mass.

Here I am reminded of Robert Yamamoto's story in Chapter Two. Robert saw himself as a change agent. He spoke of a "critical mass that is willing to look at challenges in a new way and work on solutions together." This is how social movements work. We never convert everyone. We do not need to. To move the organization where it needs to go, we need only the critical mass.

This is how social movements work. We never convert everyone. We do not need to. To move the organization where it needs to go, we need only the critical mass.

Reaching a critical mass has marvelous impacts on the organization. At his meetings, Robert declares that there is "new energy present." With this new energy, the group also seems to have new perspective and new capacity: "What previously seemed unimaginable now seems to happen with ease."

ORGANIZATIONS ARE TRANSFORMED WHEN WE TRANSFORM OURSELVES

As Robert reflected on the profound change in his organization, he wondered why it now seemed so easy and why there was now a positive culture. He then answered his own question: "I know it all happened because I confronted my own insecurity, selfishness, and lack of courage."

Robert was making one of the central claims of this book: we transform the organization by transforming ourselves. This is a highly resisted concept. When we are failing and disempowered, we "know" that bad things are happening because of the people and circumstances around us.

We are, in fact, correct. Those people around us are in the normal state. They are pursuing their own self-focused agendas, and the collective environment is one of distrust and decreasing capacity. Unfortunately, we are in the same condition. We accept the world as it is, and we become what we behold. From our normal state, we know it is nonsense to claim that we change the organization by transforming ourselves. Hence we are likely to say, "I am doing all I can, but there is no way to change the system."

Statements like these reflect the state of empowerment we are in, for it is our own state that determines the theory of change we can accept or even contemplate. To illustrate this point, let us consider various ways in which we may try to make change happen.

THREE GENERAL STRATEGIES FOR EFFECTING CHANGE IN HUMAN SYSTEMS

In the normal state, we seek equilibrium. In the normal state, we are comfort-centered, externally directed, self-focused, and internally closed. We construct a world of social exchange and economic transaction. The central purpose of anyone in such a system is to obtain status and resources while avoiding pain and punishment. When emerging reality threatens our deeply held values by suggesting we need to move into the unknown, we resist. We become self-deceptive because we say change is needed, yet we want to avoid the risk of losing what we have, so we seek to "manage" change in ways we do not find deeply threatening.

In the normal state, we typically employ two general strategies of change: Telling, that is, making logical arguments for change and Forcing, that is, using forms of leverage such as the threat of firing or ostracizing. Less often, we may use a third strategy, Participating, that is, using open dialogue and pursuing win-win strategies. (These three general strategies are a simplified version of a scheme originally offered by Chin and Benne, 1969.)

The Telling strategy assumes that people are guided by reason. If others decide it's in their best interest to change, they'll gladly do so. Any resistance to change could only be the product of ignorance and superstition. To counter that resistance, the change agent needs to educate the people to the truth, and their resistance will dissolve. But it isn't usually that simple, as most of us know.

The Telling strategy is most effective for situations in which people are not very invested. Someone tells me my tire is going flat and that I need to get it changed. I can verify this by looking at the tire. I can make a clear cost-benefit assessment: I must have a good tire to drive my car, and changing the tire is relatively easy to do. I am not emotionally tied to getting the work done, and I am quite certain that when it is done, I can drive safely again. I know what to do, and little learning is required. This is incremental change, and it's relatively easy.

Yet what if someone tells me that I must change the way I drive because it is causing undue wear and tear on my car? Changing how I drive will be a good investment, and all I have to do is attend a weekend conference. Now I am being asked to change my fundamental behavior. I have no way of immediately assessing if the other person is right or wrong. Besides, I would have to attend classes and learn a whole new way of driving. It doesn't sound like a good idea.

Telling is not as effective in situations requiring significant behavior change because it is based on a narrow, cognitive view of human systems. It fails to incorporate values, attitudes, and feelings. While people may understand why they should change, they are often not willing to make the painful changes that are necessary. When the target of change begins to resist, the change agent often becomes frustrated and turns to the second general strategy.

The Forcing strategy seeks to leverage people into changing. Usually some form of political or economic power is exerted. Efforts may range from subtle manipulation to physical force. The Forcing strategy usually evokes anger, resistance, and damage to the fundamental relationship. Thus, it not likely to result in the kind of voluntary commitment that is necessary for healthy and enthusiastic change—change that will sustain the system and, in Tom's words, "become part of the culture."

In the normal state, then, we commonly seek to create change by engaging in a two-step process: first, tell others why they need to change; second, if telling fails, figure out a way to force them to change. This two-step process is so normalized that even I, the supposed expert who should be totally aware of it, do it over and over again. Since we are seldom interested in changing ourselves, we repeat this process while refusing to recognize that in using force, we damage the relationship and seldom obtain our desired long-term outcome.

The Participating strategy involves a more collaborative approach. This approach recognizes that people are influenced by their language, habits, norms, and institutional policies and culture. Here, the change agent welcomes the input of others, who are seen as equals in the change process. Instead of trying to make change happen simply by providing information, as in the Telling strategy, the change agent focuses on surfacing, clarifying, and reconstructing people's values and on resolving hidden conflicts. The emphasis is on communication and cooperation in a search for win-win solutions. People move forward, trusting the emergent group process.

People who know the power of this strategy often use the phrase, "Trust the process." Others find the phrase preposterous. In the normal state, many people are incapable of trusting the emergent process. They need to feel that they are in control. I am reminded of a story told by Steven Covey. A disbelieving CEO told Covey, "Every time I try win-win, I lose." Covey replied, "Then you did not do win-win."

The paradox is that this strategy calls for reducing control while remaining clear and strong about one's underlying values and intent. It is a strategy not of weakness but of strength. Participatory strategies and active listening require that each person allows the other to express his or her truth while insisting that his or her own truth be heard. The exchange can then give rise to a new and more complex truth.

Over the years, it has become politically correct to advocate the Participating strategy. Many do advocate it, although few actually believe in it. In practice, it is seldom used as intended. Instead, the change agent determines a solution and then asks a group to join in a discussion. Any answer they come up with is acceptable—as long as it is the "right" one. Because so many people experience the Participating strategy as a manipulative technique, they become deeply cynical, an attitude that undermines the process. We thus get back only what we put out: distrust of the system and what passes for "proof" that the Participating strategy does not work.

A FOURTH STRATEGY

There is a fourth general strategy for effecting change. It is even less accessible when we are in the normal state than is the Participating strategy. I call it the Transcending strategy in reference to the transcending of self that occurs when we enter the fundamental state of leadership. It can be understood in relation to the first three strategies as seen in Figure 6.1. Here is an explanation.

Look at the lower-right-hand-corner of this figure, labeled Technical Perspective. The strategy at work in this quadrant (Telling) is oriented to logical explanation. This orientation tends to reflect two sets of values, "structure and control" (indicated at the bottom center) and "external alignment of the system" (indicated at the right center). Here we seek to be in control while seeking to explain the facts to others.

Now look at the upper-left-hand corner of the graph, labeled Interpersonal Perspective. The strategy at work in this quadrant (Participating) is oriented to trust. When we are working from this perspective, our core values (indicated at the left center and the top center of the graph) tend toward "preservation of the system" and "possibility and emergence." That is, we try to maintain existing relationships while orienting others to possibility and emergent processes.

If you compare the assumed values of the Technical Perspective quadrant and the Interpersonal Perspective quadrant, you will see that the two are in stark contrast. They are psychological oppositions.

Now move to the lower-left-quadrant, the Political Perspective. Note that the emphasis here is on "compliance." When we are working from this perspective, our values tend toward "structure and control" again, just as in the Technical Perspective, and toward "preservation of the system." Of all the strategies, the strategy here (Forcing) is the most focused on the preservation of the status quo. It accepts the risk of offending people in order to preserve the current order of things.

Finally, move to the upper-right-hand quadrant, the Transformational Perspective. Here the emphasis is on vision realization. When we are working from this perspective, our values tend toward "possibility

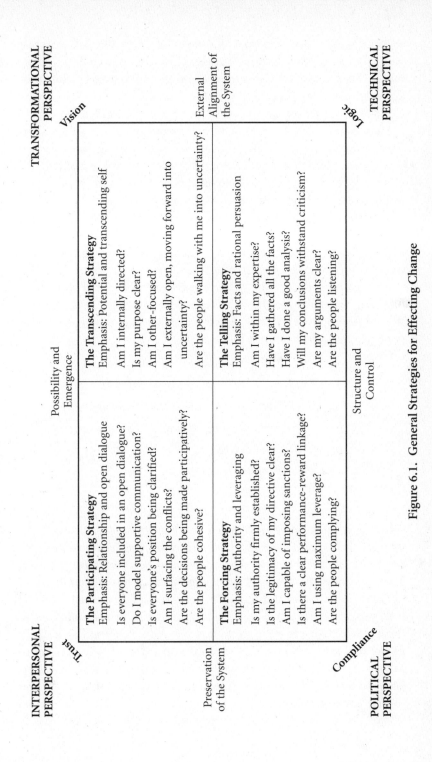

Vision

Possibility and
Emergence

External
Alignment of
the System

Logic

Trust

Preservation
of the System

Structure and
Control

Compliance

The Participating Strategy
Emphasis: Relationship and open dialogue

Is everyone included in an open dialogue?
Do I model supportive communication?
Is everyone's position being clarified?
Am I surfacing the conflicts?
Are the decisions being made participatively?
Are the people cohesive?

The Transcending Strategy
Emphasis: Potential and transcending self

Am I internally directed?
Is my purpose clear?
Am I other-focused?
Am I externally open, moving forward into
uncertainty?
Are the people walking with me into uncertainty?

The Forcing Strategy
Emphasis: Authority and leveraging

Is my authority firmly established?
Is the legitimacy of my directive clear?
Am I capable of imposing sanctions?
Is there a clear performance-reward linkage?
Am I using maximum leverage?
Are the people complying?

The Telling Strategy
Emphasis: Facts and rational persuasion

Am I within my expertise?
Have I gathered all the facts?
Have I done a good analysis?
Will my conclusions withstand criticism?
Are my arguments clear?
Are the people listening?

Figure 6.1. General Strategies for Effecting Change

and emergence" and "external alignment of the system." The associated Transcending strategy is represented in every case of deep change that we have examined. One purpose of this book is to make this strategy more clear and accessible.

The two most normally practiced strategies—Telling and Forcing—are found in the bottom two quadrants, sharing the core values identified as "structure and control." When we employ these two strategies, we believe (often erroneously) that we are in control. Even if we are totally ineffective, we tend to keep practicing them. In the end, we prefer the illusion of control to the cost of being effective.

The third strategy, Participating, is very difficult for most people to access. It means letting go of some control and trusting the interactive process. Because of our need to be in control, we often prostitute this process. We pretend to be open when we are not.

The Transcending strategy, the one that is most at the core of the fundamental state of leadership, is even less accessible. In the normal state of disempowered living, we cannot tolerate it. Yet it is the key to personal and collective transformation.

> *The Transcending strategy, the one that is most at the*
> *core of the fundamental state of leadership, is even*
> *less accessible. In the normal state of disempowered*
> *living, we cannot tolerate it. Yet it is the key to personal*
> *and collective transformation.*

It is important to recognize that each of the four change strategies resides at a higher level of cognitive and behavioral complexity. Individuals who expand their awareness from, say, the Technical Perspective to the Political Perspective are likely to become more effective. They do not give up the Technical Perspective but enrich it with a wider range of views and skills. Those who then go on to master the Interpersonal Perspective keep the tools of the Technical and Political strategies but enlarge their awareness and skill set. They have a richer perceptual map with which to see the context, and they have more skills to apply in trying to change it. As a result, they are likely to be even more effective, yet they still lack the fundamental thing they need to lead transformation.

Individuals who embrace the Transformational Perspective are the ones who are most capable of leading deep change. That is what we learn from all the people we have met so far in this book. These are the catalysts of change who have discovered that to transform the organization, they must first of all transform themselves. They must "become the change they want to see in the world." Thich Nhat Hanh, an insightful observer of change, expresses this truth in these words: "If a [community of practice] is having difficulties, the way to transform it is to begin by transforming yourself, to go back to your island of self and become more refreshed and more understanding" (1995, p. 68). This is what Tom Jones learned at CIGNA Individual Insurance. It is what we all learn when we enter the fundamental state of leadership.

PREPARATION FOR ENTERING THE FUNDAMENTAL STATE OF LEADERSHIP

Choose a quiet time when you can reflect on the meaning this chapter has for you. Strive to be as honest as you can.

Questions for Reflection

1. What does it mean to be a leader of a social movement when you work in a large organization? Can you identify an example from your own experience?

2. What is your response to Ralph Nader's statement that "I start with the premise that the function of leadership is to produce more leaders, not more followers"? What implications does this idea have for your own leadership?

3. Have you witnessed leaders who succeeded in past transformations but failed when they tried to lead a second transformation? How do you account for the failure?

4. Are you convinced that to transform the organization, you must transform yourself? If so, what are some concrete implications for you?

5. Can you identify a case of the "tyranny of competence" in an organization you know about? What might you do to prevent a similar occurrence in your own organization?

6. In your experience, how does transformational change happen? Do you agree that members of the top management team are often not a part of an early social movement within the organization?

7. Provide an example of a time when you have seen each of the four general change strategies (see Figure 6.1) employed. How often do you employ each strategy?

8. How could the information in Figure 6.1 make you a more effective leader?

Self-Improvement

1. Reflect on the concept of self-transformation as the key to transforming the organization. Then write a paragraph describing yourself as you are today.

2. Write a paragraph describing ways in which you would like to change.

Sharing Insights

If in responding to the questions above, you have an important insight or a meaningful story that you would like to share, visit www.deepchange.com and look for the links to submit stories for possible posting on the Deep Change Web site. You may thus help many people. If you would like to review such insights and stories, go to the same Web site.

CHAPTER SEVEN

A New View of Leadership

"If language is not in accordance with the truth of things, then affairs cannot be carried on to success."

—CONFUCIUS

s Confucius observed, "If language is not in accordance with the truth of things, then affairs cannot be carried on to success." In order to think more clearly, deeply, and accurately about leadership—and, more important, in order to find pathways to the fundamental state of leadership—we need a language that does justice to the "truth of things."

It is time now to pull together several of the threads that have run through the stories of transformation that we have encountered in the first six chapters. Our discussion of leadership strategies in Chapter Six brought us to the threshold of a new vision of leadership. In this chapter, I make that vision explicit.

In discussing increased awareness in Chapter Five, I noted how we see differently when we are in the fundamental state of leadership. In particular, there is less of the either-or thinking that characterizes the normal state and more of the both-and thinking in which apparent opposites are reconciled in a more comprehensive view of reality. In Part Two of this book, I will describe a set of eight practices that we can employ if we want to get into the fundamental state of leadership. The eight practices embody unusual, even paradoxical, concepts about leadership that result from both-and thinking. These concepts allow us to transcend our old categories and definitions. They provide a fuller and richer language for talking about leadership that is simultaneously more ambiguous and more accurate. Because they are so unusual, it will be necessary to extend our normal thinking tools in order to grasp them. The rest of this chapter prepares the way for these ideas by suggesting how we can view leadership in a more complex and dynamic way. Let's begin by meeting Kevin Fickenscher, a man with a profound tale to tell.

TRANSCENDING THE USUAL CATEGORIES

Kevin is a physician who is very involved in the transformation of health care. He has now led transformations in at least four organizations. Along the way, he has discovered that he must transcend the usual categories that we use to define leadership. Here he shares his observations:

> Since arriving in health care as an orderly, continuing on as a medical student, resident, and practicing physician and, now, in providing leadership as an executive in large health care organizations, I have been committed to making health care better for all people. It is this commitment that constitutes the notion of deep change. Yet I have learned that maintaining commitment is not easy. I will share two examples.
>
> When I arrived at one large organization, I discovered that the approach to information technology [IT] was adrift. There were overlapping costs, duplication, unfettered purchasing of incompatible systems, and so forth. This had been done in an era where there were sufficient funds to pay for these "systems." However, shortly before I arrived, the organization had begun to face a situation of ever tightening reimbursement that was causing it to take stock of its direction. I'll never forget my first conversation with the CEO: he told me, "Take care of IT and make it work" (a fairly clear directive).
>
> The long and short of it is that I crafted a vision for the organization, went through a process with those who were directly involved, and gained a large measure of support among the troops for the many changes required to make us a more efficient, productive, stable, and future-oriented information management organization. This was one project among many change projects that I became involved in with the organization. In fact, my moniker became "Dr. Change."

After three years and despite very positive evaluations, I was terminated. I was devastated. The organization had come to a significant financial crisis, and the CEO had laid down the rule that the corporate overhead would not exceed 0.9 percent of total operational budget—something that it had met in the years prior to a more centralized approach. He did this to placate the multiple regions and overlapping administrative structures that existed throughout the organization. In my exit interview, he stated (and I'll never forget it): "Sometimes we let the most talented go because we know that they can take care of themselves."

I was flabbergasted. I felt that it was so ironic that I was leaving and the "resisters" to change were staying. He had seemed supportive, but when the wolves were at the door, he moved to placate them by ousting me. I had felt that if we continued on the course of the corporate leaders, the board would soon take action.

Kevin had encountered the phenomenon of the resistant organization that was discussed in the preceding chapter. The resistance was more intense and more dangerous than he realized. He suffered for his commitment. This kind of painful surprise happens often to people who enter the fundamental state of leadership. Such people, focused on purpose, act from principle and pursue the transformation that the organization needs. Yet often the organization does not want what it most needs. Like Kevin, change agents are often flabbergasted when they are fired and the people who are responsible for the slow death of the organization are retained. This prospect alone is enough to keep people in the normal state. Yet as Kevin discovered, to enter the fundamental state of leadership is to see leadership in new ways. He continues:

> It turns out that I was right. My departure precipitated a crisis (not solely because of my departure, although that was a part of the crisis) that resulted in the CEO's losing his position a short six weeks after my departure. Ironically, I recently spoke with one of the individuals who had reported to me. In that conversation is an important lesson.
>
> She told me the organization went on to hire a new CEO (exactly the type of leader needed for supporting change efforts), and very few of the original "wolves" remain. She then said: "Kevin, we are doing everything that you envisioned. You had the ideas, you carried the message, you got us to the door, and the leaders slammed the door in your face. You'd be proud! We're doing everything. It's amazing. We carried the vision forward."

From this exchange Kevin derives some critical lessons about being in the fundamental state of leadership:

There is a major lesson here. Visionaries are often not present for the final institutionalization of deep change. Witness that people like Jesus, Gandhi, Martin Luther King, Martin Luther, Abraham Lincoln, George Washington, Deng Xiao Ping, and many, many others were not allowed to live out their vision. The vision, of necessity, eventually became the work of others.

In a similar vein, I visited with my former boss at another organization several years ago. He said to me: "Kevin, you'd be proud of all the seeds you planted that have come bearing not just plants but flowers." What a tribute.

There are three points to be made about my experience in leading change.

First, while it's nice to "be there" when the platitudes come and the plaques are handed out, I've come to the conclusion that the true transformational leader must frequently accept his or her results through the work of others who embraced the vision and moved it forward. In the book *Deep Change,* Quinn notes that we must "trust in our vision enough to start our journey into the chasm of uncertainty, believing that the resources will appear . . ." It is this initial step of trusting ourselves that is the most difficult. For as a leader, if we trust ourselves, it is critical that we embrace not only the vision but also those who are emboldened to walk with us. Such a step requires that we move forward knowing that the final work for a truly deep change effort may not—and frequently does not—include us. If we are truly committed to the purpose, our own exit is an acceptable outcome. If it is not, we are unlikely to succeed anyway.

A second lesson is that "walking naked" and "building the bridge while we walk on it" are core considerations for any leader who is serious about change at any level. The change is as much about us as individuals as it is about our organizations. The confidence and belief that we can go ahead without knowing how, trusting ourselves to learn, is critical. The concept is particularly relevant in a world where managerial control is frequently no longer feasible.

Control is derived from information, and with the ubiquitous availability of information—both public and proprietary—the ability to control diminishes. To be effective leaders in this new world, "walking naked" requires us to let go—to embrace the unknowable by offering followers the conceivable. Working through others, setting direction while others navigate, and maintaining personal accountability require a totally different approach to leadership.

A third lesson is about patience with adversity and resistance. I've come to the conclusion that if you truly believe in your vision, then you must be willing to accept the fact that some may not want to follow and will even resist your efforts. The tincture of time has taught me that the resistance can exceed the following—in the short term. However, what initially may seem to be failure, if it is allowed to lay fallow, grow, and mature, frequently results in the organization's moving forward—if the vision is grounded and thus compelling. To make the decision to follow your vision, then, can be very difficult. The end result is that gratification from deep change comes from the work of others who accept, embrace, and move the vision. In fact, it is through the work of others that the true contribution of a change leader is made.

"To make the decision to follow your vision, then, can be very difficult. The end result is that gratification from deep change comes from the work of others who accept, embrace, and move the vision. In fact, it is through the work of others that the true contribution of a change leader is made."

Here Kevin becomes crystal clear about what it really means to enter the fundamental state of leadership. It means being so focused on achieving the desired outcome that we are always willing to accept that it may be necessary for us to go in order for the outcome to emerge. This means we are truly focused on the collective good.

This is the observation of a complex person. It is antithetical to the thinking that characterizes the normal state. The first principle of normal living is survival of the self. The objective in a world of scarce resources is to win as much as you can. There tends to be no collective purpose worthy of self-sacrifice. In the fundamental state of leadership, our worldview changes. In every case we have so far considered in this book, we watched people clarify their purpose. We watched them make courageous decisions to pursue that purpose and to move forward to build the bridge as they walked on it. As they did so, they became other-focused, willing to make sacrifices for the common good.

SUCCEEDING WITHOUT
BEING THERE

Note that Kevin crafted a vision, enrolled his people, and engaged them in building the bridge as they walked on it. In the process, he was terminated. The explanation was political; the outcome was clearly unfair. Yet later, all that Kevin had initiated came to fruition. Why?

When we enter the fundamental state of leadership, we change. We become a source of variation, a jolt of uncertainty in the system. Once that happens, emergent organizing begins. When uncertainty goes up, people create new patterns of relationship. Control systems and status structures melt away. Leadership shifts from person to person as needed. No one is leading the process in the traditional sense, yet it leads to striking new outcomes.

We see this process at work in Kevin's story. He was in the fundamental state of leadership, and he attracted others to join him. The change he had put in motion continued even after he was gone. Although he was terminated, he was successful. In the words of his colleague, "It's amazing. We carried the vision forward."

People in the normal state read this and focus on what happened to Kevin: "Big deal; the man lost his job." In the normal state, we are externally driven, and we define success in terms of external rewards. We cannot understand Kevin or his message. But Kevin was not in the ordinary state.

When people like Kevin enter the fundamental state of leadership, they set off storms. People get divided into camps. In the process, the leaders learn much about themselves. They become people of increased capacity. They look back on the failures and injuries and now see them as important wellsprings of power and capacity.

In our usual ways of thinking about leadership, we have a difficult time accounting for stories like Kevin's. "Succeeding without being there" is, from the standpoint of the normal state, a paradoxical concept. As we probe more deeply into the characteristics of people who enter the fundamental state of leadership, we will discover more apparent paradoxes.

WHEN CATEGORIES MELT

We normally assume that thinking determines behavior. Yet behavior also determines how we think. I suspect that one reason old categories melt away for the people we have met in this book is that when they are in the fundamental state of leadership, they enter uncertainty—that which they do not yet know. They must open up and explore reality. In this state of true learning, they realize that the old categories that so defined reality were an invention, words we used to construct the reality that we experienced at an earlier time. Once those words and categories were in place, they became the containers that held us in place. Suddenly we see a new reality where the categorical differences collapse. Everything becomes one. We now have the opportunity to resee and rename things. In the process, we create a new world.

To understand this process, it may be useful to consider how we normally think. There is a pattern of human thinking that has been noted by careful observers in both the ancient and modern worlds. Sense making is characterized by splitting oppositions and polarities. Things are hot or cold, soft or hard, past or present. In making these differentiations, we also tend to make implicit judgments about good and bad. We reconstruct polarities. Our underlying differentiations take on a positive-negative structure. We speak of love or hate, action or stagnation, honesty or corruption. In this splitting process, we tend to dissociate ourselves from the negative. We embrace only the positive. By labeling the other half of reality negative, we act and construct a world that lacks dynamic balance. We lose the kind of integrity that renews itself. In denouncing stagnation and pursuing action, for example, we forget the value of stability, the positive opposition to action. We lose the capacity to embrace stability and join it with forward movement.

Because of this tendency to split the world, we endlessly generate strategies that are the seeds of their own failure. They succeed for a time and then mysteriously transform into seemingly incomprehensible, vicious cycles. As we engage in the normal process of splitting, we can no longer tolerate emerging reality. We have to cut off the feedback loops that tell us our internally split values are now attempting to split a natural world that will not be split. Because we feel insecure, we deny the messages of changing external reality until it is too late. Then we enter some form of crisis.

As the crisis expands, the ego tends to collapse. This is not a disaster but a rebirth. We shed the old categories of sense making. For a brief moment, we experience the oneness of the transformational world. We marvel at the both-and nature of things. We gain new insights. We choose to enter the fundamental state of leadership, and we become empowered and empowering. Then, because we lack the language and concepts necessary to maintain both-and thinking, we return to the need to act with intention and fall into the natural process of splitting.

SEEING THROUGH MULTIPLE LENSES

In the fundamental state of leadership, it is natural to think in both-and terms and to gain capacities that we normally split off as "not part of us." Consider an illustration.

One day one of my colleagues and I were discussing the four quadrants of the competing values model. The model articulates contrasting leadership behaviors. One quadrant of the model emphasizes the conceptualization of the future, and the quadrant opposite it emphasizes the detailed analysis of the present. A third quadrant emphasizes task achievement, and its opposite emphasizes concern for people. Most people think of the opposing quadrants in an either-or fashion.

My friend told me that he was really good at conceptualizing the future, good at task achievement, and sometimes good on concern for people. However, he said, he was terrible at details and never performs well in that area.

I told him I disagreed. He was a little offended by my willingness to intrude on his self-analysis. Our conversation continued as follows:

"You love to write music, right?"

"Right."

"You told me that sometimes you get into 'the zone' and really feel that you are doing high-level work."

"That is true."

"When you are at that high level of performance, you pay great attention to details of creating music, right?"

There was a protracted silence. First my friend looked a little shocked. Then he looked a little angry. Then he said, "I hate it when you do that." We had a good laugh.

What became clear in that conversation is that when my friend is in the normal state, he dislikes and avoids details. When he is in the creative state, he attends to details while hardly noticing that he does. In the fundamental state of leadership, we are more complete and less split in both our thinking and in our behavior. Yet when we return to normal thinking and behavior, we are limited in our ability to describe transformational reality. Nevertheless, in the fundamental state of leadership, we reflect more, feel more, learn more, and achieve more. We become liberated from self-limiting definitions and consequently more dynamic. Like Kevin, we become more complex people. Our behavior patterns do not stay in commonly defined categories but tend to stretch across boundaries. We behave in ways that seem paradoxical. We discover, for example, that it is possible to be simultaneously confident and humble, detached and interdependent, tough and loving, active and reflective, practical and visionary, responsible and free, authentic and engaged.

Usually people observing from outside the fundamental state of leadership think in either-or terms and so cannot easily describe the paradoxical characteristics of people in the fundamental state of leadership. They tend to engage in positive-negative splitting. This fact accounts for much of the confusion in the literature on leadership and the futility in lists of desired leadership characteristics. People in the normal state do not have the perceptual lenses or the language necessary to describe the increased complexity that occurs when we enter the fundamental state of leadership. But as Confucius observed, "If language is not in accordance with the truth of things, then affairs cannot be carried on to success." In order to think more clearly, deeply, and accurately about leadership—and, more important, in order to find pathways to the fundamental state of leadership—we need a language that does justice to the truth of things.

FOUR WAYS TO SEE LEADERSHIP

In the rest of this chapter, we review four increasingly complex and dynamic ways of seeing leadership. At the highest level of complexity, we will end with a view of leadership that embodies the eight practices for entering the fundamental state of leadership that will be explored in Part Two.

Level 1: The Static View

The normal or most common way to think about leadership is to use what is called the *trait approach*. In trying to improve leadership, someone tries to identify the desired traits or characteristics of a leader. This approach is illustrated in Table 7.1, which lists thirty-two positive traits.

Using the trait approach, we might say, for example, that the company wants people who are bold, self-disciplined, responsible, active, energetic, committed, and engaged. That would be a good list. We

Table 7.1.   Leadership Traits.

active	energetic	independent	realistic
adaptive	engaged	integrated	reflective
assertive	expressive	involved	responsible
bold	factual	mindful	secure
compassionate	flexible	open	self-disciplined
concerned	grounded	optimistic	spontaneous
confident	hopeful	principled	strong
constructive	humble	questioning	visionary

could build a training program to try to develop these characteristics. And in doing so, we would be developing people who are likely to have a very negative effect on the company. Why?

Our list of traits contains a strong bias toward focused action yet ignores other dimensions that are crucial to organizational success. This is a typical outcome of using the trait approach, which usually produces a list of low complexity. The trait approach assumes that leadership can be understood and developed by breaking it into parts. In reality, effective leadership tends to incorporate a dynamic whole that we usually see as contradictory qualities. We cannot see this so long as we imagine that we can analyze leadership into component parts. Moreover, leadership is not a fixed list of traits; it is a dynamic, complex, living process. A trait view keeps us from seeing leadership in this way.

Level 2: The Polar View

Normal human thinking takes the form of either-or reasoning in which we tend to split very different characteristics such as humility and confidence. We have a harder time thinking in terms of polarities, or contrary characteristics operating simultaneously in the same system. We read the list of thirty-two traits in Table 7.1, for example, and we are unlikely to pay much attention to the unseen polarities that are actually present. In Table 7.2, the same list is presented in terms of eight tensions or polarities.

This approach moves us toward both-and thinking. When we use the trait approach, we have to take the dynamic reality of leadership apart. It is like killing a butterfly and pinning it on a board to study. In the words of the poet William Wordsworth, "We murder to dissect." In this way, we can discover much about the parts of a butterfly, but our analysis loses an appreciation for what it means to be a living

Table 7.2. Leadership Traits: A Polar View.

compassionate; concerned	assertive; bold
spontaneous; expressive	self-disciplined; responsible
mindful; reflective	active; energetic
principled; integrated	engaged; involved
realistic; questioning	optimistic; constructive
grounded; factual	visionary; hopeful
independent; strong	humble; open
confident; secure	adaptive; flexible

thing. So it is with leadership. Moving from single traits to a set of polarities allows us to look at leadership from a more complete and dynamic perspective. If in observing a leader, we use positive oppositions or polarities to observe what is happening, we will see and understand more than we could with the trait approach. Let's take it to still another level of complexity.

Level 3: A Competing Values View

In a third way of viewing leadership, the polarities revealed in Table 7.2 become still more complex. The model in Figure 7.1 is called the competing values framework. It contains the thirty-two leadership traits organized into eight polarities and places each polarity next to a similar or overlapping polarity. It also articulates what happens when a leader overemphasizes some positive value: the positive becomes a negative. The leader splits the polarity apart and begins to move into the negative zone on the outer edge of the figure. So, for example, a concerned leader who practices too much concern becomes a lax leader. An overly assertive leader becomes an overbearing leader. A questioning leader becomes a cynical leader. An optimistic leader becomes a naive leader.

This observation takes us to a still more complex view, suggesting that effective leadership not only stretches across polarities, but also requires maintaining positive opposites without sliding into the negative zone shown at the outer edge of Figure 7.1.

A leader who scores high on all the positive characteristics in Figure 7.1 is said to have high behavioral complexity, or the capacity to behave in many different ways. Research shows that leaders with high behavioral complexity tend to generate more positive organizational outcomes (Hart and Quinn, 1993).

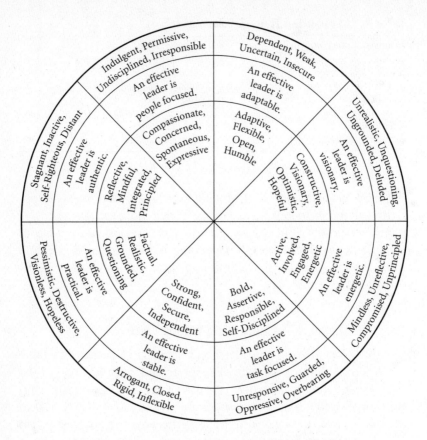

Figure 7.1. Competing Values Model of Leadership

The competing values framework helps us to see the polarities that tend to operate in the social world. Organizations are dynamic, living systems, and people must have great adaptability and exhibit a complex array of behaviors to manage or lead. Unfortunately, the normal mind employs either-or thinking to quickly reduce the competing values framework back to the trait approach. Trainers using the model, for example, tend to assume that they should assess people on the various dimensions and then educate them on their weak traits. That is natural but still hinders us from more fully understanding leadership and developing it in ourselves or in others. To achieve that fuller understanding we need to turn to a fourth level of complexity.

Level 4: An Integrated View

In the fundamental state of leadership, people become more focused, hopeful, optimistic, visionary, confident, courageous, persistent, adaptive, concerned, caring, and so on. If we look for a predetermined trait in them, we are likely to find it. If we are also practicing normal, either-or thinking, we will tend to miss the fact that they also exhibit polar, positive traits.

Yet positive traits tend not to exist in isolation. Rather, they exist and expand as part of a reciprocal system. Positive characteristics tend to cocreate and sustain each other. These internal dynamics spread to the external environment and have the potential to transform other individuals and then the entire organization. It is hard for us to see these dynamics from a normal view. Yet this is why Kevin Fickenscher succeeded without being there. The changes he initiated brought forth the emergence of a self-organizing system. His initial surprise that it had happened is a reflection of how few of us understand self-organization. It does not lend itself to normal thinking.

By integrating positive oppositions, we can create a set of eight new concepts for describing leadership. A simplified version of these concepts appears in Table 7.3. The first two columns of the table show the original thirty-two traits consolidated into the eight polarities. In the far right column, the eight polarities are linguistically integrated. These eight linguistic integrations suggest eight creative states. A person in one of these creative states would be high on both ends of a given polarity. Someone who exhibits "tough love," for example, will be both assertive/bold and compassionate/concerned.

Taken together, the creative states listed in the far right column are the basis of the eight practices described in Part Two. In the chapters

Table 7.3. Eight Polarities and Eight Creative States.

Eight Polarities	Eight Creative States
spontaneous; expressive/self-disciplined; responsible	Responsible freedom
compassionate; concerned/assertive; bold	Tough love
mindful; reflective/active; energetic	Reflective action
principled; integrated/engaged; involved	Authentic engagement
realistic; questioning/optimistic; constructive	Appreciative inquiry
grounded; factual/visionary; hopeful	Grounded vision
confident; secure/adaptive; flexible	Adaptive confidence
independent; strong/humble; open	Detached interdependence

in Part Two, I will explore more about how these concepts were derived, provide illustrations of them, and show how they suggest ways of entering the fundamental state of leadership. Here I will simply point out the ways in which they are different from normal leadership concepts.

The eight concepts are integrated in Figure 7.2. I see these concepts as overlapping and not mutually exclusive, as usually required by normal science. Normal science differentiates categories for good reason. Mutually exclusive categories facilitate measurement and prediction. Normal science is very good at breaking things down into parts. It does not readily lend itself to the integration of differentiated concepts. It took years, for example, for leadership researchers to notice that there was a high correlation between task orientation and concern for people across hundreds of studies (Schriesheim, House, and Kerr, 1976). The data were right in front of many highly trained ana-

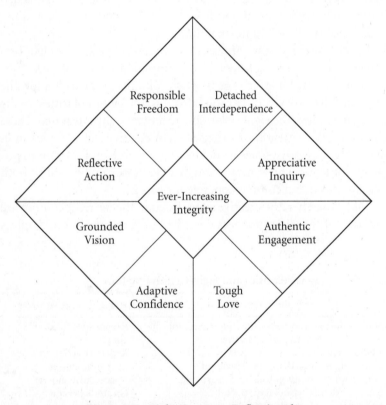

Figure 7.2. Eight Concepts Reflecting the
Fundamental State of Leadership

lysts, but their categorical thinking did not allow them to see the obvious connection. Even now that we know they are highly correlated, we tend not to examine their potential connection and overlap. Understanding this, Bernard Bass (1997) wrote:

> An almost insurmountable problem is the question of the extent to which we pour old wine into new bottles when proposing "new" theories. For instance, Julius Caesar's descriptions of his leadership style in the Gallic Wars in the first century B.C. are clear, succinct endorsements of the need for what Blake and Mouton (1964) conceived as 9–9 style—a style that Fleishman (1953) described in terms of high initiation and consideration and that in the year 2500 some new theorist will give a new name. When does the field advance? Are we beyond Caesar's understanding of how to lead infantry shock troops? [p. 16].

A general in war tends to enter the fundamental state of leadership. Caesar was complex enough to see that a real leader is high on people and on task. He was not complex enough or lacked the language to articulate that a leader is not only high—high on task and person but on many other positive polarities.

Here the new wine is, first, the articulation of that more complex view and then a distillation of that complexity into the simplicity that says the fundamental state of leadership is a state in which we are more purpose-centered, internally directed, other-focused, and externally open. Still more simply, it is the movement toward ever-increased levels of personal and collective integrity. Ever-increasing integrity is the source of life for individuals and groups. Ever-increasing integrity is the alpha and the omega of leadership. That is why it is at the center of Figure 7.2.

The fundamental state of leadership is . . . the movement toward ever-increased levels of personal and collective integrity. Ever-increasing integrity is the source of life for individuals and groups. Ever-increasing integrity is the alpha and the omega of leadership.

Each of the corresponding practices described in Part Two reflects increasing integrity in the self and results in increasing integrity in the organization. In the fundamental state of leadership, both the person and the organization have increased integrity in terms of pursuing the purposes they know they should be pursuing. Both the person and the organization have increased integrity in terms of living core values. The person has more integrity in relating to others. The people in the organization have more integrity in terms of how they relate to each other. Both the individual and the organization have increased integrity in terms of honestly recognizing changing external reality. Increasing integrity is at once the driver and the outcome of deep change. It is the antithesis of slow death, personally and collectively. It is the answer to entropy in the social world.

In addition to suggesting practices or pathways that can help us enter the fundamental state of leadership, the eight leadership concepts are lenses that allow us to look for things we cannot currently see but that might exist. Consider an analogy. In the early twentieth century, astronomers had data and theories that led to the prediction that there was a planet in our solar system that we could not see. They painstakingly looked for it and discovered Pluto.

In the social sciences, we seek to predict relationships, but we seldom do what the astronomers have done. We tend not to look for social patterns that must exist but are yet to be discovered. That is what we are doing here. We are embracing oppositional concepts for exploring the system known as the fundamental state of leadership. The concepts are tools that may help us to see things we could not see before—things that even Caesar could not see.

This list of concepts is not complete. Many other such concepts could yet be derived. It is meant only to get us started. It will be evident, however, that these concepts capture in explicit terms much of what we have learned in individual stories of deep change like those you have read so far.

MOVING ON

We now have a language or set of conceptual tools for describing and exploring the meaning of leadership in a more profound way than we could access previously. I believe this language better represents the reality of leadership as a complex, dynamic process than the typical vocabulary we find in discussions of this subject. But my purpose is not merely, or even mainly, to present a new theoretical model. Rather, it is to illuminate how we can transform ourselves and our organizations. In the chapters that follow, we will delve more deeply into the eight concepts I have just described and learn how each suggests a practice or pathway for entering the fundamental state of leadership.

PREPARATION FOR ENTERING THE FUNDAMENTAL STATE OF LEADERSHIP

Choose a quiet time when you can reflect on the meaning this chapter has for you. Strive to be as honest as you can.

Questions for Reflection

1. Why was Kevin "flabbergasted"? What did he learn from being fired? What did you learn from his being fired?

2. Have you witnessed an example of someone who "succeeded without being there"? If so, what lessons did you draw from his or her example?

3. In Table 7.2, thirty-two leadership traits are presented as eight polarities. Identify someone you admire as a leader. Use one or more of the polarities to explain why he or she is effective.

4. Which of the eight polarities in Table 7.2 do you tend to integrate?

5. Create a list of desirable leadership traits, characteristics, or behaviors that have been identified in an organization you are familiar with. Place them on the competing values framework in Figure 7.1, and then identify what is missing. What does the bias imply?

6. Which part of the negative zone in Figure 7.1 do you tend to enter most frequently? Why?

7. How does the following sentence apply to you: "Ever-increasing integrity is the alpha and the omega of leadership"?

Self-Improvement

1. Reflect on the picture of the fundamental state of leadership presented in Figure 7.2. Then write a paragraph describing yourself as you are today.

2. Write a paragraph describing ways in which you would like to change.

Sharing Insights

If in responding to the questions above, you have an important insight or a meaningful story that you would like to share, visit www.deepchange.com and look for the links to submit stories for possible posting on the Deep Change Web site. You may thus help many people. If you would like to review such insights and stories, go to the same Web site.

PART TWO

Eight Practices for Entering the Fundamental State of Leadership

"What man actually needs is not a tensionless state but rather the striving and struggling for some goal worthy of him. What he needs is not the discharge of tension at any cost, but the call of a potential meaning waiting to be fulfilled by him."
—VICTOR FRANKL (1963)

The stories in Part One led us to a new model of leadership. The model suggests that leadership is a creative state of being that we may enter, leave for a time, and reenter again. Eight concepts help us to capture the essence of the fundamental state of leadership: reflective action, authentic engagement, appreciative inquiry, grounded vision, adaptive confidence, detached interdependence, responsible freedom, and tough love. Each of these concepts embraces a dynamic tension between polar qualities, and all converge on the central idea of ever-increasing integrity.

In Part Two, we explore these eight notions not as theoretical constructs, but as practices or pathways that we may follow in order to enter the fundamental state of leadership. We will see through numerous examples of deep personal change how individuals have traveled these pathways in the direction of greater integrity. At the end of each chapter, you will be challenged to assess yourself as you are today with respect to each practice and to formulate a strategy for your own personal growth.

CHAPTER EIGHT

Reflective Action

When we take the time to integrate action and reflection, we begin to behave differently. . . . As we become more purpose-centered, internally driven, other-focused, and externally open, we more fully integrate who we are with what we are doing. At this point, what we are doing enlarges our best self, and our best self enlarges what we are doing.

Here we will examine the first of the eight practices introduced in Chapter Seven: reflective action. It was Plato who once argued that the unexamined life is not worth living. To this someone once responded, "Yes, and the unlived life is not worth examining." Reflective action is a concept that combines both arguments. It is not easy to integrate both reflection and action. In the world of business, for example, there is a tremendous imperative toward action. If we err between action and taking the time to reflect, we err on the side of action.

Given the bias toward action in modern life, let us begin our examination of the practice of reflective action from the other direction—from the viewpoint of a man who had chosen a life of reflection and contemplation.

A MONK'S TALE

Thomas Merton was one of the most influential religious writers of the last century. A convert to Catholicism, he became a Trappist monk. In 1948 he published a best-selling book, *Seven Storey Mountain*. It was the first of many successful books and the beginning of a life of high visibility in which he continued to write beautifully of the value of solitude, reflection, and contemplation.

Ten years later, on March 18, 1958, Merton had an epiphany. It occurred while he was standing on the corner of Fourth and Walnut Streets, in the middle of the shopping district in Louisville, Kentucky:

> I was suddenly overwhelmed with the realization that I loved all those people, that they were mine and I was theirs, that we could not be alien to one another even though we were total strangers. It was like waking from a dream of separateness, of spurious self-isolation in a special world, the world of renunciation and supposed holiness. The whole illusion of a separate holy existence is a dream. Not that I question the reality of my vocation, or the monastic life; but the conception of a "separation from the world" that we have in the monastery too easily presents itself as a complete illusion: the illusion that by making vows we become a different species of being, pseudo angels, "spiritual men," men of interior life, what have you [Merton, 1966, p. 156].

After this event, Merton changed. He could no longer go on just writing about meditation, even though it was of great value. He could not bury himself in typical monastic concerns. He had to begin to face what he called the big issues of life and death in the world. From that point on, he became much more involved in the social issues of his day. He did not give up reflection and meditation. Rather, he brought about an integration of reflection and action.

Most of us in the organizational world have the opposite challenge. We are engulfed in action, at the expense of contemplation and reflection. This extreme is just as isolating as the extreme of contemplation divorced from action. With a deep apology to Merton, let me rewrite his vision as it might be reported by a suddenly enlightened executive standing in the foyer of a monastery:

> *Most of us in the organizational world . . . are*
> *engulfed in action, at the expense of contemplation*
> *and reflection. This extreme is just as isolating as the*
> *extreme of contemplation divorced from action.*

I was suddenly overwhelmed with the realization that I loved all those people, they were mine and I was theirs, that we could not be alien to one another, even though we were total strangers. It was like waking from a dream of separateness, of spurious self-isolation in a special world, the world of corporate involvement and endless work. The whole illusion of a separate powerful existence is a dream. Not that I question the reality of my vocation, of the corporate life, but the conception of being in the material world that we have in the corporation too easily presents itself as a complete illusion: the illusion that by making money we become a different species of being, pseudo power figures, wealthy people of analytic genius, people of power, what have you.

In the corporate world, we often become addicted to action. We develop organizational cultures that carry the expectations that people will come in early and leave late. We reinforce the compulsive patterns of type A personalities. We complain endlessly about the loss of balance in our lives and the pain of burnout. We assume that there is no place for reflection. We dare not speak of the need for spiritual awareness and personal integration. In this distorted world where we have institutionalized the split of action and reflection, we are trapped in the vortex of slow death. People often recognize the problem but lack the courage to do anything about it. They choose slow death over deep change.

Recall from Chapter Four the story of Mark Silverberg, a frantic company president. He felt that he was trapped in the requirement for perpetual action and that there was no way out. If he stopped "jumping from crisis to crisis," the organization would surely collapse. Yet Mark made the courageous decision to change. He learned to listen to his inner voice, made time for the things that mattered to him, and he became a centered human being. Once he did this, his world changed. It reorganized to support the new Mark.

My experience suggests that nearly all of us can benefit by carefully considering Mark's story, yet most of us will not. Instead we will find a way to dissociate ourselves. We will tell ourselves that Mark must have been some kind of anomaly, that we cannot do what he did. Most of us "know" that there is no way out. We "know" this because doing what Mark did requires more faith and courage than we think we can muster. In this sense, we are like Merton before his epiphany, except that we are at the other end of the reflection/action polarity. Like Merton, we are living half a life. We need to move from constant action to an appreciation of the power of reflection. Then, like Merton, we need to integrate the two. When we take the time to integrate action and reflection, we begin to behave differently. In reflecting deeply on our behavior, we travel to "the center of our existence." There we find our best self. We also find the courage to enter the fundamental state of leadership. We then change our patterns of behavior. As we become more purpose centered, internally driven, other focused, and externally open, we more fully integrate who we are with what we are doing. At this point, what we are doing enlarges our best self, and our best self enlarges what we are doing.

REFLECTIVE ACTION

The positive tension of the state of reflective action can be seen in Table 8.1. We can be so mindful and reflective that we become stag-

Table 8.1.   Reflective Action.

Negative	Positive	Integrative	Positive	Negative
This person is so mindful and reflective as to be stagnant or inactive.	This person is mindful and reflective.	This person practices reflective action.	This person is active and energetic.	This person is so active and energetic as to be mindless or unreflective.
Stagnant; inactive	Mindful; reflective	Reflective and active	Active; energetic	Mindless; unreflective

Reflective action: This person is active and energetic while also being mindful and reflective. While deeply engaged in the world, the person also spends time in reflective contemplation. Contemplation when away from a task increases the capacity for mindfulness during the task. The person acts and learns simultaneously and is both mindful and energized while actively creating.

Personal orientation: I continually renew my understanding of who I am and why and how I am doing the things I do by learning from action and acting from an ever-expanding consciousness. I live in a reciprocal relationship between action and reflection. I practice reflective action.

nant and inactive. On the other hand, and much more commonly in organizational life, we can be so active and energetic that we become mindless and unreflective.

The challenge is to be both reflective and active. We can do this by making a practice of regularly reflecting on what is happening in our lives. At first, we make time for contemplation when we are away from our usual tasks so as to increase our capacity for mindfulness during the tasks. Eventually we act and learn simultaneously. We are both mindful and energized while creating the life we want to live.

PRACTICING REFLECTIVE ACTION

We begin by examining the group approach and then move on to the discipline of writing.

The Group Approach

The culture of the corporate world tends to drive out the possibility for deep reflection. To counteract this pattern, we often need support.

I think, for example, of a young man I have worked with for some years. During those years, he has become president of a midsized corporation. Like most other people in that role, he feels constant pressure to be in the action mode. We were discussing this when he told me how much he has come to value his membership in the Young Presidents' Organization (YPO). I asked him why. He described the typical agenda for their regular meetings. There is no content agenda. Instead, these young executives take time to identify the issues that are most on their minds, from complicated business problems to serious personal dilemmas. Each person shares an issue, and then the group spends time sharing ways to think about the issues.

My friend told me that these meetings have become the most valuable time he spends each month. He said confidentiality breeds trust, and people stretch in their efforts to be helpful. In those conversations, he can get clear about who he is and what he needs to do next. The process allows him to reflect in ways he normally does not.

After listening to his story about the structure of these meetings, I developed the following exercise.

Reflecting on Core Issues

1. Record brief answers to the following. Then prepare a three-minute report conveying your most important present concern.

   During the past month:

   What was the best thing to happen to you?

   What is the most challenging thing to happen to you?

   In the next month:

   What professional situation will be most demanding?

   What personal situation will be most demanding?

2. Each person should give his or her report in three minutes or less. Be disciplined about time. As each report is given, group members should take notes on what is said.

3. The group should identify the key themes in the presentations. The issues may include such things as marriage, divorce, taking a small company public, problems with children, how to cope with a pressing organizational issue, or a wide range of other topics. During the week, the group will have one hour each day to address the five most important topics.

4. During that hour, one person will be assigned to make a short (five-minute) presentation on the topic, and one person will be assigned as a coach to the presenter. At the conclusion of the presentation, the coach acts as the facilitator of the discussion.

5. The facilitator invites people to give advice. The facilitator is responsible to see that participants do not make "You should do" statements but rather "It has been my experience . . ." kinds of statements.

In my next week-long executive education class, I asked the participants to engage in the exercise. Afterward, they reported the very same reaction as my friend did to his experience in YPO. They were amazed that as strangers, they could achieve such intimacy. They were amazed that they could walk away from their discussions with such a sense of insight. I pointed out to them that the exercise can be executed by any group. Indeed, people in many companies have created such groups and used *Deep Change* as a tool for reflecting on daily patterns of action. One way to gain support for integrating action and reflection is through such a group approach.

The Discipline of Writing

Perhaps the most common way to integrate action and reflection is through the habit of journal writing. This entails a commitment to set aside some time each day to reflect and write about the patterns currently unfolding in your life. Some people turn activity into a process of diary writing, simply recording what happened during the day. Reflective action requires more that just recording events. It requires careful examination of who we are and how that matches with what we are doing. It often requires an exploration of the link between our present and our past. Consider an example.

I once had an opportunity to write a chapter with my son Shawn (Quinn and Quinn, forthcoming). He had just received his master's degree in organizational psychology at Columbia University, and he intended to become a consultant. The chapter was about the process of becoming a transformational change agent. It consisted of two letters. In the first letter, I wrote to Shawn explaining some of the basic concepts of transformation. The concepts, like the ones here, suggested high personal accountability and would lead almost anyone to conclude that they could not be expected to live in a transformational way, especially when just starting a career. However, I asked Shawn to do an unusual thing. I asked him to reflect deeply on action. In particular, I asked him to reflect on action that had already taken place in his life.

The key thought here is that Shawn and the rest of us carry a treasure. When most of us survey our current situation, we are sure that there is no way we can be transformational. We suspect that we never will be. Yet in our treasure trove, there often are data that contradict our tightly held position. Often there are patterns of action in our past that were in fact patterns of deep change. Reflecting on these patterns can have a great impact on how we see ourselves and how we see our situations.

In responding to my request, Shawn expressed some deeply held fears. Then he wrote insightfully about his basketball career in high school, his experiences as a missionary, and his first managerial job. Here I will quote the last of these reflections as an illustration of how reflecting on the past can lead to new learning.

My first job out of college was working for one of the country's fastest growing trucking companies. I was the assistant to the president of the

Western Division and thus had frequent opportunities to work with the CEO. After a short period the CEO and I developed a trusting relationship. I think that relationship was a function of what I learned in [my previous experiences].

At one point he decided to invest in a company offering a new information technology. They had an innovative information system that would allow for the tracking and managing of our trucks and trailers. We believed that implementing the system would greatly improve our bottom line. Yet the implementation process did not go well. There were many problems and much resistance. The utilization rate was 5%. At that point I was asked to take charge of the project.

After a couple of weeks of analysis, I decided to do two things. First, each time a driver was sent to me with questions about the system, I sent the driver back to get his manager. I would then teach the manager how to use the system. When the managers first came in, they were usually resistant, but as they gained a sense of control, they got excited about what they could do. They then went back and coached their other drivers. Second, I spent a lot of time talking to people at higher levels. I continually pushed the need for them to include competency with the system as part of their job evaluations. Gradually, this came to pass, and it helped a great deal.

Despite measurable progress, there were still a number of drivers and driver managers who were not using the technology. At first, I was tempted to blame them, but instead I decided to own the problem. If they were not using the system, I had to bear some responsibility. So this realization forced me to develop new strategies. I committed to continuously talk to everyone, at every level, about the bigger picture. I explained that if we could make the technology work, it would help the technology company go public and, since we owned part of the company, it would help our bottom line. I did this relentlessly. I also continually shared data showing the improvements in time utilization. I did interviews and distributed questionnaires seeking to learn every problem they were encountering. I made sure we took action to remedy each one. I identified the non-users and started spending my time with them. I did whatever was necessary to free them up to learn and teach the system.

Utilization rates started to climb. In four months we went from 5% to 60% utilization. As this happened, we discovered some of the real problems with the technology. Here my integrity failed. I worried a lot about pleasing the CEO. He wanted the new technology company to be successful. So I had a tendency to soften my accounts of the problems in the new technology. I also failed to confront the people in the technology company. I should have challenged them to be more honest with themselves, to embrace and deal with their real problems. They did not want to face the pain of reality, and I did not have the courage to impose the pain. In the long run, they had to drop a part of their product line. They suffered and we suffered.

In this account, Shawn works hard to be very honest with himself. He not only tells of his success, but lays bare his failure, his lack of integrity. As opposed to keeping a diary, this kind of writing leads to deep personal learning. The author begins to learn things about the author. Here are the lessons that Shawn identifies:

Lessons: In the first phase I did a lot of rational explanation, telling people why they should change. I also used political leverage by getting management to evaluate people. I used a number of participative techniques, involving people in the learning process. Yet, even after all that effort, we were still only partially successful. At that point, I very much wanted to blame others. Instead, I tried to change myself, trying to take more accountability for the results and increasing my integrity. That led to greater commitment, effort, and change from myself and from others. It brought a lot of success.

Yet in perhaps the most key area, I had a failure of integrity. I was more concerned with impressing the CEO than I was with the good of the enterprise. As I tried to move forward at the edge of chaos, my fears triumphed. I now see things in that episode that I could not see then. I see things I was denying. Being transformational is a function of our ability to constantly engage that which we least want to engage, our own hypocrisy. I think it will help me to approach such situations differently in the future.

> *"Being transformational is a function of our ability to constantly engage that which we least want to engage, our own hypocrisy."*

Shawn's comments point to a future of continued effort to engage in reflective action. He concludes his letter with further reflections on all he has learned and what these lessons mean for him as he moves forward:

In trying to become a professional change agent, I have had the experience of negotiating and designing some interventions. In these initial interventions, I have felt very much like a novice. I found myself saying and doing things that a novice would do. I have been too worried about what authority figures think. I have tried to say what I think they want to hear. Other times I have tried to do what I thought was right but made statements that only led to discomfort. I was challenging but not supportive. . . . I need to stop describing and trying to sell the process model. Instead I need to live it.

When I consider the insights derived here, I see myself behaving differently in the future. I know that by being more internally driven and other-focused I will begin to make decisions that can benefit more people than myself. I will try to look past my deceptions and the deceptions of others. I will constantly need to ask myself, what can I change to improve a relationship or situation? I will seek to free myself of the rules and scripts so that I can learn to live in a state of cocreation. I know these things are far easier to say than to do. However, recognizing that I have taken these steps in a few cases in the past should help me move forward.

Last week I watched a movie. The movie is about a woman living a superficial life, and denying the pain associated with such a life. She finds out she is going to die and begins to clarify what matters. She begins to make choices at work that most people are afraid to make. She immediately becomes more authentic. She takes risks and creates relationships. She ends up getting great new offers.

My challenge is to do what she did, without death to motivate me. I need to live authentically because I choose to do so. I hope to move closer to becoming a transformational change agent, because, if I am growing, it may also help others to grow.

ENTERING THE FUNDAMENTAL STATE OF LEADERSHIP

As Thomas Merton discovered, we must integrate reflection and contemplation with engagement in the realities of life. My friend found that joining with others in a group process helped him to do this. Shawn found that analyzing his present in the light of his past helped him to do it. Here you might reflect on what technique might best help you.

PREPARATION FOR ENTERING THE FUNDAMENTAL STATE OF LEADERSHIP

Choose a quiet time when you can reflect on the meaning this chapter has for you. Begin by assessing where you are today, as honestly as you can.

Questions for Reflection

1. Check each item that describes you as you are today.

___ I take the time to meditate.

___ I learn from every experience.

___ I carefully evaluate each victory and failure.

___ I have identified the transformational moments in my past.

___ I have articulated the lessons of my transformational moments.

___ I have a personal, experience-based theory of change.

___ I continually clarify my values.

___ I know who I am.

___ I recognize the greatness in me.

___ I recognize the greatness in others.

___ I am centered and productive.

___ I am peaceful and focused.

___ I am very active.

___ I am full of energy.

___ I get lots of things done.

___ I see the potential in every situation.

___ I am shaping the unfolding future.

___ I choose my own emotional state.

___ I am living with deep conviction.

___ I love what I am doing.

2. Now assess yourself on the following scale by circling the number under the characteristics that currently describe you. Note that the "negative" areas of the scale represent the overemphasis of a positive characteristic so that it becomes a negative. The "integrative" part of the scale represents the integration of opposing positives. If you feel you model the integration of mindful reflection and energetic action, circle one of the numbers under "Integrative." Otherwise circle two numbers, one on each side of the scale.

Negative	Positive	Integrative	Positive	Negative
Stagnant; inactive	Mindful; reflective	Reflective and active	Active; energetic	Mindless; unreflective
−3 −2 −1	1 2 3	4 5 4	3 2 1	−1 −2 −3

Self-Improvement

1. Based on the assessments you have completed, write a one-paragraph self-description on the theme of reflective action. In your own words, describe where you are today with respect to this aspect of the fundamental state of leadership.

2. Write a strategy for self-improvement in the area of reflective action. Try to be as concrete as possible in describing steps you are willing to take beginning today.

Helpful Hints for Practicing Reflective Action

Treat time as a precious resource.

Maximize the time you spend doing what only you can do.

Minimize the time you spend doing what others can do.

Have a daily, weekly, monthly, and yearly plan for accomplishing your goals.

Analyze your past daily, weekly, monthly, and yearly plans, and learn from them.

Design every action to a clear objective.

Leave no action open-ended. Connect every action to a next step.

When you begin to feel intuitive unease, seek to understand why. Do a root cause analysis of your misgivings.

Take time every day to ask who you are and who you are becoming.

Continually clarify your values.

Examine the link between your values and your current behavior.

Do not give in to taking the easiest way out.

Demand productive action from yourself.

Analyze the relationships in your life.

Establish a group for discussing key life issues.

Have a sacred time devoted to reflection.

Develop spiritual disciplines.

Have a regular physical workout.

Do something every day that gives you joy.

Schedule play into your life.

Understand your weaknesses, and work to improve them.

Understand your strengths, and work to build on them.

Challenge yourself to consider alternative routes.

Constantly monitor your level of vitality.

See that your values and behavior are always aligned.

Sharing Insights

If in responding to the questions above, you have an important insight or a meaningful story that you would like to share, visit www.deepchange.com and look for the links to submit stories for possible posting on the Deep Change Web site. You may thus help many people. If you would like to review such insights and stories, go to the same Web site.

CHAPTER NINE

Authentic Engagement

"Self-actualizing people are, without one single exception, involved in a cause outside their own skin, in something outside of themselves. They are devoted, working at something, something which is very precious to them—some calling or vocation in the old sense, the priestly sense."
—A. Dean Byrd and Mark D. Chamberlain
   (1995)

Reflective action involves the capacity to integrate the realm of action with the realm of personal identity. When we reflect deeply on our patterns of action, we clarify who we really are and what we are really doing. We can then integrate our actions and inner selves in a creative way. A sister concept to reflective action is authentic engagement.

In considering authentic engagement, I will begin with a story about a mother and a daughter. I do so because I believe the story of family intimacy provides a model for transforming a marriage, a classroom, a Fortune 500 company, or an entire society.

TRANSCENDING OUR SELF-DECEPTIONS

Terry Warner (2001) tells a story of an eight-year-old girl, Erin, who cared nothing about doing her schoolwork and even cheated. Her mother insisted that Erin complete her homework and spent hours working with her. Erin complained. The mother tried to be cheerful, frequently giving Erin warm hugs and assuring her that she was loved. Over time, however, the mother became increasingly irritated. It took all her self-discipline to avoid comparing Erin with her sister, who was a good student and highly motivated. The mother states, "The trouble with Erin is especially frustrating because for years I have given her my best efforts." She describes drilling Erin with flash cards and Erin's seemingly perverse efforts to frustrate the effort by knowingly giving wrong answers. The mother recounts the feeling of being "kicked in the teeth" and her feelings of helplessness.

Reaching out for help, Erin's mother attended a self-help workshop run by Warner and was encouraged to look more deeply into herself. This experience had considerable impact. She went through a personal change that altered how she saw the world. In reflecting on her relationship with Erin, she noted considerable self-deception in her protestations of love and concern and how she implicitly communicated her own negative feelings: "I was outwardly encouraging, but inwardly I mistrusted her. She felt that message from me."

With her new and more complex worldview, the mother took on a higher level of concern for her daughter: "I cried when I realized the price she had to pay for my inability to love her without reservation." With a new vision for the relationship, the mother stopped micromanaging it. Instead, she started modeling the importance of self-discipline, encouraging Erin to come to her for help when she was ready. The relationship dramatically changed. Erin began to perform well in school. Her mother reports a particularly interesting moment:

> But this time I pulled her up on my lap and looked at her, and I had this overwhelming feeling of love for her that just seemed to flow between us. I hugged her tightly, and told her how much I loved her. I realized that for the very first time in eight years, I was expressing true love for her. Previously, I had hugged her, but the love didn't flow. This time, the love just flowed. It was as if I was holding a new baby for the

first time. Tears were streaming down, and she looked at me and said, "Are you crying because you love me, Mommy?" I nodded. She whispered, "Mommy, I want to stay with you forever."

> "I realized that for the very first time in eight years, I was expressing true love for her. Previously, I had hugged her, but the love didn't flow. This time, the love just flowed. It was as if I was holding a new baby for the first time."

WHAT HAPPENED?

Some people read the story about Erin and her mother and say, "So the mother just withdrew and let her daughter make her own decisions. Is that the technique you are suggesting?" My answer is a resounding no! But if that is not it, what did occur here?

Read the story carefully. A mother (think "manager") defines a problem: the unwillingness of an eight year old to study. She describes the purity of her own motives, the logic of her strategy, the resistance in the change target, and the frustration she felt. These behaviors and feelings are common to people in the normal state. What happens next is not. It is uncommon and transformational.

The mother (manager) finds herself in a situation where she is able to lower her defenses and examine her motives, her thought processes, and her behaviors. She makes the discovery that she has been self-deceptive. Her motives have not been so pure, and her analysis of the problem has not been accurate. Because of her own negativity, her strategies for changing Erin were far more punitive than she could originally see. With her new vision, she enters the fundamental state of leadership, becoming more internally directed and externally open, purpose-centered, and other-focused. As a result, her behaviors changed, and the changed behaviors sent a new message to her daughter. These variations caused Erin to be more mindful. She had to pay attention and make sense of the new patterns. She interpreted the new behaviors accurately: she was no longer being judged as a problem. Now she felt loved. In the warmth and safety of that love, Erin found increased confidence and felt safe to experiment with new behaviors of her own.

At this point, the relationship was altered, and so were both Erin and her mother. Erin could now grow more effectively because her mother was growing more effectively. Her mother was growing more effectively because she had confronted and altered her self-deceptions. She had closed the gap between her script and the emergent reality in her life. She could now look beyond her interpretations of Erin's behaviors and relate to her daughter in the reality of the moment. Because she could better trust and love herself, she could better trust and love her daughter, and Erin responded accordingly.

This is the story of a transformational change. At first, the would-be change agent was behaving according to a script she carried in her head. In changing, she had to transcend her old script, and she became more authentically engaged with her daughter. This led to a new pattern of interaction. Erin now encountered a mother with a new self. She saw the doors opening to a more intimate kind of contact. She responded to this new opportunity, and mother and daughter became more richly connected than ever before. In this interaction, there were new feedback loops. The child began to change, and the mother continued to change. They reinforced each other. The relationship now consisted of two people who each had a sense of their own individuality and freedom to make their own choices within this new, more integrated system.

AUTHENTIC ENGAGEMENT

The situation involving Erin and her mother was transformed when the mother became more authentically engaged. Authentic engagement means being engaged in the world of action with love for what we are doing. That love usually comes from increased integrity. To increase integrity is to live a more principled life, to be more virtuous, to be a more authentic or real person. Here the emphasis is not on achieving a state of complete integrity; it is on gaining more integrity than we had before.

In many spiritual traditions, it is suggested that we find our integrity by withdrawing from the world: retreating to the nunnery or the Buddhist monastery or, like Jesus, to the wilderness. The assumption is that we become pure by withdrawing from the corruption of the world. As Thomas Merton discovered, the problem with this perspective, when taken alone, is that we may so cherish our integrity that we lose our connectedness. In attempting to maintain our purity, we may become unengaged, uncommitted, aloof, withdrawn, or detached.

The opposite of avoidance is engagement. A person who is engaged is involved, connected, and committed. A person who is too involved, however, may lose perspective and integrity. That person may become corrupted and compromised. This negative state is the opposite of integrity.

Once again, the challenge is to integrate highly differentiated positive values—to be at once principled and involved, virtuous and engaged, authentic and committed. As many spiritual traditions state, the challenge is to be "in the world but not of the world."

The tension between the positive values of integrity and engagement can be seen in Table 9.1. At the extreme left is the person who, in the name of integrity, has become uncommitted and unengaged. At the far right is the person who goes too far in being engaged with the world, losing his or her ethical rudder and becoming unprincipled and compromised. The transformational condition of authentic engagement is shown in the center column. Here, like Erin's mother, the person is both principled and engaged. This state was well described by Byrd and Chamberlain in *Willpower Is Not Enough*, where it was related to the concept of self-actualization:

Table 9.1. Authentic Engagement.

Negative	Positive	Integrative	Positive	Negative
This person is so principled and ethical as to be uncommitted and unengaged.	This person is principled and ethical.	This person practices authentic engagement.	This person is committed and engaged.	This person is so committed and engaged as to be unprincipled and unethical.
Self-righteous; withdrawn	Principled; integrated	Principled and engaged	Engaged; involved	Compromised; unprincipled

Authentic engagement: This person is principled and ethical while also involved and engaged. The person thus brings a more integrated, whole, or authentic self to his or her activity. When this happens, he or she experiences increased awareness and accesses resources not available in a less integrated state. The person loves what he or she does, which becomes a calling or labor of love.

Personal orientation: I continually close the gaps between my self-interests and the interests of the collective, thus bringing an evolving and authentic self to a passionately held, shared purpose. I am both principled and fully engaged. I love what I do. I practice authentic engagement.

Self-actualizing people are, without one single exception, involved in a cause outside their own skin, in something outside of themselves. They are devoted, working at something, something which is very precious to them—some calling or vocation in the old sense, the priestly sense. They are working at something which fate has called them to somehow and which they work at and which they love, so that the work-joy dichotomy in them disappears [pp. 29–30].

In other words, self-actualizing people are internally directed, other-focused, purpose-centered, and externally open. They have entered the fundamental state of leadership.

SELF-DECEPTION AND AUTHENTIC ENGAGEMENT IN THE EXECUTIVE EXPERIENCE

When I use illustrations like the one about Erin and her mother in talking to executives, they often recoil. The example is a story about family, they think, and does not apply at work. Here is a case that illustrates just how much the concept of authentic engagement does apply to the world of work, even at the highest levels of the organization.

Once a company president was attending my week-long Leading Change course. During the first three days of the course, he said very little. On Thursday morning, he asked if we might have lunch together. Over lunch, he told me that if he had attended my course any time in the past five years, he would have been wasting his time because he knew everything there was to know about leading change. He backed up this bold claim by explaining that he had successfully turned around two companies.

Then he acknowledged that he was now a lot more humble. There were five companies in his corporation. He had turned two of them around and was seen as the shining star among the corporate presidents. Six months before our talk, he had been told that he had earned the right to lead the largest company in the corporation when the current president retired in eighteen months. In the meantime, he had been asked to try his hand at one more turnaround. There was a company in the corporation that was considered hopeless. It had once commanded a large market share for its product. Now it had only a small percentage of the market and was still shrinking. Nobody believed this company could be turned around, so if he failed in his efforts, no one would hold it against him.

It had now been twelve months since he took on the challenge. He felt defeated. Everything that had worked for him before, everything his past had taught him, had failed. Morale was dismal. The numbers were dismal. The outlook for the future was dismal.

I asked him what he thought he would do next. On a paper napkin, he listed his short-term objectives. He began to draw an organizational chart. He described the people in each of the senior positions and the changes he was going to make in regard to each person on the chart. I found his answer unexciting. There was no engagement or passion in what he was telling me. If he thought he was genuinely committed to this challenge, he was deceiving himself. Yet it was clear that he was a man of character with a sincere desire to succeed. I took a deep breath and asked a hard question:

> What would happen if you went back and told those people the truth? Suppose you told them that you have been assigned as a caretaker for a year and a half. No one believes the company can succeed and no one really expects you to succeed. You have been promised the presidency of the largest company, and the plan is to put you into the plum job. You have, however, made a fundamental choice. You have decided to give up that plum job. Instead, you are going to stay with them. You are going to bet your career on them, and you invite them to commit all the energy and goodwill they can muster into making the company succeed.

I was worried that I might have offended him, and I half expected an angry response. He looked at me for a moment, and then it was his turn to take a deep breath. To my surprise and relief, he said, "That is pretty much what I have been thinking." He paused, and in that moment I watched him make the fundamental decision. Almost immediately, he picked up the napkin and started doing a reanalysis. He said, "If I am going to stay, then this person will have to go; this person will have to be moved over here; and this person . . ."

As he talked, there was an air of excitement in his words. His earlier plans to move on to the larger company were suddenly scrapped. He had made a fundamental choice to close off his exits and commit to the challenge before him, and as a result he had a new life stance, a new outlook, and a new way to behave. The organizational chart that had made sense a few moments before now made no sense at all. He had entered the state of authentic engagement, and he was seeing a new reality. None of the original problems had changed, but he had changed, and that made all the difference.

> *He had made a fundamental choice to close off his*
> *exits and commit to the challenge before him, and as*
> *a result he had a new life stance, a new outlook, and a*
> *new way to behave. The organizational chart that*
> *had made sense a few moments before now made no*
> *sense at all. He had entered the state of authentic*
> *engagement, and he was seeing a new reality.*

ENTERING THE FUNDAMENTAL STATE OF LEADERSHIP

Authentic engagement usually increases when we make a fundamental choice. The term *fundamental choice* comes from the work of Robert Fritz (1989). He tells us that a fundamental choice has to do with our state of being or our basic life orientation. It is a choice to live in a certain way. It is different from what he calls primary and secondary choices. Primary choices are about specific results. Secondary choices are about the means to achieve the results.

There are many people who have chosen the religious path (primary choice), without making the fundamental choice to live in accordance with their highest spiritual truths. There are many people who have chosen to be married (primary choice), without making the fundamental choice to live from within a committed relationship. . . . Fundamental choices are not subject to changes in internal or external circumstances. If you make the fundamental choice to be true to yourself, then you will act in ways that are true to yourself whether you feel inspired or depressed, whether you feel fulfilled or frustrated, whether you are at home, at work, with your friends, or with your enemies. . . . When you make a fundamental choice, convenience and comfort are not ever at issue, for you always take action based on what is consistent with your fundamental choice [Fritz, 1989, p. 193].

To make a fundamental choice is to enter the state of authentic engagement. To be authentic is to be genuine, actual, legitimate, true, real, pure, and uncorrupted. We become authentic by being true to what is highest in us. We do this by committing to live by principle, to do what is right even when it is not pleasurable. In the normal state, we flee pain and pursue pleasure. It is unnatural to do otherwise. Yet when we make fundamental commitments, we are choosing to be unnatural. We choose, if our commitment requires it, to embrace pain and sacrifice pleasure. We become positive deviants, extraordinary people.

The decision to increase our authenticity while remaining engaged has profound impacts. Note the sentence, "When people make a fundamental choice to be true to what is highest in them or when they make a choice to fulfill a purpose in their life, they can easily accomplish many changes that seemed impossible or improbable in the past." This is what we saw in the cases in Part One and again in the examples of Erin's mother and the company president in this chapter. When we enter the fundamental state of leadership, we can accomplish things we could not accomplish before. We can accomplish things that we were sure could not be accomplished.

PREPARATION FOR ENTERING THE FUNDAMENTAL STATE OF LEADERSHIP

Choose a quiet time when you can reflect on the meaning this chapter has for you. Begin by assessing where you are today, as honestly as you can.

Questions for Reflection

1. Check each item that describes you as you are today.

    __ I am fully engaged.

    __ I listen to my conscience.

    __ I am at peace with who I am.

    __ I have a feeling of increasing integrity.

    __ I am not really working for money but for the joy in what I do.

___ I love what I am doing.

___ I am fully involved with each task.

___ I am fully involved with the people around me.

___ I am present when people speak to me.

___ I energize others.

___ I am positive.

___ I am creative.

___ I am committed to the common good.

___ People experience me as having no personal agenda.

___ People experience me as authentic and sincere.

___ People tend to quickly trust me.

___ I keep my defenses down.

___ My words and my actions are congruent.

___ I am continually growing.

___ I help others to grow.

___ My work reflects my purpose in life.

2. Now assess yourself on the following scale by circling the number under the characteristics that currently describe you. Note that the "negative" areas of the scale represent the overemphasis of a positive characteristic so that it becomes a negative. The "integrative" part of the scale represents the integration of opposing positives. If you feel you model the integration of principled integrity and involved engagement, circle one of the numbers under "Integrative." Otherwise circle two numbers—one on each side of the scale.

Negative	*Positive*	*Integrative*	*Positive*	*Negative*
Self-righteous; withdrawn	Principled; integrated	Principled and engaged	Engaged; involved	Compromised; unprincipled
−3 −2 −1	1 2 3	4 5 4	3 2 1	−1 −2 −3

Self-Improvement

1. Based on the assessments you have completed, write a one-paragraph self-description on the theme of authentic

engagement. In your own words, describe where you are today with respect to this aspect of the fundamental state of leadership.

2. Write a strategy for self-improvement in the area of authentic engagement. Try to be as concrete as possible in describing steps you are willing to take beginning today.

Helpful Hints for Practicing Authentic Engagement

To maintain authentic engagement, you have to grow in integrity.

Know that everyone, including you, is by nature a hypocrite.

Deal with your hypocrisy by knowing it is destroying you and your relationships.

Understand that monitoring and reducing hypocrisy is your greatest source of power.

Take time every day to reflect on the match between your values and behaviors.

Monitor the level of vitality in your patterns of engagement.

Have a written set of operating principles, and keep rewriting them as you grow.

Carefully observe the political games, but refuse to play them.

Know that you must compromise while knowing what you will not compromise.

Challenge authority figures who stray from the collective good.

Find loving ways to support authority figures to find the courage they need.

Be ready to suffer for your integrity.

See that you encounter every person with authenticity and energy.

Remember that when we practice authentic engagement, we are full of enthusiasm.

Choose to live with faith, hope, and love.

Lead by example: do things you do not want to do.

Embrace reality by getting the feedback that most people are afraid to seek.

Take into account the needs of all the actors; then overlay the needs of the organization.

If you do not love what you are doing, ask why not.

Commit to keep reinventing yourself until your work becomes your calling.

Sharing Insights

If in responding to the questions above, you have an important insight or a meaningful story that you would like to share, visit www.deepchange.com and look for the links to submit stories for possible posting on the Deep Change Web site. You may thus help many people. If you would like to review such insights and stories, go to the same Web site.

CHAPTER TEN

Appreciative Inquiry

"It could be argued that all leadership is appreciative leadership. It's the capacity to see the best in the world around us, in our colleagues, and in the groups we are trying to lead. . . . It's the capacity to see with an appreciative eye the true and the good, the better and the possible."
—DAVID L. COOPERRIDER (CREELMAN, 2001)

In this chapter, we turn to the concept of appreciative inquiry. The term *appreciative inquiry* currently is used to describe a rapidly evolving transformational method, a form of intervention originated by David Cooperrider that is revolutionizing the field of organizational development. While I am using the term in a somewhat broader sense to describe a facet of the fundamental state of leadership, the concept presented here is a direct reflection of the intervention method that Cooperrider described. As a first illustration of both the method and the concept, consider the following story.

ASKING A TRANSFORMATIONAL QUESTION

Kurt Wright (1998) tells of working as a consultant for a huge software project that involved a $100 million government contract. There were four hundred engineers, and they were thirty-eight months into a sixty-month schedule. The technical requirements were highly complex, and the schedule slipped every month. The project was already eighteen months behind. Anxiety was reaching a peak because of a clause in the contract: a $30 million penalty if the contract was eighteen months behind at the forty-eighth month milestone. Disaster lurked a mere ten months in the future.

Pause and ask yourself how you would approach this situation. If you operate by normal logic, your list of ideas will reflect a single underlying assumption: there is a problem that needs to be solved. This, of course, is the underlying assumption in most organizational actions. Nearly every discussion is designed to identify and solve a problem. In fact, the single question that drives most organizational meetings is, "What is wrong, and how do we fix it?"

Wright says his objective was to change the foundation of the organization. He would do this by changing the meaning system, that is, the way people make sense or meaning of what they do. What was needed was to get every person operating on a new, positive vision. He needed to galvanize everyone's efforts. Wright believed that the key was to change the underlying question. From the perspective of the normal state, he made an absurd assumption: if he could simply find a good question, he could transform the organization and move it into the creative state.

The question had to be creative, outside the established logic of problem identification. It had to be engaging enough to "capture everyone's imagination and lead to *wholehearted* commitment" (p. 9). Such a question would not come from his thinking about it. It required that he engage in and trust an interactive process.

To get things started, Wright held a series of two-day retreats with eighteen to twenty engineers in each one. In the second week, the question he was seeking dawned on him: "What will it take to finish this project a week early?"

On the surface, this was a ridiculous question. The project was eighteen months behind as it was—that, according to the normal view, was the "problem." Yet Wright went about asking his new question of everyone.

Wright's behavior was not well accepted. After a time, angry managers began to summon him to their offices. They would explain that he was losing his credibility and was going to get himself into trouble. Each time, he thanked them for their concern. Then he went back into the halls and asked the same question.

What was the outcome? Wright finished his consulting work in six weeks, using only $90,000 of his $150,000 budget. Months later, the project finished on time and was $15 million under budget. Since the $30 million penalty was also avoided, Wright claims that his "ridiculous" question was worth $45 million.

In fact, Wright's question was brilliant. It disturbed the collective script. He does not share the details, but we know what must have happened. A very few people began to take his question seriously. They began to ask, What will it take for us to finish a week early? The question had captured their imaginations. It invited them to join one another on a journey of common commitment. In a spontaneous, informal manner, that commitment grew. Once that unspoken commitment reached a critical mass, the effort became self-organizing.

Wright's question was indeed transformational. Yet where did it come from? How did it arise?

The question emerged from the searching mind of a man who had entered the fundamental state of leadership. Notice that Wright did not do a complex rational analysis of the problems in the systems and structures. Instead, he simply searched for the right question. Yet how did he search? He held some retreats and engaged in dialogue until he discovered what he was looking for. He surrendered himself to being externally open. He practiced action learning. He then modeled the process of entering the fundamental state of leadership. He focused on his purpose even in the face of resistance, trusting his internal direction and remaining other-focused in putting the good of the company ahead of his own short-term gain. He modeled what he wanted the system to do.

Because he was externally open, purpose-centered, other-focused, and internally directed, Wright was able to draw on all of his integrated and expanding personal resources. When we live with increased integrity, our conscious and unconscious minds begin to integrate better. We seem to be given what we need in the very moment of need.

In this case, Wright accessed a transformational tool. Although his question seemed foolish, it tapped into the latent strengths of the organization. Instead of dwelling on everything that was going wrong and asking how it could be fixed, it changed a problem into a quest. As others were attracted to the quest, a new vision emerged that called forth the creativity needed to achieve it.

> *Although his question seemed foolish, it tapped into the latent strengths of the organization. Instead of dwelling on everything that was going wrong and asking how it could be fixed, it changed a problem into a quest.*

It is important to note that having discovered the power of changing the question, Wright reports that he never uses the same question in different situations. In each intervention, he seeks to become one with the system, to understand what assumptions are actually driving behavior, and then he waits for a new question to emerge that will change the assumptions. He does not try to repeat his own thinking or the thinking of anyone else. He searches for the unique question that will give rise to shared vision and the self-organizing processes that follow.

APPRECIATIVE INQUIRY

The example of Kurt Wright illustrates the practice of appreciative inquiry. To understand the tension that appreciative inquiry represents, consider the polarities of constructive optimism and realistic questioning (see Table 10.1). It is a positive value to be optimistic and constructive. Yet taken too far, these characteristics can cause us to become unrealistic and unquestioning. And although it is a positive value to be realistic and questioning (or analytic), these characteristics, if taken too far, can cause us to become pessimistic and destructive. The challenge is to be constructively optimistic at the same time that we are realistic and analytic.

This integrative state is what I mean by appreciative inquiry. In this state, we are grounded in reality; we are realistic and questioning. But

Table 10.1.   Appreciative Inquiry.

Negative	Positive	Integrative	Positive	Negative
This person is so optimistic as to become unrealistic and naive.	This person is optimistic and looks for what is constructive.	This person practices appreciative inquiry.	This person is analytic and questions surface assumptions.	This person is so analytic as to become pessimistic and destructive.
Unrealistic; unquestioning	Optimistic; constructive	Constructive and analytic	Realistic; questioning	Pessimistic; destructive

Appreciative inquiry: This person is optimistic and constructive while also being realistic and questioning. The person seeks to find the most enabling and constructive aspects of the current reality. Appreciative questions tap into the issues people care about most deeply and surface possibilities that have been outside their consciousness. In this way, they unleash energy and move self and others to a more creative state.

Personal orientation: I use questions to surface the most enabling past realities in myself and in others, thus initiating the dynamics of possibility, increased connectedness, and emergent organization. I thus integrate optimism and realism. I practice appreciative inquiry.

instead of being pessimistic and destructive, our analysis is highly optimistic and constructive. It is focused on what is good in the past and present and what is possible in the future. This is not a simple task.

Wright spent weeks doing retreats because he needed to listen deeply to hundreds of conversations. He was tapping the core of the culture, listening to the collective voice of the organization in order to access the essence of the existing system. In the process, he trusted his intuition to deliver that question about the future that would have transformational impact. As he walked up and down those hallways, tapping into the potential around him instead of focusing on the "problem," Wright was leading the organization. I suspect few of the executives realized this fact. In reflecting back on those days, I suspect they would tell the story of the turnaround without even mentioning Wright.

In the normal problem-solving state, the questions we ask are often discouraging. They limit us by focusing on everything that is "wrong" and by narrowing our attention to available "fixes." In contrast, appreciative inquiry is the kind of constructive questioning that surfaces what people care most about, inviting their commitment and releasing energy and creativity. The questions we ask in appreciative inquiry tap into everything that is right. They expand our consciousness and lead us collectively into the creative state. To David Cooperrider, this is the essence of leadership:

> It could be argued that all leadership is appreciative leadership. It's the capacity to see the best in the world around us, in our colleagues, and in the groups we are trying to lead. It's the capacity to see the most creative and improbable opportunities in the marketplace. It's the capacity to see with an appreciative eye the true and the good, the better and the possible [quoted in Creelman, 2001].

A RADICAL APPLICATION

Cooperrider and his colleagues have developed appreciative inquiry into a specific method of organizational development. Since our purpose here is to consider appreciative inquiry as a tool for getting into the fundamental state of leadership, I will not go into a discussion of the details of the Cooperrider method (for details, see Cameron, Dutton, and Quinn, 2003). Instead I will move to a most unusual application of the notion. Instead of thinking in terms of how to transform an organization, let us consider how we might apply appreciative inquiry so as to call forth and expand our own personal core. Consider an example.

Bert Whitehead is a financial adviser. A few years ago, two colleagues and I invited him to consult with us as we considered the possibility of launching a company. Bert is no ordinary finance guy. He defies all the stereotypes. That day was no exception. He began by telling us that if we were going to be entrepreneurs, we should run our lives so that we have 180 days a year free of any work obligations. That statement seemed absurd. We listened as he explained his philosophy.

Finally he got to his key point. He told us that all three of us were unique and masterful creators of value. He also explained that each of us was *incompetent* at some things and asked us to identify our areas of incompetence. We made our lists and presented them. Next, he said that we were each good to excellent at some things and asked us to identify those. We did. Then he said we each have some unique skills that we use to create value in extraordinary ways. He asked us to identify these, and we did, or at least we thought we did.

Bert then spent some time talking about how success breeds failure. He said we succeed because of the skills we have developed, but our success leads to new expectations. We get drawn away from our high-value-added activities and get trapped into doing things we are only good or even incompetent at doing. The key, he argued, is to structure our lives so that we are spending as much time as possible using our unique skills to create value.

We were just starting to agree with him and accept these ideas when he moved on to a shocking assertion. He told us the lists we had made of our unique skills were not any good. He told us that we were self-deceptive and could not trust our own lists. He then gave us a home-work assignment: we were to contact some of the people who know us best and ask them to help us identify our unique skills.

All three of us were uncomfortable with the assignment. I decided that if I was uncomfortable about it, it was probably worth doing.

After the meeting, I went home and made a list of about thirty-five people from different areas of my life: family members, long-time friends, and professional colleagues. Some came from the past, others from the present. They shared two characteristics: they all knew me well, and they would give me their honest opinions. I then sent them all e-mails explaining the assignment I had been given and asked them to share some feedback on how I most create value or what my unique, positive characteristics seem to be.

The responses started to roll in. I read them with great interest. In fact, I could not put them down. Some were very brief. Some were very long. Some told stories. I saved them all because they told me things about myself that I did not know. Those insights energized me in new ways.

I had often received formal feedback, but it was usually pretty su-perficial compared to what I was getting here. This feedback was rich, and it was focused on what people most valued about me. I found it almost overwhelming. Why? It was an intense form of appreciation. In reading what these people had written, I felt approved and received. I felt thanks and gratitude. I felt understood and that people were aware of the best parts of me. The feedback simultaneously humbled and up-lifted me; it made me want to be my best self as often as possible.

There was more. As I reflected on the responses, I was struck by something else when people gave examples of particular incidents: helping a woman understand her daughter, telling a story in a depart-ment meeting, teaching in a certain way, not getting mad at a woman for disagreeing with me, asking an angry administrator to tell us what we were doing wrong and thus opening honest communication. Most of these incidents I had long forgotten. Even when they occurred, I had not considered them particularly unusual. I was just doing what seemed like the natural thing to do at the time. I thought it strange that people would remember these incidents much later and place such great value on them.

There is another interesting thing. As I read through the statements, I noticed a great deal of overlap. People seemed to recognize my patterns of value creation in fairly consistent ways. This surprised me. People in very different contexts were seeing my best self in the same way.

A SEARCH FOR MY BEST SELF

Energized by the feedback I had been given, I took the responses and began an analysis. I pulled out all the descriptive statements and tried to organize them. I spent many hours creating categories. Gradually a structure began to emerge. In the language of appreciative inquiry, I was finding my positive core. Finally I boiled the analysis down to the following statement. Note that it is not a description of me in my normal state. It is a description of me when I am at my very best:

> In enacting my best self, I tend to be creative. I am enthusiastic about ideas and craft bold visions. I am an innovative builder who perseveres in the pursuit of the new. I do not waste energy thinking about missed opportunities or past failures nor do I take on the negative energy of the insecure nor do I worry about the critics. I do not waste energy in defensive routines. I stay centered and focus on what is possible and important.
>
> I have frameworks that allow me to make sense of complex issues. I get to the essence. I can see disparate ideas and integrate them through "yes, and" thinking. So I make points others do not readily see. I tend to be inner directed, so my message comes from an authentic level. I think deeply and speak with conviction. In doing so I frame experiences in compelling and engaging ways. I paint visions and provide new ways for people to see. I use metaphors and stories to do this. I find the stories in everyday experiences, and people find it easy to understand them. The new images that follow help people to take action.
>
> In helping others, I see the possibility for greatness in people. I calm them while I energize them. I help people identify their own core ideas, core emotions, and core values, and it has a catalytic effect on how they feel and think. They see new possibilities, and the excitement helps

them find the courage to act. I give them my attention and energy, but I allow them to be in charge.

In exercising influence, I do not try to think others into action. I try to enroll them in new directions. I do not try to sell but to invite people into my own journeys. In pursuing the journey, I seek reality. This means seeking honest dialogue. I do not get defensive or reject others if they are uninterested or otherwise minded. I make it clear that the relationship is more important than a conflict and that honest dialogue will improve things. At such times, I surrender my ego and invite criticism.

As a teacher and interventionist I do not seek to inform but to transform. I use dialogue to help people surface their ideas, and then I weave them together with others until we create knowledge in real time. In doing so, I move them from the abstract to the concrete and from the objective to the intimate. I ignore symptoms and focus on the deep causes. I ask piercing questions. I help people and groups surface the darkest realities and the most painful conflicts. From these emergent tensions comes the energy for transformation. I liberate people from their fears and help them embrace new paths. In all of this I try to model the message of integrity, growth, and transformation.

You might be offended by this description. You may feel that it is illegitimate for someone to talk about himself in this manner. You are right in that our culture normally forbids such expression.

Yet there was something about writing these statements that was unusually powerful for me. Previously I had made lots of assumptions about my strengths. Yet I had never asked anyone else how he or she saw my strengths. To do so had seemed unacceptable because to me it violated the norms of humility. What these people gave me in their statements was unusual and had a unique impact on me. Even now, I feel energized every time I reread their responses. The appreciation and love of the people making those comments seems to pull me out of my ordinary patterns. I become filled with energy and want to initiate new projects. I feel elevated and motivated.

There is another reason that this feedback was so powerful. It was not just that people were appreciating me. There was something else. The information provided was not about my ordinary, reactive self. Usually we focus on our weaknesses and failures. I tend to spend plenty of time seeing myself negatively. So do you. So does everyone else. When we do see ourselves negatively, our self becomes a problem to be solved. In contrast, this very personal information was about my successes and my contributions. It was about when I was adding value. All of this material gave me hints about my purpose and how I best enact my values. It pulled me into the realm of possibility and hope. It provided me with clues for making a greater and more positive difference in the world. This is exactly what appreciative inquiry does and why it is so much more powerful and liberating than our normal problem-solving mentality.

As powerful as the process of appreciative inquiry can be when it is applied to ourselves, I have become increasingly aware of some hidden incentives in our lives that work against it. Usually we use feedback about ourselves as a way of identifying problems so we can work on them. It is amazing how pervasive this problem-solving perspective is. We need to abandon that perspective to engage in appreciative inquiry. That is, we need to integrate analysis and questioning with optimism and constructive purpose.

There is another obstacle. When we begin to explore our positive core, the issue of humility comes up. Identifying the ways we do well is viewed as a form of bragging. It is prideful. What I am describing here is different. When I am prideful, when I brag about something, it is usually because I feel insecure. I feel the need to impress someone. I want them to admire me, and I am manipulating them. What I felt when I got the feedback from other people about what makes me unique was quite distinct from this type of hubris. Rather than increasing my self-focus, asking for and receiving feedback moved me further toward being focused on others. The feedback made me feel that I sometimes do make a positive difference. It also made me feel connected to other people. I could feel love and appreciation in the words I was reading. In that connection and love, I could feel a form of greatness—not greatness from within me but greatness moving through me.

Being humble is often associated with weakness or lack of power. Real humility comes when we see the world as it really is. The real world is a world of connectedness, of moving flows of power. When we transcend our own egos, when our outer self and our inner self connect, we experience increased integrity, increased oneness, and greater connectedness. At such moments, we feel greatness. Yet we recognize that the greatness does not emanate from within us, as we assume it does when we brag. It emanates from connectedness with resources outside our conscious self. Robert A. Johnson, a Jungian analyst, expresses this insight in writing about love: ". . . When I say that

'I love,' it is not I who love, but, in reality, Love who acts through me. Love is not so much something I do as something that I am" (1997, pp. 189–190).

> *Being humble is often associated with weakness or lack of power. Real humility comes when we see the world as it really is. The real world is a world of connectedness, of moving flows of power. When we transcend our own egos, when our outer self and our inner self connect, we experience increased integrity, increased oneness, greater connectedness. At such moments, we feel greatness.*

I think that is one of the things that "best-self" feedback demonstrates to the person who receives it. We contribute our greatest added value by doing the things that we do naturally when we are in caring relationships and in pursuit of a genuine purpose because we are connected to unconscious gifts.

ENTERING THE FUNDAMENTAL STATE OF LEADERSHIP

In recent years, I have taught the "best-self" process and had students engage in it. The outcomes are usually rewarding. One day I gave a talk to the support staff at the University of Michigan Business School. Two weeks later, I was in the cafeteria when a woman approached me and told me she had done the exercise, but with a wonderful twist. She first identified thirty people and contacted them. When they responded to her request for best-self feedback, she gave *them* unsolicited best-self feedback. She told me this usually led to an exchange and claimed she was having the most meaningful dialogues of her life. As she wiped away her tears, she looked up, smiled, and told me her husband had just announced that he too was going to engage in the exercise. This wonderful woman, who has a back-office staff job, was in the fundamental state of leadership. She was transforming herself, and others were following.

PREPARATION FOR ENTERING THE FUNDAMENTAL STATE OF LEADERSHIP

Choose a quiet time when you can reflect on the meaning this chapter has for you. Begin by assessing where you are today, as honestly as you can.

Questions for Reflection

1. Check each item that describes you as you are today.

___ I am optimistic and constructive.

___ I am realistic and questioning.

___ I know my mission in life.

___ I know my own greatest strengths.

___ I can explain the unique ways in which I create value.

___ I continually integrate my potential with changing external reality.

___ I spend little time in the reactive state.

___ I search for the potential in every situation.

___ I trust my intuition to provide me with transformational questions.

___ I pull others into the constructive creative state.

___ I ask questions designed to appreciate and surface potential.

___ I ask such questions even when they make people uncomfortable.

___ I capture people's imaginations.

___ I align people with a powerful purpose.

___ I help people find compelling strategic intent.

___ I encourage people to transcend old, collective scripts.

___ I encourage people to connect, cooperate, and co-create.

___ I seek to stimulate the process of emergent organizing.

2. Now assess yourself on the following scale by circling the number under the characteristics that currently describe you. Note that the "negative" areas of the scale represent the overemphasis of a positive characteristic so that it becomes a negative. The "integrative" part of the scale represents the integration of opposing positives. If you feel you model the integration of constructive optimism and realistic questioning, circle one of the numbers under "Integrative." Otherwise circle two numbers, one on each side of the scale.

Negative	Positive	Integrative	Positive	Negative
Unrealistic; unquestioning	Optimistic; constructive	Constructive and analytic	Realistic; questioning	Pessimistic; destructive
−3 −2 −1	1 2 3	4 5 4	3 2 1	−1 −2 −3

Self-Improvement

1. Based on the assessments you have completed, write a one-paragraph self-description on the theme of appreciative inquiry. In your own words, describe where you are today with respect to this aspect of the fundamental state of leadership.

2. Write a strategy for self-improvement in the area of appreciative inquiry. Try to be as concrete as possible in describing steps you are willing to take beginning today.

Helpful Hints for Practicing Appreciative Inquiry

Practice appreciative inquiry on yourself.

Identify your best value creation patterns.

Explore your own peak performance episodes.

Write a statement describing your best self.

Write a "life statement" that defines who you are and where you are going.

Return to your life statement often.

Continually connect your best-self past with your best-self future.

Live with high purpose.

Continually integrate reality with possibility.

Remember that the objective is to surface optimism founded in reality.

Always insist on dealing with reality.

Recognize that there is both a positive and a negative reality.

Focus on clarifying the result that needs to be created.

Recognize that there is untapped energy in every person, relationship, and system.

Remove yourself from the expert role and take the role of positive inquirer.

Ask questions directed at surfacing that which is most valued and most loved.

Encourage people to contemplate the best of their past.

Encourage people to interview one another and share the good they see in the relationship or organization.

While debriefing the interviews, help them to articulate and capture the positive.

Allow them to spontaneously organize and pursue the desired future.

Let go of your fears and your need to control. Trust the process.

The group will lead itself better than you can manage it.

Sharing Insights

If in responding to the questions above, you have an important insight or a meaningful story that you would like to share, visit www.deepchange.com and look for the links to submit stories for possible posting on the Deep Change Web site. You may thus help many people. If you would like to review such insights and stories, go to the same Web site.

CHAPTER ELEVEN

Grounded Vision

Even when a vision seems to come from the leader, as in the case of Gandhi, the vision moves others because it is deeply in touch with their reality and their hopes. That is why they respond. And the vision is credible because they can see that it is not a castle in the air, but a vision that is grounded in their lived experience, in bread and salt.

Appreciative inquiry allows us to surface the positive core in a human system and in ourselves. In so doing, we unleash hope. Here we consider a complement to appreciative inquiry: grounded vision.

FINDING THE BREAD AND SALT

Over the past twenty years, most organizations have become more tumultuous, creating greater uncertainty for everyone inside them. When uncertainty increases, so does the need for vision. In the face of uncertainty and change, people need a meaning system that allows them to connect and move forward in a productive way. Yet most organizations suffer from a lack of vision. I remember a visit I made to a large company. A task force composed of the company's top executives had been given three months to generate a vision statement. I met with the members of this group and read the nearly completed statement. They asked me what I thought of their vision. I simply responded, "Who is willing to die for this vision?" No one spoke up. My question had surprised them and made them somewhat uncomfortable. Why? Because as a politically segmented group, they had executed an exercise in rational compromise and forged some abstract generalities into a statement to which no one could object. They did not generate a document with power.

I also know an executive who heard middle managers regularly claim that they did not know the company vision. After some time, he met with his top management team and spent several days coming up with a statement of the company's vision and values. They then put the vision and values on plastic cards and distributed them to every employee. Within a week, the message circulated again: "We don't know the vision." Finally, in frustration, the executive turned to one of his vice presidents and said, "Go tell them to stop saying that."

I tell this story not in derision but with empathy. I have tried to convey a vision to others. It was a frustrating experience. It is much easier to focus on solving today's problems than it is to mold the future. It is easier to be an operational analyzer and taskmaster than it is to be a person of grounded vision. Yet how does one find a vision?

When I encounter the yearning for vision in a organization, it often leads to a discussion with the senior leaders. Frustrated, they show me their official vision documents and ask me why they are not effective. Sometimes I respond by saying that their documents do not reflect bread and salt. I then share with them a story from the movie *Gandhi.*

In the early part of his career, Mohandas Gandhi successfully confronted some forms of discrimination in South Africa. When his work was completed, he returned home to India. Although he was encouraged to become involved in politics, he instead went on a long journey through his homeland. His travels led him through the countryside, where he visited many villages and farms. Gandhi endured many unpleasant conditions as he patiently listened to the peasants and observed their surroundings.

Shortly after, a political convention was held. The country's top politicians attended and gave rousing speeches calling for home rule and expulsion of the British. The audience was largely in agreement and loudly expressed support. Finally, the unpretentious Gandhi was given a chance to speak. When he was introduced, people left their seats and began to wander around the convention floor. They were not interested in this small stranger.

Gandhi began his low-key speech by talking about the "real" India. The issue facing India, he argued, was not about home rule. The citizens of India did not really care who was ruling the country. What they did care about was bread and salt. Unless the politicians understood the issues of bread and salt, which they did not, the voters would simply be replacing British tyrants with Indian tyrants.

> *The issue facing India, Gandhi argued, was not about home rule. The citizens of India did not really care who was ruling the country. What they did care about was bread and salt.*

As Gandhi continued speaking, people gradually returned to their seats and began to listen because they were hearing something unusual—and something of great importance. This small, unassuming man had journeyed through their heartland and captured the essence of India. He was now vocalizing it in a way they could feel and understand. Such articulation is often at the heart of radical, deep change.

The term *radical* is derived from the Latin word for root. In mathematics, for example, we use the radical sign to indicate the square root. To make radical change, one must move to the root—the origin or archetype. An influential vision reflects the insight of an individual or group that has deeply contemplated the core issues. Gandhi's vision was such a reflection. It was rooted in both facts and values. It inspired passion.

A visionary leader delves into the core of the organization or group and touches the issues of bread and salt. Few senior executives ever do so. They are thus greatly hindered in the process of aligning the operational present with the developmental future.

It is sometimes difficult to touch the issues of bread and salt because of the upward filtering process in the organization. Almost every message an executive receives from subordinates is finely filtered and highly polished. In a hierarchy, we seldom really know what is going on below us. Sometimes we are uncomfortable being around "the masses." I remember hearing stories about particular auto executives who could not stand to be in meetings with auto dealers whom they called "slimy." Similar snobbishness exists in most large organizations. As people thus dissociate, the organization disintegrates. In the midst of this slow death process, everyone continues to act as if there is a healthy organization. This deception allows everyone to avoid the work of entering the fundamental state of leadership.

Isolated and insulated people cannot succeed in motivating others. When they finally generate a vision document, its message will be frail and uninspirational. Usually the "walk" of such people will not match their "talk," and the real message is clear. Nothing happens, and the vision document soon slides into decay and obsolescence.

A powerful vision does not emanate from the solitary musings of the supposed leader. Nor does it reflect only the "leader's" conception of the future. A vision that truly enlists and inspires others wells up from their deep needs and aspirations. Often, as we shall see, the way to achieve such a vision is by working with and through the people for whom it is intended. Even when a vision seems to come from the leader, as in the case of Gandhi, the vision moves others because it is deeply in touch with their reality and their hopes. That is why they respond. And the vision is credible because they can see that it is not a castle in the air, but a vision that is grounded in their lived experience, in bread and salt.

GROUNDED VISION

I think of a visit I made to large bank that was in crisis. The CEO stood up and articulated a list of devastating events and external pressures. The feeling was very dark, and the possibility of organizational death was real. A person in the audience raised his hand and asked, "What is your vision?" The CEO responded, "The stock price at this time next year will be forty dollars." There was an embarrassing silence. The people looked at each other in disbelief. The CEO seemed not to notice that he had just destroyed their last glimmer of hope.

A stock price of forty dollars is indeed an image of the future. It is even a grounded image in that it is a measurable thing. Yet it is not grounded in the present reality of the people, in the emotional facts of their current situation. It is not a vision that they can feel in their bones and commit to.

At that moment, this man needed to have his people reorganize. They needed an emergent process. They need to engage in new behaviors. They needed a form of hope that would allow them to connect with each other in new ways. They needed to build a new bridge and do it while they were walking on it. For this process to happen, they needed someone, anyone, to be in the fundamental state of leadership.

The CEO was far from this state. When he most needed to have a grounded vision, he had none. What he offered produced the exact opposite of what was needed. Instead of generating hope, he generated increased fear, depression, and inaction.

In times of transition a grounded vision is essential. We practice grounded vision when we integrate the present with an image of a positive future. The creative tension can be seen in Table 11.1. It is a positive quality to be hopeful and visionary, yet if this is taken too far, we become ungrounded and deluded. Similarly, it is positive and necessary to be grounded and factual, but if this is taken too far, we become visionless and bereft of hope. The challenge is to have a grounded, positive image of the future. A grounded image is an image that people cannot only see but feel, believe, commit to, and act on.

A CEO FINDS A VISION

We have considered a situation in which there was high uncertainty and the CEO was unable to provide a grounded vision. Now consider a similar case with a very different outcome.

Table 11.1.   Grounded Vision.

Negative	Positive	Integrative	Positive	Negative
This person is so visionary as to be ungrounded and deluded.	This person conceptualizes a compelling and hopeful vision of the future.	This person practices grounded vision.	This person is grounded in the facts of current reality.	This person is so grounded in the facts of the past and present as to be without hope or vision.
Ungrounded; deluded	Visionary; hopeful	Grounded and visionary	Grounded; factual	Visionless; hopeless

Grounded vision: This person is grounded and factual while also hopeful and visionary. The person conceptualizes and communicates a future that emerges from the realities of the existing system. The integration of reality and possibility creates an image that attracts self and others outside the comfort zone and into a state of active creation.

Personal orientation: I use conceptual images of the future embedded in the language and facts of the past to help myself and others recognize the reality that life is a continuous stream of change, and I seek to empower myself and empower others in shaping an emerging future. I thus integrate fact and hope, past and future. I practice grounded vision.

One large company I am familiar with had a long record of financial success. But when the economy turned bad, the company began to struggle. A new president was elected, and the federal government began to initiate policies that had devastating impacts. The company's financial performance then began to deteriorate rapidly. Everything that had made the company successful was now in question. The organization's people were frustrated. They were looking for a new vision from their new CEO. But despite a great personal effort, the CEO declared that he had no new vision statement.

In the light of the deteriorating situation, the company's top management decided that an immediate intervention was necessary. I was one of several professors who were brought in to design a program. Our top priority was to see that the company confronted and resolved real issues. Yet in this company, there was seldom any kind of public conflict. This made the design of our intervention difficult.

We decided on a series of four week-long meetings. Each week-long session would be held with one hundred of the company's top executives—four hundred in all. The proposed intervention would begin with introductory presentations on finance and strategy. Then there would be a number of discussions of the issues facing the company.

The CEO attended the first meeting. We advised him to listen to everything but to say very little, even when he knew that certain statements were not factual. It was a time for others to speak and feel safe. He needed to listen.

During the week, the exchange of ideas and opinions was intense and constructive. My colleagues encouraged the participants to speak candidly. For the first few days, the CEO was blamed for nearly every problem. Gradually, however, the tone of the sessions began to change. People began to look closely at themselves and to assume some responsibility for the organization's undiscussable issues.

The final session of the first week-long meeting was a speech by the CEO. Despite the fact that he still had no vision for the corporation, he conveyed empathy for his listeners' struggles. This alone was a step forward, and the speech was well received.

Subsequently, the CEO made an interesting decision. He cleared his calendar and allocated three weeks to attending the three remaining sessions. On the Friday of the third week, he stood up and told the group he had a vision. The faculty was stunned. He proceeded to analyze the company's dependence on research and development and the general failure of that function. He called his vision the billion-dollar challenge. He said he wanted to move a billion dollars into R&D, and he wanted it from the budgets of the people in the room.

Many of us assume that when a CEO makes such a demand, people respond. This is not true. In most cases, so challenging a demand is met with passive resistance. Yet in this case, the people came up with the billion dollars. The reason they did is that this CEO had found the bread and salt of his organization. He had squarely confronted the reality that people were living, and they recognized it. The problems in R&D were indeed the most central block to making the transformation that the emergent world was imposing on this company.

But how did the CEO find this bread and salt? For three weeks, he had listened to people complain, moan, and fight over key issues. In the process of listening, he heard the inner voice of the organization. The inner voice always exists beneath all of those self-interested conversations. If we do the work to listen, we will hear it.

ENTERING THE FUNDAMENTAL STATE OF LEADERSHIP

I was once invited to a church meeting at which a family was making a presentation. I was particularly interested when I listened to the teenage daughter. In the middle of her talk, she held up a large, framed document and said, "This is our family vision. Whenever we have contention or if we have to make a decision, we go back and read it, and then we know what to do." She read the vision. I thought it unusual for a family to have a vision and later asked her father about it. Her father, Rick DeVries, a bank president at the time, told me that the family vision had its roots in an experience he had had at work.

When he had first arrived in Ypsilanti, Michigan, Rick could see enormous potential for moving his branch banks forward. He believed that if he could better align his branches with the opportunities emerging in the local economy, they could make a lot more money. Yet his employees did not seem connected to such notions, and so he knew that he had to change the culture of the branches. He talked with his people about the potential he saw, but nothing seemed to change. The manager who was directly over the first-line people, or personal bankers, seemed to have particular difficulty catching the vision of what might be possible. Rick tried to help her set meaningful goals, but the process did not lead to change. There was no tangible connection, no profound contact between the present and the future.

One day in a meeting, it dawned on him to try something new. He asked everyone to close their eyes. In very concrete terms, he described the branch that he saw as it was at that time. Next, he asked them to imagine that they were walking into the best branch bank in the world. He asked, "What do you see?" Each person was asked to share his or her mental picture. He recorded what each person said. Then he went into his office and wrote down what he had just heard in a two-page document integrating their various views on what an ideal branch is like. His statement described what the customer experienced as he or she walked in. It described what the facility looked like. It described what each employee was doing. The two pages contained an image of an ideal future that was grounded. It was something the people could understand, own, and act on. It was something that could guide their behavior as they tried to make contact between the present and the future, the actual and the potential.

When Rick shared his statement with the staff, it particularly influenced the key manager, who had been struggling to understand what Rick was trying to tell her. She now understood and became excited and committed. The staff provided additional feedback about the vision, and Rick made appropriate adjustments. Slowly but steadily, things began to move forward.

Notice that in this simple process, Rick was doing the same thing that the CEO did when he finally announced the billion-dollar challenge. Rick was not dictating an abstract vision from on high. He was interacting with his people so that together, they were creating meaning. Eventually they articulated a vision that was grounded in the lived experience and the hopes of everyone involved.

> *Rick was not dictating an abstract vision from on high. He was interacting with his people so that together, they were creating meaning. Eventually they articulated a vision that was grounded in the lived experience and the hopes of everyone involved.*

This process had a profound impact on Rick's people and on Rick. He was struck by how much difference it made. He found himself often contemplating what had happened, and he talked about it a great deal. When he told his peers about it, they showed only limited interest. This baffled him. Yet that is consistent with my experience: people are not anxious to deal with grounded vision. Most people resist deep clarification of purpose; they prefer to spend their time problem solving. Engaging in problem solving requires less accountability, less personal authenticity. This is another way in which people prefer the process of slow death. They are not anxious to enter the fundamental state of leadership, in which they leave their comfort zone and put themselves on the line. People are not naturally drawn to build the bridge as they walk on it. Someone must show the way.

I began this story by saying that Rick's experience led to a fundamental change in his own home. Rick and his wife have five children. Raising a family of that size is a challenge. On one particularly contentious day, it struck him that what had worked at the bank might work at home. He told his family that on that night, he would like to hold a family meeting. When the time came, he put on some music, arranged some snacks on the table, and called them together. He told them he had played a game at the bank and that he would like to play it with the family. He then asked the family to close their eyes. From that exercise came the vision that his daughter held up in church and that she said guided the family in times of contention. Rick had entered the state of leadership, and his family was following.

PREPARATION FOR ENTERING THE FUNDAMENTAL STATE OF LEADERSHIP

Choose a quiet time when you can reflect on the meaning this chapter has for you. Begin by assessing where you are today, as honestly as you can.

Questions for Reflection

1. Check each item that describes you as you are today.

   __ I analyze the emotional facts in my organization.

   __ I envision what is possible.

   __ I understand that everyone prefers to stay inside his or her zone of comfort.

   __ I understand the power of potent visual images.

__ I realize that radical change requires connecting with root issues.

__ I continually monitor the concerns of my people.

__ I continually surface their fears, hopes, and dreams.

__ I pay attention to the unexpressed needs that are beneath the existing conflicts.

__ I mold visions that people feel, understand, and respond to.

__ I go to great lengths to see that I live the values I advocate.

__ I understand that a vision is not announced but co-created.

__ I insist on accurately monitoring progress.

__ I understand that most executives do not want a real vision.

2. Now assess yourself on the following scale by circling the number under the characteristics that currently describe you. Note that the "negative" areas of the scale represent the overemphasis of a positive characteristic so that it becomes a negative. The "integrative" part of the scale represents the integration of opposing positives. If you feel you model the integration of hopeful vision and a grounded, factual approach, circle one of the numbers under "Integrative." Otherwise circle two numbers, one on each side of the scale.

Negative	Positive	Integrative	Positive	Negative
Ungrounded; deluded	Visionary; hopeful	Grounded and visionary	Grounded; factual	Visionless; hopeless
−3 −2 −1	1 2 3	4 5 4	3 2 1	−1 −2 −3

Self-Improvement

1. Based on the assessments you have completed, write a one-paragraph self-description on the theme of grounded vision. In your own words, describe where you are today with respect to this aspect of the fundamental state of leadership.

2. Write a strategy for self-improvement in the area of grounded vision. Try to be as concrete as possible in describing steps you are willing to take beginning today.

Helpful Hints for Practicing Grounded Vision

Reality without vision destroys possibility; vision without reality destroys credibility.

Recognize that excellence does not derive from problem solving.

Focus on the result you want to create.

Be sure you are willing to sacrifice for the desired result.

Recognize that your integrity around the vision is being continuously examined.

Be sure the final result is attractive enough that people are willing to fail to get there.

Produce a film in your mind of the group achieving the desired result.

Keep playing and editing the film; describe the film to others.

Focus everyone on the desired future.

Do not explain the desired future. Help people see, feel, hear, and taste it.

Gain a deep understanding of the history of the unit and the people in it.

Ground the future in the past.

To enlist people in the quest, show them how they have been on such journeys before.

Tell stories that bring the vision to life.

Communicate visual images that capture the imagination.

Listen carefully to the arguments of resistance. Hear the deeper messages.

Transform the deeper fears by surfacing and exploring them.

Model the process by surfacing your own fears.

Never flee from the pain of reality.

Help people relate the pain of change to the big picture.

Continuously identify, surface, and discuss the realities of what is happening.

Recognize the factual constraints.

Show which constraints must be accepted and which must be transcended.

You do not have to have answers to the problems. Just keep focusing on the result.

Trust the process of honest dialogue and keep learning.

Focus on the early small wins, and celebrate when they are accomplished.

Sharing Insights

If in responding to the questions above, you have an important insight or a meaningful story that you would like to share, visit www.deepchange.com and look for the links to submit stories for possible posting on the Deep Change Web site. You may thus help many people. If you would like to review such insights and stories, go to the same Web site.

CHAPTER TWELVE

Adaptive Confidence

The practice of adaptive confidence means that we are willing to enter uncertain situations because we have a higher purpose and we are confident that we can learn and adapt as we move forward.

E veryone avoids deep change because deep change is terrifying. It is terrifying because it requires letting go of control. It requires moving into a state of action learning. Action learning is not like classroom learning. It is far more demanding. To successfully engage the process, we have to practice something called adaptive confidence.

A WOMAN WITH PURPOSE

I once sat next to a woman on a plane. She began to tell me about herself. Brought up in a blue-collar home, she had eventually become a salesperson and after a long period of struggle began to have extraordinary success. She told me of the struggle. She worked long hours and put herself in every sales presentation setting she could. Her failures greatly outnumbered her successes, yet she persisted. She kept putting herself in the terrible position of discomfort. I asked her why. She indicated that she was convinced she could learn her way to success. In telling me her story, she did not say much at all about the pain of failure. It was as if it did not matter.

Then she described what she did. She deeply analyzed every inter-action with customers. Over time, she identified patterns and ran con-tinual informal experiments to test her conclusions. Eventually she developed an inductive theory of selling that was based on principles of discipline and accountability. For example, she believed that she should know everything there is to know about the customer before she ever went in, and she described the extraordinary lengths she went to in order to live this principle. As she described such principles and practices, it suddenly became clear why she was so successful: she was operating at a level of discipline that few salespeople ever think about.

She laughed as she told me, "My peers take bagels to the customer, thinking they can bribe their way to a sale." I asked her if she ever shared her theory with her peers. She replied, "I have tried, but they do not want to hear what I am telling them. They find it much easier to keep buying the bagels."

As I thought about her story, it struck me that this was a woman who knew what it meant to practice reflective action and live in au-thentic engagement. She was continually working, but she was also continually deeply analyzing everything she did. She integrated action and reflection. From her analysis came powerful insights and a per-sonal theory of practice.

Yet this woman was also practicing another transformational dis-cipline. It became clear as she shared an intimate story.

She told me she had been in an abusive marriage. After seven years, she had decided to walk out. It was a terrifying thing for her to do. She indicated that in her neighborhood, there are many women in abu-sive marriages who stay in the relationship rather than face the un-certainty of being on their own. I was very struck by this and thought about how natural it is for us to cling to that which we know, even at the most punishing costs. We all seek to keep ourselves in our com-fort zone. We all tend to live in the reactive, problem-solving state.

Then she told me that a few women do leave, but most of them can only think about getting out of the terror, so they quickly get married again, often to another abusive man. This also impressed me. Just leav-ing the comfort zone is not enough. Why? I thought about executives who quit a job in disgust and go to another company. After some months, they often begin to experience the same problems. What they cannot see is that they are the carriers of the disease they so hate. They claim the disease is "out there" in the organizational community. In fact, the disease is in them.

Because we all tend to project our problems onto the world, it is not enough for us to just leave the comfort zone. Something else is also required. Using a most unusual example, this woman was about to illustrate the requirement.

She told me that she did a lot of dating. Many of the men she dated were "high rollers" who did not hesitate to spend two hundred dollars on a bottle of wine. She said it would have been easy to be impressed, but she stayed grounded. In fact, she said that she had developed rules to guide her. For example, she would not date a man a second time unless he offered to pay for her babysitter the first time. Then she said, "He did not have to pay for the babysitter, but he did have to offer."

Given the norms of our day and the obvious strength of this woman, I could not comprehend what she was telling me and shared my confusion. She said, "If he offered to pay, that meant he *saw me.* He did not see a sex object, he *saw me,* the human being in my unique situation."

Suddenly it all clicked.

This woman had experienced the pain of an abusive marriage. In leaving that marriage, she was not fleeing the pain. That is the natural thing to do. She was pursuing a purpose. She was willing to leave what she knew and enter the state of terrifying uncertainty. She would not rush back to the comfort zone with the first man who had resources and showed interest. She intended to create an abundant life with someone. She knew that this required finding a man who was capable of living in an effective relationship. She also knew that it required her to build the bridge as she walked on it, learning and growing as she moved forward. In the process, she would become a more capable and authentic human being, one able to co-create the kind of relationship she envisioned.

Her rules were brilliant. They were a counterintuitive set of guidelines that would help her stay the course, to remain in the anxiety of

---

Her rules were brilliant. They were a counterintuitive set of guidelines that would help her stay the course, to remain in the anxiety of uncertainty while pushing ahead in the process of real-time learning. . . . She was a practitioner of adaptive confidence.

---

uncertainty while pushing ahead in the process of real-time learning. Just as she had an intuitive, inductive theory of selling, she had an intuitive, inductive theory of personal transformation. She was a practitioner of adaptive confidence.

ADAPTIVE CONFIDENCE

The creative tension that is adaptive confidence can be seen in Table 12.1. It is a positive value to be adaptive and flexible, yet if that characteristic is taken too far, we become uncertain and insecure. To be confident and secure is similarly a positive value, and yet if that characteristic is taken too far, we become rigid and inflexible. The challenge is to be both adaptive and confident. The practice of adaptive confidence means that we are willing to enter uncertain situations because we have a higher purpose and we are confident that we can learn and adapt as we move forward.

The concept of adaptive confidence is a marriage between confidence and flexibility. Being flexible means being open to learning and change. People with adaptive confidence understand that the most powerful

Table 12.1.   Adaptive Confidence.

Negative	Positive	Integrative	Positive	Negative
This person is so adaptive as to be dependent and weak, without the strength to move forward.	This person is adaptive and flexible.	This person practices adaptive confidence.	This person is confident and secure.	This person is so confident as to be rigid and inflexible, incapable of learning.
Uncertain; insecure	Adaptive; flexible	Adaptive and confident	Confident; secure	Rigid; inflexible

Adaptive confidence: This person is adaptable and flexible while also confident and secure. The person has the confidence to learn from experience, moving forward into uncertain situations knowing that self and others can adapt and learn in real time. He or she maintains a focus on purpose while experimenting and remaining open to feedback about failure as well as success.

Personal orientation: I exhibit the confidence to enter uncertainty, knowing that I, and others, will successfully evolve to more complex levels of order through improvisational trial-and-error learning. I thus model a sense of security and confidence in the midst of risky adaptation. I am both secure and flexible. I practice adaptive confidence.

learning is found in improvisation. They are secure enough to push forward into uncertainty while seeking feedback on their successes as well as their failures. Instead of being frozen by uncertainty and doubt, they can move forward in most situations, taking initiative while remaining open to feedback and learning while they move. They are simultaneously stable and changing. They live in a positive, creative tension with their changing environment.

MONITORING OUR HYPOCRISY

Bill Torbert (1987) has written about confidence. He argues that most forms of professional knowledge result in conditional confidence—confidence that we will act well as long as the situation does not violate our assumptions about it. In other words, all of us are trained in our jobs and professions. We learn what to do in a given situation. We learn how to be in control. If the situation changes, we are not in control. This usually leads to panic. Most people live to be in control, to be in their comfort zone. Yet if we want to be adaptable to changing circumstances, we must learn how to move outside our comfort zone.

Torbert claims that the alternative to conditional confidence is unconditional confidence. I consider it synonymous with adaptive confidence. According to Torbert, unconditional confidence means that we are capable of discarding inaccurate assumptions and ineffective strategies even in the midst of an ongoing action. We are confident enough to act and humble enough to learn at the same time. Torbert also has a recommendation on how to develop such confidence. He says unconditional confidence increases as our integrity increases and that we increase integrity *by* constantly monitoring our lack of integrity.

I find this a very striking observation. As I have remarked previously in this book, we are all hypocrites. We all have values we do not live. We also have enormously powerful mechanisms for denial. We refuse to see our hypocrisy. Yet seeing our hypocrisy is the potential motor of change. When we engage our hypocrisy, there is so much pain that we are often willing to begin to close our integrity gaps. When we do, we exercise the courage to change. We finally leave a particular comfort zone and begin a process of transformation. Now we can move forward with confidence, whereas before, we were prisoners of our own need to be in control. Instead of fearing uncertainty, we welcome it.

I believe that many people have experienced adaptive confidence but do not realize it. That is why in the invitation to reflective action, I asked my son Shawn to examine the transformational moments in his own past, as I described in Chapter Eight. I believed he would recognize that he had been transformational in the past and could be in the future.

If you truly excel in an area, it is likely that you have practiced adaptive confidence. The woman I spoke with on the plane excelled in sales because she spent time moving forward in the face of uncertainty and learning from her failures. She thus internalized new competencies—competencies that others do not have. She was able to sell far more in far less time than others. She was a master. She could go into any situation and create as she moved forward in the conversation. Her theory of sales was actually a theory of co-creation of shared learning and discovery. She was focused on the good of the client and looking to create a win-win result.

THE CAPACITY TO LEARN IN REAL TIME

In the language of this book, adaptive confidence is the capacity to walk naked into the land of uncertainty and build the bridge as we walk on it. Consider an extreme example.

I once attended a professional meeting in which Warren Bennis, a noted leadership scholar, showed a video clip of an interview he had conducted with the former president of a Quaker college. Because it was a Quaker institution, a core value of the college was nonviolence. In the middle of the interview, the president talked of a particularly important moment in his tenure.

It was the height of the Vietnam War. Protests were frequent, and they often turned violent. The fatal shooting of the students at Kent State had already occurred. Word came to the president that a group of his students were going to hold a protest. They were going to take down the American flag and burn it. He also heard that his football team had gathered around the flagpole to prevent the burning.

Imagine his feeling at that moment. Nonviolence, a core value of his institution, is about to be violated. He wants to preserve that value and prevent the conflict from taking place. What would you do in this situation?

Most people would suggest taking control, perhaps calling in security and a large police backup. Yet all such alternatives are likely to increase the probability of conflict and violence. Another normal reaction is to accept the reality that conflict happens and withdraw. Stay out of it, and let nature take its course. There are many arguments that could be made for that alternative.

So what did the college president do? He walked out of his office and toward the flagpole. He had no intended strategy. He did not know what to do. He felt helpless and vulnerable, but he knew that to be true to himself, he had to go to the flagpole and try to enact the value for which he and the institution stood.

At that moment, he was exercising adaptive confidence. He was moving forward into uncertainty not knowing what he was going to do. Because he lived in authentic engagement and because he was willing to put the good of the institution ahead of his own well-being, he moved forward. He would learn and adapt in real time.

THE REST OF THE STORY

In the interview, the president appears to be a strong-minded man. Yet as he comes to this moment in the story, he begins to weep. He says that as he arrived on the tumultuous scene, he heard a voice say to him, "Tell them to wash the flag."

He turned to the demonstrators and said, "Why don't you get a box of detergent and a bucket of water and wash the flag. Then when it is clean, run it back up the flagpole." Both the demonstrators and the football players found this to be an acceptable option. The flag was washed and put back up.

This was one of those moments of inspiration that often occur when we are in the state of authentic engagement and are moving forward in adaptive confidence. The initiator or leader articulates an image that transcends differences. It is a moment of extraordinary impact. But where does the key idea come from? It comes from outside his conscious mind. The president hears a voice in his head. At that moment, he knows he is connected to something greater than himself. He knows that greatness is not "in us but through us." That is the reason for his tears when he tells the story. When we experience that flow of revelatory greatness, the memory moves us even years afterward. When such greatness flows through us, we tend to become an instrument of integration and oneness. The extraordinary person integrates that which is differentiated. He or she provides some form of integration as atonement. In this case the image of the flag needing washing lifts the conflicted actors toward a more integrated and complex way of seeing and being. They too have a transformational experience.

When we experience that flow of revelatory greatness,
the memory moves us even years afterward. When
such greatness flows through us, we tend to become
an instrument of integration and oneness.

ENTERING THE FUNDAMENTAL STATE OF LEADERSHIP

When I share a series of cases containing moments like the one I have just described, even dubious executives are sometimes convinced. When they are, they often ask, "How can I learn to think like that person did?" Teachers ask, "How can we teach people to think like that?" When I turn their own question back on them, they often suggest exercises in which they use stories like the above as analogies. Then they say, "Let's take the problem confronting this business and try to think in this same transformational way." Occasionally this strategy is actually applied in an organizational workshop. It seldom works.

There is a reason for this failure. The entire educational strategy is based on the wrong question. The wrong question is, "How can we get people to think like that?" The right question is, "How can we get people to *be* like that?" We come to be like that when we reduce our integrity gaps, when we live with increased courage, moving forward in the face of uncertainty. It is our increased integrity that allows us to practice adaptive confidence and thereby enter the fundamental state of leadership. As the director of nursing told us in Chapter One, it is not what we do that matters; what matters is who we are.

PREPARATION FOR ENTERING THE FUNDAMENTAL STATE OF LEADERSHIP

Choose a quiet time when you can reflect on the meaning this chapter has for you. Begin by assessing where you are today, as honestly as you can.

Questions for Reflection

1. Check each item that describes you as you are today.

    ___ I am confident and secure.

    ___ I am adaptive and flexible.

    ___ I continually clarify my purpose.

    ___ I am willing to enter uncertainty and build the bridge while I walk on it.

    ___ I know that in high uncertainty, the only way out is real-time learning.

    ___ I am willing to stay in the crucible of anxiety until I learn my way to the desired result.

    ___ I focus on the purpose, not the pain.

    ___ I make a few simple, strategic rules to structure my journey through uncertainty.

    ___ I launch many informal experiments.

    ___ I cherish bad news as well as good.

    ___ I make it possible for people to tell me the truth.

    ___ Failure is my friend. I surface and carefully examine each failure.

    ___ I continually seek to identify patterns and discover insights.

    ___ I continually work at reducing my integrity gaps.

    ___ When I close my integrity gaps, I experience increased creativity.

    ___ I find courage by reflecting on my transformational experiences in the past.

2. Now assess yourself on the following scale by circling the number under the characteristics that currently describe you. Note that the "negative" areas of the scale represent the overemphasis of a positive characteristic so that it becomes a negative. The "integrative" part of the scale represents the integration of opposing positives. If you feel you model the integration of adaptive flexibility and secure confidence, circle one of the numbers under "Integrative." Otherwise circle two numbers, one on each side of the scale.

Negative	Positive	Integrative	Positive	Negative
Uncertain; insecure	Adaptive; flexible	Adaptive and confident	Confident; secure	Rigid; inflexible
-3 -2 -1	1 2 3	4 5 4	3 2 1	-1 -2 -3

Self-Improvement

1. Based on the assessments you have completed, write a one-paragraph self-description on the theme of adaptive confidence. In your own words, describe where you are today with respect to this aspect of the fundamental state of leadership.

2. Write a strategy for self-improvement in the area of adaptive confidence. Try to be as concrete as possible in describing steps you are willing to take beginning today.

Helpful Hints for Practicing Adaptive Confidence

Recognize that excellence requires you to go where you have not been before.

Understand that leaving the comfort zone is terrifying.

In high uncertainty, you cannot rely on knowledge.

You must surrender your sense of control and begin to learn in real time.

In uncertainty and learning, you must continually clarify the desired result.

Keep it simple. Establish a few simple operating rules, and move forward.

The learning process is improvisational; you must create as you go.

You launch a thousand ships knowing most will sink.

It is normal to be scared.

Act on intuition, and learn from what happens.

Failure is not an enemy but a teacher.

You must be committed to gathering disconfirming feedback.

Model the process of encouraging people to criticize what you are doing.

Listen carefully to the criticism, and draw out more than they want to say.

Trust is a major asset. To maintain support, you must have complete credibility.

Forget self-interest, and focus on collective success.

There will be many conflicting opinions.

There will be strong emotions.

Frequent sense-making meetings are necessary.

Be disciplined about personal stress management.

Give yourself time to process feedback and get through the emotions.

Trust yourself and trust others.

Sharing Insights

If in responding to the questions above, you have an important insight or a meaningful story that you would like to share, visit www.deepchange.com and look for the links to submit stories for possible posting on the Deep Change Web site. You may thus help many people. If you would like to review such insights and stories, go to the same Web site.

CHAPTER THIRTEEN

Detached Interdependence

"I've discovered that when you free players to use all their resources—mental, physical, and spiritual—an interesting shift in awareness occurs. When players practice what is known as mindfulness—simply paying attention to what's actually happening—not only do they play better and win more, they also become more attuned with each other. And the joy they experience working in harmony is a powerful motivating force that comes from deep within."

—PHIL JACKSON (1995)

---

he concept of detached interdependence is one of the most elusive of the eight considered in Part Two. It requires that we consider our relationships from a very high level of maturity. When we do, extraordinary things are likely to happen.

POLARITIES

Author and philosopher Peter Koestenbaum sees a dynamic world of contrasting tensions and speaks of them as polarities—two contrasting or opposing things that are linked in a relationship. In Part One, we considered the competing values framework of leadership, for example, and identified many of the polarities within leadership traits. There are many such polarities in organizational life, such as the need to maintain stability and change, concern for people and for task, for internal cooperation and external competitiveness, for hierarchical control and for innovative flexibility. It is normal for the human mind to split off such polarities, to value only one end and negate the other. Koestenbaum argues that in an organization, "every interaction is a form of confrontation—a clash of priorities, a struggle of dignities, a battle of beliefs" (quoted in Labarre, 2000, p. 222). When we are in the normal state, and most of the time we all are, we often allow polar tensions to turn into deep conflicts.

Koestenbaum (in Labarre, 2000) shares a case in which a young couple found themselves in such a conflict. The husband was promoted and transferred to Cairo. He went home and excitedly told his wife, but she was not so positive. She told him that she was not taking her new baby to Cairo. If he wanted to go, he would have to go alone. It was a serious conflict. If he gave up his promotion, he would be forever resentful of her for injuring his career. If she went to Cairo, she would be ever resentful for his insensitivity to her and their baby. What should people do in such an impossible situation?

Koestenbaum suggests that the solution is found by changing perspective. We move from the surface issues that seem to be deeply important to more fundamental concerns. In this case, it is done by focusing on the higher collective good. "Is it *my* career, or is it *our* career? Is it *your* baby, or is it *our* baby? Are we *individuals,* or do we operate as a *team*? What are our values?"

Such questions are transformational. In asking these questions, the husband and wife came to a new awareness. His career was important to her. Their child was important to him. Once these things became clear, a change took place. They were more connected, more trusting. There was more willingness to change. From this point, they might have decided the issue either way. As it happens, they went to Cairo, but the important thing is that they were able to make the decision without resentment because they were operating on a new and more solid foundation.

This case illustrates a key point. We are all separate individuals, with our own being and values, and yet we all depend on one another. In organizations as well as in our family lives, none of us succeeds alone. Too often in our self-focus, we care most about getting a conflict resolved to our own satisfaction. But what matters is not how we resolve a conflict but how we maintain the relationship in resolving it.

Usually it takes courage to explore and define who we are. The process of honest exploration, through openness, self-trust, and trust of others, builds us. We enter a more authentic level of engagement. When we change ourselves so we are more authentic, the original conflict becomes of less consequence. I love this sentence from Koestenbaum: "When you grapple with polarities in your life, you lose your arrogant, self-indulgent illusions, and you realize the joke is on you" (quoted in Labarre, 2000, p. 222). I think that means that when we see the polarities, tensions, and conflicts that are inherent in our lives, we see a larger reality. We lose some of our self-focus and discover our interdependence. As a result, our perspective changes, and the immediate problem tends to seem less important than our fundamental purpose and the larger network of relationships that sustains us. The joke really is on us. I have often defined humility as seeing things as they really are. In this case, humility means seeing that our reality is dynamic and interdependent.

> *"When you grapple with polarities in your life, you lose your arrogant, self-indulgent illusions, and you realize the joke is on you."*

In keeping with such notions, Koestenbaum shares a particularly provocative insight about what he calls the key polarity of leadership: "It's the existential paradox of holding yourself 100% responsible for the fate of your organization, on the one hand, and assuming absolutely no responsibility for the choices made by other people, on the other hand" (quoted in Labarre, 2000, p. 222). This is a very challenging notion. I call it detached interdependence.

DETACHED INTERDEPENDENCE

This notion of detached interdependence is well captured in the following quotation from Phil Jackson, a professional basketball coach:

Yet even in this highly competitive world, I've discovered that when you free players to use *all* their resources—mental, physical, and spiritual—an interesting shift in awareness occurs. When players practice what is known as mindfulness—simply paying attention to what's actually happening—not only do they play better and win more, they also become more attuned with each other. And the joy they experience working in harmony is a powerful motivating force that comes from deep within, not from some frenzied coach pacing along the sidelines, shouting obscenities into the air [Jackson and Delehanty, 1995, pp. 5–6].

In this quotation, Jackson paints two contrasting pictures. In one picture, there is a "frenzied coach pacing the sidelines, shouting obscenities into the air." This image represents what we often think of when we speak of good, hard-nosed leadership. In the other picture, a group of people with large egos have surrendered their egos. They have become internally directed and other-focused. They are highly attuned to one another, and they work in harmony while winning more games. This picture seems like the dream of someone who does not understand the "real" world. Yet we might note that it represents the philosophy advocated by a man who has more National Basketball Association championship rings than he has fingers to wear them on.

In Jackson's preferred picture, we see the fruit of detached interdependence. When we practice detached interdependence, we transcend our own need to be in control, to pace "the sidelines, shouting obscenities into the air." Instead we model a process that allows others to find and express their full capacities. All of this begins with recognizing and transcending polarity.

The tension and integration represented by the notion of detached interdependence can be seen in Table 13.1. We can be humble and open, yet if these qualities are taken too far, we become dependent and weak. Or we can be independent and strong, yet if these qualities are taken too far, we become arrogant and closed. The challenge is to integrate being humble and strong. When I am in the state of detached interdependence, I am in a relationship in which both parties can create and draw rich meaning, but because of my clarity of purpose, I am not defined and determined by the relationship. I am both internally driven and other-focused. As a result, I have high authenticity and credibility.

MOVING TOWARD DETACHED INTERDEPENDENCE

Here is a story that illustrates the difficulty and the power of moving to a state of detached interdependence. One day, I received a telephone call from my daughter, Shauri. She was distraught. She had been get-

Table 13.1. Detached Interdependence.

Negative	Positive	Integrative	Positive	Negative
This person is so humble as to be weak and dependent.	This person is humble and open to influence.	This person practices detached interdependence.	This person is independent and strong.	This person is so strong as to be arrogant and isolated.
Dependent; weak	Humble; open	Humble and strong	Independent; strong	Arrogant; closed

Detached interdependence: This person combines independence and strength with humility and openness. The person has a strong sense of purpose and belief that provides an inner strength. He or she is thus open but not determined by the relationship. Such detached interdependence allows for rich relationships in which people enable each other in co-creating a future that is best for both. That future may include continuation or separation.

Personal orientation: I hold myself open to the influence of others while taking accountability for the evolution of my own uniqueness, happiness, and physical well-being. I model independent strength while recognizing my need for others. I am both strong and humble. I practice detached interdependence.

ting serious about a relationship with a young man in which she had invested a great deal emotionally. He had just told her he was going to break off their relationship, and now there was only pain. She felt rejected and hurt and churning with negative feelings. She announced she was coming home to recover.

The next morning, Shauri climbed into the car and immediately started talking about her situation. She was flooded with negative emotions, and we talked at length about the agony of relationships and attraction. Nothing seemed to ease her pain. She was in a deep emotional hole, and as she agonized, the hole seemed to get deeper and darker. Finally I asked her, "Are you problem solving or purpose finding?" The question jolted her, and she looked at me quizzically.

I suggested to Shauri that most people tend to live their lives in a reactive mode. They are always trying to solve their problems. Their problems are a source of pain, and they want the pain to disappear. Their problems ebb and flow in intensity but tend not to go away. People are then sad or happy depending on where they are in the ebb and flow.

Shauri asked what the alternative was. I suggested that instead of being reactors, we can be actors, initiators, or creators. When we initiate, we tend to create value eventually, and we tend to feel good about ourselves. If we continually clarify our basic purpose, it becomes a magnet. We are drawn toward the purpose and begin to pursue it. As we do so, our negative emotions tend to disappear. We experience victory over the reactive self, and we feel good about who we are. We feel better because we literally begin to have a more valuable self. We then relate to others in a very different way. We become empowered and empowering to others.

Shauri was not buying it. She ignored what I had tried to say and spent another fifteen minutes complaining about how unfair life can be. She paused for a breath, and I again asked her if she was problem solving or purpose finding. She ignored my question and continued venting. We repeated this pattern four times. The last time I asked, she stopped talking and just looked at me. I could tell a big challenge was coming. In order to stop my insensitive questions, she asked, "How would I ever use purpose finding in this situation?"

"You can use it in any situation," I replied.

She asked, "How do you do it?"

I said, "Whenever I am feeling lost or filled with negative emotions, I get out my life statement and I rewrite it."

Just then we were turning into the driveway. She asked me, "What is a life statement?"

I explained that it is a short document in which I try to capture the essence of who I am and what my purpose is in life.

"You have an actual document that does that?" She seemed truly surprised.

Something had changed. She was expressing genuine curiosity. For a moment, she had changed her focus from her bad fortune, and she wanted to know more. This was a window. She was momentarily open. If we could stay on this track, our souls might begin to touch more deeply. We might more openly exchange ideas and feelings. New images might emerge, and a transformation might take place.

I said, "Let me show you my life statement."

She followed me into my study. I reached into a file, pulled out a sheet of paper, and handed it to her.

Shauri read the document carefully and then looked up. She was fascinated. She asked, "When you feel bad, you read this and it makes you feel better?"

"No, when I feel really bad, I take my life statement out, read it carefully, and try to rewrite any part of it that I feel needs revision. Or I add something that was not there before. The document is always evolving. When I finish rewriting it, I feel clearer about who I am. By knowing what I most value, I become stable. To make change, I have to become stable at one level so that I can change at some other level. If my values are clear, then I can confront the issues that previously made me feel confused and fearful. My being state changes. I become more proactive. I have the energy to move forward no matter how negative my emotions. In fact, my negative emotions tend to disappear before I even start to act. Just clarifying who I am and what I want to create seems to energize me. Even the thought of movement becomes purifying."

I paused for a moment as Shauri took in my words. Then I continued: "There is another reason for rewriting the statement. People think that values are permanent, like cement. Clear values can stabilize us, yet they are living systems and need to be allowed to evolve. Each time we face a new situation and reinterpret our values, they change a little bit. Rewriting a statement like this one allows us to integrate what we have learned. Hence, our values also evolve with us. We co-create each other."

Shauri asked how she might apply what I was saying to her own situation. I suggested that instead of spending the weekend moping about what had happened and working through all her reactions to the event, she might spend the time writing her own life statement. She would thus move from being a reactor to becoming an actor.

Shauri indicated she would start writing her own life statement, and she did. By the end of the weekend, she was ready to return to her home. A few days later, she sent me a copy of an amazing letter. She has given me permission to share it.

REACHING DETACHED INTERDEPENDENCE

Shauri began by recounting our conversation. She confessed that despite her claims to the contrary, what she really wanted to do was wallow in self-pity. She wanted to play the victim role. I had caused her to rethink what she was doing. She then ties purpose finding to the notion of purifying herself and states, "In working to purify my life I would be focusing on service and things of higher purpose rather than on my day-to-day problems."

After describing these insights, Shauri's letter took a surprising turn. She shared an e-mail message she had recently sent to the young man who had cut off the relationship. It turns out he had contacted her and indicated he missed her. In response, she wrote the following:

I was really sad after our talk—more than I thought I would be. I still can't totally pinpoint why. I think a lot of it was because even though I was never 100 percent sure of whether we were right, I still put more into our relationship than I ever have with anyone else. I opened myself up to hurt, and I don't usually do that. It was a good growing time for me, though. I also think rejection hurts regardless of how you feel for someone or why they do it, so I probably felt bad that you didn't *love* me. Finally I think it hurt because I spent a good bulk of my time with you since May, and I felt I wasn't just losing a potential relationship, but also a good friend. Separation is not my strong point.

. . . I was just excited to make some changes and find a vision. The reason I'm sharing all of this with you is because I feel like the process of deciding how we felt about each other actually deepened our relationship. I learned to communicate more effectively because of you and opened myself up and shared all kinds of feelings, so the outcome is that I feel as if I can still share anything with you. I hope you feel the same about me. I think we've established a great friendship, and I hope you feel the same. I think we may have tried to force feelings a little that weren't there—maybe timing was off, maybe it just isn't right now or ever, but I definitely want to keep our friendship. I hope you feel like you can tell me anything and that I will be here for you no matter what, because I will. I appreciate your honesty with me about your feelings. I think what you felt is right. I hope you know I love you!

Shauri told me how she had decided to share this message with her roommates. They all had the same strong reaction. They argued that the message was too honest! They could never imagine opening themselves up like that to someone who had just rejected them. I suspect that previous to this moment, Shauri might have agreed with them. Yet something had changed. She was suddenly less reactive then before. What Shauri writes to me next is of great consequence:

The funny thing is I felt a huge sense of peace about it all. It was liberating. . . . I was no longer worried about his response or reaction to me or to what I told him. I chose to act rather than react. Because I did, it freed me and empowered me. By giving up control in this situation, I gained control of the situation. I wasn't worried about his response. I had been completely honest with him, and strangely, it gave me confidence. My purpose is to purify myself and serve others. Since I began working toward that purpose I have been set free from my problems, and they are resolving themselves. I feel filled with light, and

I know that as I continue in my purpose, my light will grow brighter and brighter and I will lose myself in it.

> *"The funny thing is I felt a huge sense of peace about it all. It was liberating. . . . I was no longer worried about his response or reaction to me or to what I told him. I chose to act rather than react. Because I did, it freed me and empowered me. By giving up control in this situation, I gained control of the situation."*

ENTERING THE FUNDAMENTAL STATE OF LEADERSHIP

Shauri's experience illustrates many important points. First, it is normal to be reactive and have negative emotions. We are all pulled in this direction. Although most of us would claim that we hate the negative emotions we are feeling, we do not behave as if we do. In fact, we often choose to stay in our negative state. We seem to become addicted to the process of wallowing in the problem. It is natural, and in a strange way, it is comfortable to be in such pain. At such times, this victim role is our path of least resistance, and we willingly take it, perhaps because it is a role we know how to play. We make a long list of the things that are wrong and then complain that nothing can be done.

Second, we can control our being state. We do not have to stay in the victim role. We can choose our own response. We do this by leaving the "external world," where it can seem to us the problem is located. We go inside ourselves, not to the problem or our feelings about it, but to our purpose. When we go inside to clarify our purpose, our perception is altered dramatically. The original problem does not necessarily go away, but it becomes much less relevant. We outgrow the problem.

Third, our being state changes the world. As soon as Shauri started to clarify her purpose, she felt a sense of progress. Her negative emotions turned positive. She started to feel faith, hope, strength, confidence, and love. The new positive emotions empowered her and made her empowering. She became inner-directed and other-focused.

Shauri was practicing detached interdependence. She was combining independence and strength with openness and humility. With clarified purpose, she was open to the relationship but not determined by it. Instead of withdrawing, she could share her most honest and vulnerable feelings with complete confidence. She could not be hurt. As she explained to her roommates, how her former boyfriend reacted did not matter. It was now a richer relationship in which they could co-create a future best for both. That future could be a future of connection or separation. Detached interdependence is a powerful, loving, and generative state.

After this experience, there was a dramatic change in Shauri's life. At the professional level, her career suddenly took off. She went from frustration and fear to a bold job change. Her performance on that job has been full of creativity, and she has become a successful young professional. She now loves what she is doing. She presents herself in a much more potent yet peaceful and confident way. Shauri clarified her purpose and made a change in her being state, and now her external world is dramatically different. She has begun to learn how to live in the state of detached interdependence. She is more frequently living in the fundamental state of leadership.

PREPARATION FOR ENTERING THE FUNDAMENTAL STATE OF LEADERSHIP

Choose a quiet time when you can reflect on the meaning this chapter has for you. Begin by assessing where you are today, as honestly as you can.

Questions for Reflection

1. Check each item that describes you as you are today.

___ I am humble and open.

___ I am independent and strong.

___ I know who I am and where I am going.

___ I do not take the victim role.

___ I hold myself 100 percent accountable for the fate of the organization.

___ I assume no accountability for the choices of others.

___ I have clear boundaries between my identity and those of others.

___ I am deeply committed to the welfare of others.

___ I am able to absorb personal attacks because I do not take them personally

___ When conflict occurs, I do not withdraw or attack.

___ When conflict occurs, I focus on the overall value of the relationship.

___ I can maintain relationships during conflicts.

___ I avoid getting caught up in surface concerns and seek to help people clarify their values.

___ I help people discover their interdependencies.

___ I move people from self-concern to the collective concern.

2. Now assess yourself on the following scale by circling the number under the characteristics that currently describe you. Note that the "negative" areas of the scale represent the overemphasis of a positive characteristic so that it becomes a negative. The "integrative" part of the scale represents the integration of opposing positives. If you feel you model the integration of openness and humility and independent strength, circle one of the numbers under "Integrative." Otherwise circle two numbers, one on each side of the scale.

Negative	*Positive*	*Integrative*	*Positive*	*Negative*
Dependent; weak	Humble; open	Humble and strong	Independent; strong	Arrogant; closed
−3 −2 −1	1 2 3	4 5 4	3 2 1	−1 −2 −3

Self-Improvement

1. Based on the assessments you have completed, write a one-paragraph self-description on the theme of detached interdependence. In your own words, describe where you are today with respect to this aspect of the fundamental state of leadership.

2. Write a strategy for self-improvement in the area of detached interdependence. Try to be as concrete as possible in describing steps you are willing to take beginning today.

Helpful Hints for Practicing Detached Interdependence

Accept that you are accountable for your own happiness.

Recognize that you are a totally unique human being.

Resolve to know your best self better.

Know that joy follows personal growth.

Take responsibility for yourself by exercising increased self-discipline physically, intellectually, socially, and spiritually.

Increase your time in the creative state, and reduce your time in the reactive state.

Clarify your values.

Clarify the result you want to create.

Resolve to face adversity with positive coping mechanisms.

Look beyond your self-concern to the collective good, and seek to engage others in pursuing it.

Know who you are and what is not negotiable.

Realize that you are a part of many larger systems.

Realize the need to continually transcend the ego.

Accept that you are not in control.

Remember that excellence requires relationship.

Examine the potential in high interdependence.

Realize that collective excellence increases as trust goes up.

Recognize that everyone else is a free agent with the right to choose.

Resolve to be ever loving and ever learning.

Sharing Insights

If in responding to the questions above, you have an important insight or a meaningful story that you would like to share, visit www.deepchange.com and look for the links to submit stories for possible posting on the Deep Change Web site. You may thus help many people. If you would like to review such insights and stories, go to the same Web site.

CHAPTER FOURTEEN

Responsible Freedom

"For me, the ego-death and subsequent 'rebirth' was a wonderfully and powerfully transformative event. I experienced a sort of 'awakening' in which I realized in a flash of insight that 'I' was not my ego or the external trappings of my life. 'I' was still all that had ever been, my true self. Nothing that was real and certain had changed, just superficial aspects of my environment."

—MARK YOUNGBLOOD (1997)

The next practice is responsible freedom. Freedom is one of the most central human values. Without it, people cannot become what they are capable of becoming. We know this intuitively, and we often go to great lengths to protect our freedom. But we do not always understand what freedom really is. In particular, we fail to grasp the intimate connection between freedom and responsibility.

A CASE OF PHILOSOPHY AND PRACTICE

Viktor Frankl gave much thought to the notions of responsibility and freedom. He was concerned that in our culture, freedom was in danger of degenerating into "mere arbitrariness." In fact, he suggested that the Statue of Liberty on the East Coast of the United States should be balanced by a statue of responsibility on the West Coast.

The path that gave rise to Frankl's thinking about responsible freedom is most interesting. Frankl was a psychotherapist in Vienna. In 1942 he was arrested, and he spent the next three years in Nazi concentration camps. He survived the horrendous ordeal and afterward wrote a book about his experiences, *Man's Search for Meaning* (1963). The book has sold more than nine million copies.

In the first portion of the book, Frankl recounts the daily horrors of the camps. In the second portion, he describes the philosophy of human meaning that he derived from his experience. One of the reasons that the book has sold so well is that it contains so many profound observations that we would not necessarily expect to come from such extreme suffering.

A central assumption of most academic disciplines is that humans are determined by their context. When we examine a random sample of behavior patterns, we tend to find that given a particular context, most people do what is expected. This is consistent with the claim of this book that in the normal state, people tend to be externally determined.

Frankl noted that behavior in the brutal environment of the camps was consistent with this assumption. Under severe external duress, many ordinary people quickly turned to animal-like behaviors. Yet what caught Frankl's attention were the positive deviants. Even in the extreme conditions of the camps, they were people who chose to live not like animals but like saints. At great personal cost, they stretched themselves to do unexpectedly good things. He concluded that even in the most constrained circumstances, there is always the freedom to choose one's attitude, to empower oneself.

Humans are inherently free and inherently responsible. They are free to choose, and they are responsible to "actualize the potential meaning" in their lives. Mental health is not a tensionless state of comfort but rather a state of tension in which the person is "struggling for a worthwhile goal, a freely chosen task."

After witnessing how different people responded to suffering, Frankl (1963) came to believe that the central motivating force in human life is not mere survival; it is finding meaning. Humans are inherently free and inherently responsible. They are free to choose, and they are responsible to "actualize the potential meaning" in their lives. Mental health is not a tensionless state of comfort but rather a state of tension in which the person is "struggling for a worthwhile goal, a freely chosen task."

For Frankl, to be fully human is to choose a meaningful purpose and pursue it. In this act, we choose our own unique course. Our purpose may involve work and achievement, or connection and love, or finding the meaning in suffering that cannot be avoided. Frankl believed that extending ourselves in the pursuit of purposeful action leads to self-transcendence. When we experience victory over the normal self, the ego dies, and a new self begins to emerge. In this process of self-transcendence, awareness is altered. The visual field widens. We come to "see the world as it really is." We see a "whole spectrum of potential meanings." As a result, we are more free and more potent.

After the war, Frankl lived for twenty-five years in Vienna and for twenty years in the United States. He engaged in mountain climbing, and in his sixty-seventh year he took up flying. When asked about these unusual pursuits, he indicated that both activities were a source of fear. Why, then, would a sixty-seven-year-old man freely choose to engage in activities that he found fearful?

Frankl was living what he fundamentally believed: the necessity to always be in the process of becoming, to forsake his zone of comfort. His life thus carries a message for us. In both his philosophy and his behavior, Frankl calls on us to practice responsible freedom.

RESPONSIBLE FREEDOM

The book *Changing for Good: A Revolutionary Six-Stage Program for Overcoming Bad Habits and Moving Your Life Positively Forward* (Prochaska, Norcross, and DiClemente, 1994) is a marvelous volume based on years of research on how people make self-change. Of the many powerful insights in the book, one is particularly important. The authors indicate how shocking it is that we otherwise intelligent human beings resist becoming aware of the problems that are endangering or destroying us. We seemingly prefer to suffer rather than give up the illusion of control. No one is going to tell me what to do, no matter what the consequences are. They call this orientation foolish freedom, as opposed to responsible freedom.

Foolish freedom is the obsessive pursuit of independence. In trying to prevent or to flee a state of bondage, we often go too far and seek to avoid all structure and responsibility. We prize being "independent" at all costs. We think that freedom means "letting it all hang out," expressing ourselves without restraint. This is actually hubris, or vain pride. In such a state, our focus is entirely on ourselves; other people are mere obstacles to our "freedom." But instead of liberating and energizing us, foolish freedom tends to result in a depletion of energy and resources. It robs us of the sense of meaning we crave.

I believe that we all tend to practice foolish freedom because it is difficult to practice responsible freedom. Responsible freedom is a form of work that leads to the unfolding of a more complex and capable self.

Frankl discovered that responsible freedom entails internalizing a commitment to higher purpose and to richer connections. When suffering is imposed on us, we become free by finding the meaning in it. In a similar way, even in more ordinary circumstances, we become free by committing to continual personal renewal. In so doing, we lose our focus on preserving the self, and paradoxically we discover our true selves. This is the essence of responsible freedom. It is the key to transcending the entropy toward which we tend to move when we are in the normal state of fleeing pain and seeking to preserve our comfort.

I think of responsible freedom as an integrative state or creative tension, as depicted in Table 14.1. The tension is between being spontaneous and expressive and being self-disciplined and responsible. Each of these pairs of qualities has its undesirable extreme. A person who overdoes being spontaneous and expressive becomes undisciplined and irresponsible. A person who overdoes being self-disciplined and responsible becomes less expressive and more guarded.

In the negative zone on the left, we become undisciplined and irresponsible. We are seemingly free of structure. Some people are so impulsive that they do things to destroy their own resources, like the rock musician who smashes his instrument on the stage. But impulsive, chaotic, and random actions cannot bring sustained growth and development. We are not free when we lack purpose and structure. In order to practice responsible freedom, we must have purpose and see meaning in our choices. If we enter the negative zone on the right, we

Table 14.1. Responsible Freedom.

Negative	Positive	Integrative	Positive	Negative
This person is so spontaneous and expressive as to be undisciplined and irresponsible.	This person is free-flowing, spontaneous, and expressive.	This person practices responsible freedom.	This person is structured, self-disciplined, and responsible.	This person is so structured as to be unexpressive and guarded.
Undisciplined; irresponsible	Spontaneous; expressive	Self-disciplined and spontaneous	Self-disciplined; responsible	Unexpressive; guarded

Responsible freedom: The person who practices responsible freedom is spontaneous and expressive while also self-disciplined and responsible. Rather than fleeing purpose, discipline, or structure, this person is self-structuring and tends to be ever elevated to higher levels of awareness and capacity. In obtaining this higher state, the person becomes more complex and capable, more empowered and empowering to others.

Personal orientation: I discipline myself to engage in purposes and disciplines that require me to grow in awareness, knowledge, and self-confidence. I thus become increasingly capable and free to express a uniquely emerging self. I model both self-control and expressive spontaneity. I practice responsible freedom.

try to maintain our freedom or independence by becoming obsessed with structure and control. In relationships, we are distant and guarded, not expressive. We tend not to trust others and show no signs of spontaneity or feeling. Our relationships are not enriching. We live without meaningful connections.

Consider highly structured professionals who hide behind their analytic ability or those persons who stay forever distant and try to do everything themselves. Such people tend to be seen as the opposite of impulsive, yet they are actually engaging in a self-defeating quest for foolish freedom. By remaining distant, striving to be in control, and overly structuring life, they destroy their own resources. They seek to establish relationships of escape or domination, either of which preserves the illusion of control. Such relationships seldom flourish.

The challenge is not only to avoid the extremes in Table 14.1 but to integrate the positive qualities of being self-disciplined and spontaneous. A person who reaches this integrated state becomes self-structuring and self-empowering. Disciplined action based on principles of higher purpose transforms us. As we change, we enter a higher state of awareness. We begin to see that what we had previously thought of as freedom was in reality a form of bondage to our own fears and our attachment to our own zone of comfort.

Consider the case of Mark Youngblood, who has written eloquently of his own experience of profound suffering and deep personal change. Mark spent a year trying to launch a company. He spent his life savings, went into debt, and exhausted himself trying to make the business successful. Finally he had to admit what all the data had been telling him: the business was not going to make it. He writes:

> With it went everything that defined who I was to the world. I could no longer say that I "was" my job, because I had none. I couldn't rely on my wealth to create a sense of worth and identity, for I had no money and loads of debt. I could not look to social standing, for a failed entrepreneur has no social standing. And the failure of my love relationship, a month earlier, ensured that I could not find myself through the love of another. I had nothing, therefore I was nothing. I had died [1997, p. 208].

As we read Mark's words, we can feel his pain. No one would ever want to enter such an emotional space. Yet a great lesson emerged from what Mark experienced as a "death." Consider his next observation:

> Until that point, I had lived my life through the eyes of other people. I had defined myself through object-reference—my sense of identity and my feelings of self-worth were tied directly to the outer circumstances of my life—all of these external references were stripped away. When I looked in the mirror, I did not know who I was. For me, the ego-death and subsequent "rebirth" was a wonderfully and powerfully transformative event. I experienced a sort of "awakening" in which I realized in a flash of insight that "I" was not my ego or the external trappings of my life. "I" was still all that had ever been, my true self. Nothing that was real and certain had changed, just superficial aspects of my environment [Youngblood, 1997, p. 208].

In the depths of his suffering, Mark attained a new level of awareness. He awakened to the fact that his life was much more than recognition from others and the accumulation of material objects in the world. He was not an object. Other people are not objects. Underneath it all, he had a lasting self. The only things that had really changed were the "superficial aspects of his environment."

How do we explain such a remarkable reversal? Whenever we make deep personal change, we take the journey, in the words of Joseph Campbell (1949), to the "center of our own existence." At the center of our existence is not the "abomination" we feared before, but an authentic and unique self, striving to link with others and evolve together toward greater complexity.

> *Whenever we make deep personal change, we take the journey, in the words of Joseph Campbell, to the "center of our own existence." At the center of our existence is not the "abomination" we feared before, but an authentic and unique self, striving to link with others and evolve together toward greater complexity.*

This state of increased awareness is often referred to as the truth that will make us free. It comes to us as we embrace disciplines that lead to the transcendence of self, that lead us away from the normal state. As we become purpose-centered, internally directed, other-focused, and externally open, we give up foolish freedom. We find greater meaning and a more lovable and connected self.

THE DAILY PRACTICE OF RESPONSIBLE FREEDOM

In attempting to practice responsible freedom, there are dramatic approaches, like taking up flying when we are afraid of flying. There are also less dramatic approaches. In my own life, I often find myself moving toward entropy. When this happens, I begin to have feelings of depression. I then have a choice: I can give in to these feelings, or I can train myself to recognize them as an internal signal that I need to change.

There is a paradox about change. In order to be able to change, we must stabilize ourselves at one level so that we can change ourselves at another. We need to find the elusive middle ground that integrates the positive opposites of being stable and being adaptive. In this sense, we need to engage in the positive organizing of the self.

This is where the role of routines comes into play. A routine is an activity or practice that has become regimented or internalized. An example can be seen in the lives of people who participate in a formal sports program. Many of us have had a coach who insisted that we regularly practice some difficult task, like working out in a weight room. That requirement was a discipline that became a routine. It helped us grow in terms of muscular capacity. As we more fully stabilized that routine in our life, we kept increasing in that capacity. That increased capacity made us more adaptive when it came time to play our sport. Because we were stronger, we had more things we could do and more choices we could make. Ultimately, then, the "constraining" routine increased our freedom to create and contribute.

Often when I start feeling depressed, I find that I have slipped out of some positive routines that are important to me. At such times, I try to evaluate myself and give myself a report card on how I am doing in terms of my key routines. I actually keep a daily life strategy checklist. It reads as follows:

I am:

__ Exercising

__ Controlling diet

__ Evolving physically

__ Studying

__ Praying

__ Closing integrity gaps

__ Experiencing inspiration

__ Tending to family

__ Tending to others

__ Protecting mornings for creative demands

__ Controlling commitments

__ Focusing professionally

__ Disciplining finances

__ Playing

The daily life strategy checklist allows me to quickly determine whether I have all my routines in place. If I do, I am likely to be simultaneously more stable and more adaptive. If I find I have slipped in some of my routines, I go back and make a course correction, reconnecting with the disciplines I have been neglecting. I confess that there are times when I get more deeply stuck, and my checklist is not enough. I then have to ask whether I am truly purpose-centered, internally directed, other-focused, and externally open. Often I am not.

ENTERING THE FUNDAMENTAL STATE OF LEADERSHIP

One of the highest forms of responsibility is the responsibility to be free. One of the highest forms of freedom is the freedom to be responsible. These things sound simple, yet many people have difficulty enacting them. There is a natural tendency to avoid responsible freedom and enact foolish freedom. Patterns of foolish freedom often turn to addiction to alcohol, drugs, smoking, overeating, sleep, money, power, status, sex, pornography, gambling, procrastination, and so forth. We may claim that in choosing to pursue these things, we are making our own choices—we are being free. In reality, those things we cannot help but pursue become demons ruling our lives, and we surrender our freedom to them, literally becoming their slaves. That is often when we start compartmentalizing our lives. That is often when we begin feeling hopelessness. We have reduced self-control and reduced capacity to perform and contribute. We tend to lose meaning, experience depression, and move more deeply into entropy and slow death. To become free of these patterns requires a deep commitment to practices that may seem constraining yet paradoxically restore our freedom.

Many people will say that they do not suffer from addictions. Yet if we examine our lives closely, most of us will find that we are slaves to something that defines our zone of comfort—whether it is the approval of others, a need for status, a need to avoid conflict, or any one of a thousand other things that keep us from being truly committed to a purpose. When we confront our demons, as Viktor Frankl confronted his fear of flying, we free ourselves for the pursuit of meaning and purpose.

The practice of responsible freedom ensures the continuous evolution of the self. To practice responsible freedom is to refuse to live in the victim mode. Liberated from our self-concern, we feel more empowered. In that empowered state, we reach new levels of creativity in both purpose and relationship. We also become empowering in that we tend to draw others out of the victim role and into the state of productive community, so that together we build the bridge as we walk on it.

PREPARATION FOR ENTERING THE FUNDAMENTAL STATE OF LEADERSHIP

Choose a quiet time when you can reflect on the meaning this chapter has for you. Begin by assessing where you are today, as honestly as you can.

Questions for Reflection

1. Check each item that describes you as you are today.

___ I am self-disciplined.

___ I take responsibility for my own growth.

___ I always have a purpose larger than self.

___ I strive to live in relationships of love.

___ When I cannot avoid suffering, I find meaning in the suffering.

___ I know what it means to transcend self.

___ I know what it means to have increased awareness.

___ I know what it means to see an increased range of possibilities.

___ I have a daily checklist of routines that give me life.

___ I exercise personal physical discipline.

___ I exercise personal social discipline.

___ I exercise personal intellectual discipline.

___ I exercise personal spiritual discipline.

___ I am currently moving to ever higher levels of consciousness.

___ I see the potential in everyone.

___ I am spontaneous and open with people.

___ People know how I feel.

___ I am empowering in that I draw people outside the victim role.

___ I live in a world of abundant connection and possibility.

___ I inspire people to take charge of their own lives.

2. Now assess yourself on the following scale by circling the number of the characteristics that currently describe you. Note that the "negative" areas of the scale represent the overemphasis of a positive characteristic so that it becomes a negative. The "integrative" part of the scale represents the integration of opposing positives. If you feel you model the integration of responsible self-control and expressive spontaneity, circle one of the numbers under "Integrative." Otherwise circle two numbers, one on each side of the scale.

Negative	Positive	Integrative	Positive	Negative
Undisciplined; irresponsible	Spontaneous; expressive	Self-disciplined and spontaneous	Self-disciplined; responsible	Unexpressive; guarded
−3 −2 −1	1 2 3	4 5 4	3 2 1	−1 −2 −3

Self-Improvement

1. Based on the assessments you have completed, write a one-paragraph self-description on the theme of responsible freedom. In your own words, describe where you are today with respect to this aspect of the fundamental state of leadership.

2. Write a strategy for self-improvement in the area of responsible freedom. Try to be as concrete as possible in describing steps you are willing to take beginning today.

Helpful Hints for Practicing Responsible Freedom

Recognize that foolish freedom is the unbridled exercise of hubris.

Understand that foolish freedom leads people to destroy their own resources.

Know that self-discipline is choosing to reach a higher good or to find meaning in suffering.

Realize that sacrifice and delayed gratification lead to growth and development.

Recognize that responsible freedom means choosing to become more than you are now.

Know that when you are not becoming more than you are, you are actually in decay.

Focus on the result you want to create.

Articulate the disciplines you need to exercise every day.

Specify rewards you will give yourself for practicing those disciplines.

Allow yourself to be joyful in your self-discipline.

Realize that you do not need to be an extrovert to be expressive.

Know that when you are growing, your confidence increases.

Realize that only when you are growing can you know your best self.

Understand that when you encounter your best self, you feel increased self-love.

Realize that when you feel self-love, you have no need to hide your core.

When you know and express your core, there is no worry about others' reactions.

When you can express your core, you are no longer externally determined.

When you stop being externally determined, you enter the creative state.

In the creative state, you can better trust yourself to improvise and learn with others.

You can trust others to join you in the creative process.

Sharing Insights

If in responding to the questions above, you have an important insight or a meaningful story that you would like to share, visit www.deepchange.com and look for the links to submit stories for possible posting on the Deep Change Web site. You may thus help many people. If you would like to review such insights and stories, go to the same Web site.

CHAPTER FIFTEEN

Tough Love

"Bo is the only person in the world I will let kick me in the butt—because I know he loves me."
—UNIVERSITY OF MICHIGAN FOOTBALL PLAYER

Practicing responsible freedom tends to alter how we see and treat other people. Because we discover the goodness in ourselves, we better love ourselves. In this state of love, we see the world differently, and we see other people differently. We begin to enact a more mature kind of love. We begin to practice something called tough love.

FINDING LOVE WHERE WE LEAST EXPECT IT

I once had a conversation with a student who played football for Bo Schembechler, the charismatic coach at the University of Michigan. The young man was a very big lineman. I asked him what he thought of Bo. He replied, "Bo is the only person in the world that I will let kick me in the butt—because I know he loves me."

We expect authoritative discipline from leaders on the football field, but we seldom think of the football field as a place of caring. We do not expect a big, tough lineman to use the word *love*. Yet he did. He even implies that it is the love that makes the confrontation acceptable.

In sports, we readily recognize the need to be tough, but we often fail to see the need for love. Yet love is necessary because a coach usually has to transform a group from patterns of self-interested conflict to cohesive, focused effort. We call those coaches who succeed transformational leaders because they turn groups into high-performing teams. A great team, like a great leader, maintains both a tough, disciplined focus on the task and a cohesive set of relationships full of trust and love.

A good example is the story of Pat Riley while coaching the New York Knicks, a basketball team that was riddled with internal competition and composed of warring cliques. The competition between the cliques led the players to define each other negatively and provided justification for more competition between them. They became trapped in a vicious cycle (Riley, 1993).

One day Riley made a tough intervention that transformed the team. He stood up and named the members and characteristics of each clique. Then he had the players rearrange their chairs and sit in their cliques. The exercise was simple but very graphic. Riley was communicating his message at a level that everyone could understand. He was showing them the emergent reality that they were choosing to create but did not want to see.

This kind of feedback usually stimulates anger—and Riley's players were angry. They did not enjoy looking at their own foolish freedom. Instead of chastising them, Riley talked to them about positive values like tolerance, openness, and team spirit—values akin to love. Before this moment, the Knicks were surviving, but they were heading toward slow death. They needed to be reinvented. Riley's intervention was one dramatic moment that was part of a much larger pattern in which he transformed the team and led them into the playoffs.

TOUGH LOVE

Living with tough love means living in the balance of a positive creative tension. A person can be compassionate and caring, but when these positive qualities are taken too far, the person becomes indulgent and permissive. Similarly, a person who is assertive and bold becomes, in the extreme, oppressive and overbearing. The challenge is to be simultaneously compassionate and assertive, to practice tough love (see Table 15.1).

Table 15.1.   Tough Love.

Negative	Positive	Integrative	Positive	Negative
This person shows so much compassion as to be indulgent.	This person shows compassion for people.	This person practices tough love.	This person challenges people to stretch to high standards.	This person challenges people so much as to be oppressive.
Indulgent; permissive	Compassionate; concerned	Compassionate and assertive	Assertive; bold	Oppressive; overbearing

Tough love: This person is assertive and bold yet compassionate and concerned. This person calls others to higher objectives and standards while also showing empathic, relational support. Others are lifted by the loving recognition of their potential and the challenging call to enact it in a more creative state of purpose.

Personal orientation: I continually challenge myself and challenge others to higher levels of commitment while providing continuous, concerned support for the necessary risk taking. I thus integrate assertiveness and compassion. I practice tough love.

It is difficult to hold two positive opposites in mind and grasp the nature of creative tension. Of the eight concepts or practices presented in this book, tough love is the one most often used in common vocabulary. Yet when I hear it, I often conclude that the person using it fails to understand the phrase. One major tendency is that people tend to split off "tough" from "love" or "love" from "tough."

Recently I heard a speaker who was a strong advocate of love. He declared that there was no such thing as tough love. Love, he said, is about caring concern and sweetness. He said there is no place for tough in the domain of love. Others make the opposite mistake. Many coaches, for example, justify extreme discipline that destroys individual self-esteem and team cohesion in the name of tough love. They are not practicing love; they are simply practicing an obsessive need for control and authority. Pat Riley could make the painful intervention he did and have it succeed because the players knew that his concern for the team as a whole and for them as individuals was real. In an encounter with Bo Schembechler, one recognizes that one is in the presence of a very strong personality, but it is also clear that the man is capable of putting the good of a relationship ahead of his own needs.

Toughness and love must be integrated. When others practice tough love toward me, they support me, and I can feel their genuine love and concern. Yet they do not baby me. They want to call forth my greatness. For this to happen, I must become a more independent actor and take increased accountability for some aspect of my life. For me to transform, I must be attracted outside my comfort zone. Those who treat me with tough love disturb the habitual way in which I choose to see myself by asking me tough questions or making tough statements.

> *When others practice tough love toward me, they support me, and I can feel their genuine love and concern. Yet they do not baby me. They want to call forth my greatness.*

Such challenges cause me to think deeply and to see my own stagnation. Like everyone else, I continually run from pain, so I choose slow death. I shut down in some part of my life. Change agents challenge me to awaken, to stretch to my full limits. People in the fundamental state of leadership, whether they are parents, coaches, CEOs, or leaders within the ranks, tend to do this continually. They try to get individuals and the collective to stretch and grow, to become a more productive community, a winning team in the process of positive organizing.

Tough love is particularly important in times of deep change. If we want to change an organization, we must help people cope with the dread of uncertainty. The role of the leader is to provide the integration of tough and love that empowers people to move forward. During deep change, people have to move outside the comfort zone and learn new behaviors. This means surrendering control, and no one wants to do it. At such times people need both purpose and support. That is what tough love does.

TOUGH LOVE AT THE TOP

Although his popularity tends to ebb and flow, no one questions that Jack Welch transformed General Electric (GE). Everyone recognizes that he was tough. Many, however, would question whether he was a loving leader.

The president of NBC, a GE company, once observed, "Jack and I have been friends for eight years, and our wives see each other all the time. If I started down a path where I made four incredibly bad decisions, I know he would fire me" (Welch and Byrne, 2001, p. 168).

Taken alone, this might sound like the description of a vicious man. Amazingly, the president of NBC does not seem to be saying that at all. He likes Jack Welch. He is simply making clear that a caring individual relationship does not supersede the collective good. High-performing systems tend to be productive communities. In high-performing systems, people both live values and produce outcomes. Both are necessary. A person in the fundamental state of leadership understands this and uses tough love to call people to greatness. The leader does this by modeling the process. Tough love is one of the highest manifestations of responsible freedom.

I once did a PBS television show with Welch. I was one of two faculty who were designated to ask him questions. Before the show, he attended a class and interacted with our students. For several hours, I watched him carefully and asked myself what I felt when I was around him. The answer was passion and authenticity. Being with Welch was like being with Bo Schembechler. He was clearly an intense personality, but it was also clear that he could put the good of the collective ahead of his own personal good.

During the show, there were many discussions of his demanding management tools and techniques. After many tools were discussed, I told him I had two questions. In the first I told him of my personal assessment of him and accused him of loving the people at GE. He thought about this and agreed that it was true. He provided a number of convincing examples.

Then I asked if his tools and techniques worked not because they were good tools that could be applied elsewhere, but because the people at GE felt challenged by his tough standards and supported by his love and that they therefore were willing to work with tools that others would reject. I asked whether other companies, having leaders that do not practice tough love, are likely to imitate the techniques used at GE and then fail.

He had a much more difficult time with this second proposition. Most of us would. In discussing techniques, we forget the importance of relationship. I think this is why so many management fads fail. People imitate the technique originated elsewhere but fail to live in the fundamental state of leadership as did the person who originated the technique. The techniques are valuable, but people cannot learn to make them work if they are not challenged and supported in the process of learning how to make them work. People who need to learn need to be lifted by the power of tough love.

Welch clearly cared about his purpose and about his people. He argues, for example, that when people make a mistake, they do not need to be disciplined; rather, they need encouragement and confidence building. He notes that in large organizations, there is a tendency to do the former. The result, he argues, is a vortex in which the vulnerable person panics and begins to "spiral downward into a hole of self-doubt" (Welch and Byrne, 2001, p. 29).

I believe Welch was about creating upward spirals of value creation, and he understood that the process involved disciplined integration of opposing values. Nowhere was his understanding and practice of tough love better exemplified than in the standards by which he evaluated managers. To succeed at GE, managers had to deliver the hard numbers and live the soft values. If they failed on either one, they got a second chance. If they did neither, they were gone. If they did both, they were rewarded extensively. As a business leader, Jack Welch lived tough love, and he transferred the practice to others. He was requiring everyone to live in tough love. Yet I would not recommend that his evaluation system be imitated in other companies unless the leaders of those companies are first willing to model what the system requires.

TOUGH LOVE AT OTHER LEVELS

When I talk to executives, many of them reject a story about someone like Welch. They indicate a CEO may be able to practice tough love, but someone at their level cannot. This is simply wrong. An ordinary manager who makes deep change will enter the fundamental state of leadership and will then tend to practice tough love.

Roman Walley, whom we met in Chapter One, provides a good example. Roman reported that he had always been afraid to make waves. Then he experienced a crisis: he lost two loved ones, his son and his wife. For months he was "raw and empty" inside. He reported a need to increase the meaning in his life. He read a book and attended a seminar. Then he assessed his life. He concluded that he was in the process of slow death. He decided that if he put his self-respect first, the respect of others would naturally follow. He made a commitment to live as a complete person. Soon he began to ask tough questions of senior people. Instead of being fired, he was rewarded. Now, consider a part of his story that we have not yet reviewed:

I was asked to coach a team that was not meeting its deadlines. After opening a meeting with the team, I asked them what was holding the project back. The answers came back quickly: upper management kept changing the target. They weren't empowered to make decisions. They were hamstrung. There was no guidance. There were too many demands on their time. I listened for about five minutes and then reflected back what I heard. I told them that I didn't have any answers, but as an outside observer, I felt I could provide an accurate reflection of their current reality.

Their language was the language of victims. Did they want to own the problem and the outcome? Or did they want someone else to make the decisions for them? Did they want to be creative and come up with solutions that hadn't been considered before, or did they want to arrive at predictable outcomes? There was an uncomfortable silence in the room, and the unspoken question hung in the air: Slow death or deep change? The team was staffed by ambitious and bright managers who worked very hard but hadn't confronted their collective behavior yet. One by one, they all admitted they hadn't dedicated themselves to the project. A new energy flowed into the room. After a series of meetings, the team came to realize its potential. We completed the project on time and to high praise from the executive sponsors.

> *"The unspoken question hung in the air: Slow death or deep change? The team was staffed by ambitious and bright managers who worked very hard but hadn't confronted their collective behavior yet. One by one, they all admitted they hadn't dedicated themselves to the project. A new energy flowed into the room."*

The man making this report is not a CEO. He is not a natural born leader. He is a man who just a short time before felt uncomfortable making waves. Where did he find the audacity to challenge the group in this way? More important, why did it work?

Walley could be tough, even with authority figures, because he had taken the responsibility to make the journey to the "center of his own existence." Having done so, he was now free of his fears and filled with love. Now free, he was able to put the good of the company first. That choice gave him moral power.

ENTERING THE FUNDAMENTAL STATE OF LEADERSHIP

Again I must emphasize that it is very difficult to maintain the integration of positive opposites. I once did an exercise with two hundred bank executives. I explained the concept of tough love in detail and then asked them to write a paragraph about how they could increase their own level of tough love. When they were done, we had ten people read what they had written. In every case, the paragraph contained a plan to become more demanding, tougher. In no case was there any indication of becoming more supportive, more loving.

Why was the "instruction" inadequate? I had "informed" them about the idea of tough love. Yet when it came to implementing the concept, they could conceive only of being tougher. They had fallen back on the natural tendency to split oppositions instead of creatively holding them.

I had made a mistake. I had tried to change them by altering their minds. Teaching them the concept was not the key. The key was to challenge them and support them in choosing to enter the fundamental state of leadership. I cannot inform people into tough love. I must *be* the change I want to see. Only then can I invite others into that creative state.

This is why the eight transformational practices are important. The concepts we are considering ask us to look at ourselves in ways that are not natural. They ask us if we are in the normal state of slow death. We do not get into the transformational state by "learning" the concepts. We get there by committing to higher purpose. We examine our hypocrisy and loss of meaning. We commit to live with purpose and increased authenticity. When we make this commitment, we naturally become more oriented to the needs of others. We naturally become more externally open. We exhibit the characteristics that define the fundamental state of leadership.

PREPARATION FOR ENTERING THE FUNDAMENTAL STATE OF LEADERSHIP

Choose a quiet time when you can reflect on the meaning this chapter has for you. Begin by assessing where you are today, as honestly as you can.

Questions for Reflection

1. Check each item that describes you as you are today.

___ I hold high standards focused on the collective good.

___ I regularly clarify what is best for the relationship, the group, or the company.

___ People see me as having no personal agenda.

___ The people around me tend to sacrifice for the collective good.

___ The people around me tend to trust me.

___ I trust people enough to display my vulnerability.

___ I surface the uncomfortable issues no one wants to talk about.

___ I help groups transcend the uncomfortable issues and become more cohesive.

___ I do not waver from the standards I set.

___ I model the standards for others.

___ I hold those below me to my standards.

___ I hold those above me to my standards.

___ I challenge people to perform beyond their abilities.

___ People tend to respond when I issue such challenges.

___ When I issue a challenge, I extend myself to support the people involved.

___ I allow people to fail.

___ I do not let people slip into self-doubt and depression.

___ I live in a network of trusting and productive relationships.

___ The people around me tend to love what they are doing.

2. Now assess yourself on the following scale by circling the numbers under the characteristics that currently describe you. Note that the "negative" areas of the scale represent the overemphasis of a positive characteristic so that it becomes a negative. The "integrative" part of the scale represents the integration of opposing positives. If you feel you

model the integration of compassionate concern and bold assertiveness, circle one of the numbers under "Integrative." Otherwise circle two numbers, one on each side of the scale.

Negative	Positive	Integrative	Positive	Negative
Indulgent; permissive	Compassionate concerned	Compassionate and assertive	Assertive; bold	Oppressive; overbearing
−3 −2 −1	1 2 3	4 5 4	3 2 1	−1 −2 −3

Self-Improvement

1. Based on the assessments you have completed, write a one-paragraph self-description on the theme of tough love. In your own words, describe where you are today with respect to this aspect of the fundamental state of leadership.

2. Write a strategy for self-improvement in the area of tough love. Try to be as concrete as possible in describing steps you are willing to take beginning today.

Helpful Hints for Practicing Tough Love

Tough means strong, firm, having a high, unwavering standard.

Know what collective result you want to create.

Know what difficult standards are necessary to create that result.

Model complete integrity around the standard.

Hold everyone to the same standard that you are modeling.

Make no exceptions.

Let people go if they cannot live the standard.

No one is more important than the collective good.

See the potential in others that they cannot see in themselves.

Challenge others to exceed their current capacities.

Love means being attracted to, feeling affection for, being genuinely concerned.

Be completely supportive of people even as you challenge them to live up to the standard.

Spend time with the people you seek to lead.

Understand the risks they are facing from their point of view.

Analyze their struggles.

Experience their most difficult tasks.

Know their deepest needs.

Show genuine concern for their needs.

Make personal sacrifices in their behalf.

Express your vulnerability and need for them.

Recognize the necessity of failure in learning to create a new result.

Spend increased time with the people who are trying to change.

Increase your intimacy with the people who are trying to change.

Make all topics discussable, including your own behavior.

Sharing Insights

If in responding to the questions above, you have an important insight or a meaningful story that you would like to share, visit www.deepchange.com and look for the links to submit stories for possible posting on the Deep Change Web site. You may thus help many people. If you would like to review such insights and stories, go to the same Web site.

PART THREE

Developing Leaders

> *"Otherness, taken seriously, always invites transfor-mation, calling us not only to new facts and theories and values, but also to new ways of living our lives—and that is the most daunting threat of all."*
> —PARKER PALMER (1998)

The chapters in Part Two explored eight practices, each of them a pathway that can help you enter the fundamental state of leadership. By now it should be clear that these practices are not separate and distinct. Rather, like the colors in a prism that all flow from a single source of light, they are a manifold expression of what it means to be in a certain state of being.

Becoming a leader is not a matter of becoming adept at a certain set of "behaviors" or learning a particular set of leadership "principles" or "tools." Behaviors, principles, and tools all have their place, but they will not make transformational leaders of us without a process of deep inner change. When we develop a better self, we create a better world.

By the same token, to develop leaders is not to impart a set of concepts or to teach a toolkit of strategies and behaviors. It is to engage the process of deep change in oneself and thereby invite others to do the same. When this happens, we truly engage in otherness, and we soon begin to transform one another. The challenges these pose are the subject of Part Three.

CHAPTER SIXTEEN

The Stages of Self-Change

All change is self-change. Even if we are seeing a professional therapist, change still requires personal choice. In the end, we must make a choice to change.

In this final part of the book, we turn to the issue of developing leadership. The fundamental argument is that we develop leaders by enticing them to enter the fundamental state of leadership. In order to this, we must engage in a two-step process. First, we must change ourselves by choosing to enter the fundamental state of leadership. Second, we help others to change themselves by helping them to enter the fundamental state of leadership. Although the first step naturally gives rise to the second, our experience in Step One alters how we understand and go about the process in Step Two. In this chapter, we meet a woman who understands the two steps, and we review some research that gives great insight into how people make self-change. From these two sources, we will derive a very different way to think about the development of leaders.

A WOMAN WHO KNOWS

In Part One, we met many people who exercised the courage to enter the fundamental state of leadership. One of the surprises in those cases is that people do not have to hold a position at the top of an organization to lead change. We met unlikely people like Roman Walley, who began to lead in ways no one would have expected. We learned how he stepped outside the prison of his own fears and empowered himself. In the process, he became empowering to others.

We also learned that not all people at the top of an organization are in the fundamental state of leadership. In fact, most of the time, most are not. We call such people "leaders" because of the formal position they hold, but holding a position is not the same as leading. Most of the time, most top executives are simply administering. They are living in the normal state, doing what is normally expected.

A woman we'll call Joan describes herself in exactly this way. Joan has spent a decade as vice president of human resources in a Fortune 200 company. The company is well regarded. It is a global company of diverse businesses and boasts a record of continuous financial success. Joan herself has been well regarded, regularly receiving outstanding personal evaluations. Her situation is one that many people dream about being in. Yet Joan writes of some concerns:

> For more years than I care to admit, I have strongly desired to take action to change my behavior and that of my organization, but until recently haven't garnered the personal courage to do so.
>
> Despite our financial success, there have been many things wrong, in my view, with management-team interactions. Team and personal dysfunctions are alive and well in corporate America. The problems include everything from petty jealousy, to ego and personality clashes, to dishonesty, to withholding or distorting mission-critical information, and beyond. Such behaviors are natural to most top management teams. Such behavior tends to be normal, expected, hardly noticed.
>
> For a long time, I sought to influence change but gained only minor successes. I was very busy and delivering a significant quantity of valuable administrative work that certainly needed to be accomplished. But the real challenges of being an influential leader on the management team, and leveraging human resources for maximum benefit, were not being fully addressed.
>
> My performance was perceived as outstanding by my boss and by my colleagues. Yet in my view, I was falling short because I was not doing much to enhance work interactions and processes. Trust was often low. Divisions fought among themselves and with the corporate office. And our values statement looked fine on the wall, but it was not being acted out in reality.

Here Joan provides a marvelous description of what happens to many senior executives. Like Tom Jones at CIGNA, she is living in a company with a successful financial record. She has plenty of normal work to do. She does this work very well, and she is recognized for excellence in doing it. Joan's comfort zone is very comfortable indeed.

Yet Joan is plagued by the realization that the system is not a productive community. Like most other corporations, this one has a politically fragmented management system that could be much more than it is. At times, she has tried to do something about this issue, but she has been less than successful. As she notes, her courage has been insufficient. Instead of entering the fundamental state of leadership, she learned to protect herself and simply live in the normal state.

Most senior people do exactly this. Like the lower-level people whom they often condemn for lack of commitment, those at the top often choose to live for "peace and pay." They do this while calling others to live in deep commitment. As Leo Tolstoy once wrote, "Everyone thinks of changing the world, but no one thinks of changing himself." Is it any wonder that others fail to respond to the double message?

While senior executives, like the rest of us, cannot see the hypocrisy in themselves, they see it clearly in the people around them. They condemn it in private and ignore it in the endless meetings where it is manifest. As a result, organizations tend to stay in the same normal state as the people who run them.

Joan goes on with her story. She describes working for a new boss, a man who is "more demanding" and has "a different and more energizing set of expectations." The presence of this man was revitalizing but highly challenging. In facing the challenge, Joan was exposed to the fundamental notions in *Deep Change*. After some continued wrestling, she writes:

> I internalized the message that I couldn't change the business or organization until I myself changed. I became more strongly committed to being a leader and making a difference in the corporation. I knew I needed to make different decisions and behave in new ways. So I have turned inside. I have an inner voice that helps me stay on course and that keeps me focused and balanced. Mostly, the voice speaks in a whisper, but it has occasionally been a yell and a forceful call to action.
>
> My personal changes have been dramatic, and I feel much better about my professional life and workplace impact. I work hard, but I experience less stress. I have a stronger focus and think more clearly. I

have been more prone to aim for vital goals and less prone to simply do task after task, with no clear vision in mind.

> *"I have an inner voice that helps me stay on course and that keeps me focused and balanced. Mostly, the voice speaks in a whisper, but it has occasionally been a yell and a forceful call to action."*

Once Joan confronted her hypocrisy, she began to make deep change. Instead of continuing on an externally driven path, she became truly purpose-centered, internally directed, other-focused, and externally open. In her new state, she reported doing hard things. She began both "delivering and receiving difficult messages that previously would have been off-limits for honest discourse." She revitalized an important management team. She started operating in a more open and strategic fashion, "drafting a human resource strategy with meaningful insight from every corporate officer and every business division." She developed a new process for division-led decision making and cooperation. The overall result was more open and candid communication. Most important, the company has progressed in "moving the values statement off the wall and into the everyday work lives of our managers and employees." Joan concludes:

> Based on my firsthand experience, I understand the importance of personal change as it relates to influencing organization change. I am building new bridges at the same time I walk on them, and our corporation is adopting new ways of behavior and interaction, pathways that will support our continued success in the future.

Joan has learned what most managers do not want to hear: organizations do not change significantly unless someone inside the organization changes significantly. Self-change is the key to organizational change. The real issues in any organization are not the problems in the systems and processes. The real problem is human commitment and courage. When we enter the fundamental state of leadership and thereby invite others to join us, the systems and processes begin to change in a natural way.

In order to be able to help other people make such self-change, we need to have a deeper understanding of how self-change actually occurs. To gain such understanding, we will briefly turn our attention to an instructive program of research.

THE PROCESSES THAT PRECEDE SELF-CHANGE

In Chapter Eight I referred to the book *Changing for Good: A Revolutionary Six-Stage Program for Overcoming Bad Habits and Moving Your Life Positively Forward,* in which Prochaska, Norcross, and DiClemente (1994) report on a research program at the University of Rhode Island. The researchers spent years studying what people do to pull out of negative routines and addictions. They found that all change is self-change. Even if we are seeing a professional therapist, change still requires personal choice. In the end, we must make a choice to change.

The insights that come from this research are very useful. Here are some of the high points.

When interviewed, most people who have made successful self-changes describe the process in simplistic terms. They may say, for example, that they woke up one morning and just decided to stop smoking. They believe what they are saying, but much more is actually involved.

The researchers found that these people tend to go through six stages: precontemplation, contemplation, preparation, action, maintenance, and termination. In making self-change, everyone has to go through these stages. Someone who is depressed must go through them. Someone who wants to quit smoking or wants to lose weight must go through them. Part of the reason we tend not to see the six stages is that most of us equate change with action. But it's important to keep in mind that even while we are moving toward change, we are in the nonaction stages 80 percent of the time.

A further insight is that each stage requires different change strategies. If we try to use strategies that do not belong with the stage we are in, we are setting ourselves up to fail.

The six stages and their associated strategies are shown in Table 16.1. Here is an outline of how the stages work.

Stage One: Precontemplation

In this stage, we may have a problem but do not yet see it as a problem. Every one of us is perpetually in this stage in regard to at least some of our negative routines or self-defeating behaviors. Other people may see the problem clearly, but the person with the problem does not. In this stage, people have no intention of changing behavior. For example, a

Table 16.1. Stages and Strategies in Self-Change.

Process	Goals	Techniques*
Consciousness-Raising	Increasing information about self and problem	Observations, confrontations, interpretations, bibliotherapy
Social Liberation	Increasing social alternatives for behaviors that are not problematic	Advocating for rights of repressed, empowering, policy interventions
Emotional Arousal	Experiencing and expressing feelings about one's problems and solutions	Psychodrama, grieving losses, role playing
Self-Reevaluation	Assessing feelings and thoughts about self with respect to a problem	Value clarification, imagery, corrective emotional experience
Commitment	Choosing and committing to act, or belief in ability to change	Decision-making therapy, New Year's resolutions, logotherapy
Countering	Substituting alternatives for problem behaviors	Relaxation, desensitization, assertion, positive self-statements
Environment Control	Avoiding stimuli that elicit problem behaviors	Environmental restructuring (e.g., removing alcohol or fatterning foods), avoiding high-risk cures
Reward	Rewarding self, or being rewarded by others, for making changes	Contingency contracts, overt and covert reinforments
Helping Relationships	Enlisting the help of someone who cares	Therapeutic alliance, social support, self-help groups

*These are primarily professional techniques used by psychotherapists.

Source: Changing for Good by James O. Prochaska, John C. Norcross, and Carlo C. Di-Clemente. Copyright © 1994 by James O. Prochaska, John C. Norcross, and Carlo C. DiClemente. Reprinted with permission of HarperCollins Publishers Inc., p. 33.

man comes home from work every night, eats, watches television, and falls asleep. He has no interest in anything else, including family members and visitors. In the precontemplation stage, he does not see that his behavior is causing problems for others. He denies any suggestion that he might have a problem. If he perceives any need for change, it is only that he would like people to stop criticizing him.

Resistance and denial are normal in this stage. If individuals end up in therapy at this point, it is only because they have been pressured by the boss, a spouse, or a peer—in short, somebody who has leveraged them into going. In therapy, they are uncooperative and usually stop going as soon as they can reasonably do so.

Joan, for example, spent ten years doing what was expected. In the early stages of her experience, it is likely that she was not aware of any need for self-change, and no one was anyone asking her to change herself. Like most other executives, she was not even thinking about it. She was in the normal state. Some people believe that reaching people in the precontemplation stage is impossible. They believe that the best thing to do is to wait until the problem gets worse. The trouble is that some problems can snowball, making it increasingly difficult for the person to change. For people in this stage, there are only two strategies that seem to be useful: (1) consciousness-raising (getting more information about the problem) and (2) social liberation (finding positive, uplifting social situations).

When it comes to making the self-change that is required to enter the fundamental state of leadership, many people are going to be in the precontemplation stage. Trying to get them to embrace self-change is very difficult. We can keep exposing them to various kinds of information about why they might want to. We can also put them in social settings that are conducive to such a change. Yet many will not be ready. In transforming organizations, we do not reach everyone. We reach a few. If we create a critical mass, that is enough to begin to move the organization. As it moves, still others change. Yet seldom do we reach everyone.

Stage Two: Contemplation

The contemplation stage occurs when we start to think about taking action. We begin to want to change how we feel about ourselves and begin to open up to new information. We may know the end result we want to create, and we may even know the path we plan to take, but we are not ready to leave on the trip.

It is interesting that on average, smokers spend about two years in the contemplation stage. The fear of failure is a big factor, accounting for endless excuses and procrastination. It is also interesting that the clearest sign of moving out of this stage is the movement away from problem solving. The focus changes. In the language of this book, the person is beginning to become purpose-centered.

Joan spent considerable time in the contemplation state. She wrestled often with the notion that she should change. She wanted to feel better about herself. She kept gathering information and thinking about what she might do differently. She was not ready to act, but she was thinking about it.

Four coping strategies are effective in this stage: (1) consciousness-raising, (2) social liberation, (3) emotional arousal, and (4) self-reevaluation. Emotional arousal means moving from thinking to feeling, experiencing, and expressing feelings about the problem. Self-reevaluation means analyzing feelings and thoughts about oneself in relation to the problem.

In making self-change or in helping others to do so, it is important to understand the contemplation stage. Here it is appropriate to reduce the emphasis on analysis and rational persuasion. We have to move to the level of feeling. We have to recognize our feelings and those of the people whose self-change we want to encourage. In the helping role, our message has to be authentic and congruent. It is usually when we model living at the feeling level that other people find the courage to more fully contemplate change, to engage in self-reevaluation. Recall that Joan described working for a new boss, a man who was "more demanding" and who had "a different and more energizing set of expectations." This man did not communicate at only the rational level. He radiated energy. He communicated feelings. He modeled being fully alive and drew Joan into a closer examination of herself.

Stage Three: Preparation

In this stage, we are planning to take action within a month. We have commitment and readiness but also great ambivalence. At this stage, we tend to find ourselves going through the final preparations to begin the journey. We have already made some changes. We have stopped denying the need to change, we have gathered some information, and usually we have made some adjustments in our behavior. Yet we are not quite ready. This stage is an important step in the process of getting ready.

Consciousness-raising has by now fallen away as a coping mechanism. Social liberation, emotional arousal, and self-reevaluation are still effective. The additional effective strategy is commitment. Commitment means believing in one's ability to change and making the choice to act.

In coming to make self-change or in helping others make self-change, there must be movement to commitment. Joan went through this process. As she continued to churn, she was exposed to the concepts of deep change. She came to a new recognition: "I couldn't change the business or organization until I myself changed. I became more strongly committed to being a leader, and making a difference in the corporation. I knew I needed to make different decisions and behave in new ways."

Stage Four: Action

We are in the action stage when we start engaging in new patterns of behavior. Obvious examples are when a smoker throws all her cigarettes away or an alcoholic pours all his alcohol down the drain. Since these patterns are visible, other people finally see some change taking place and start giving encouragement and support. For those who are standing outside the action as objective observers, it is difficult to understand that the change started before this stage or that more will continue after it. Understanding this, we can see how important it is to get or give support.

When Joan entered the action stage, she began to engage in new patterns of behavior. For example, she began "delivering and receiving difficult messages that previously would have been off-limits" and operating in a more open and strategic fashion, ultimately developing a new process for decision making and cooperation. In the action stage, information and self-evaluation become less important than social liberation and commitment. Four additional processes also become relevant at this point: reward, countering, environmental control, and helping relationships:

- *Reward* simply means setting up ways to acknowledge our accomplishments as we make self-change. These could come from ourselves or others; ideally they come from both. We might, for example, identify some touchstones of progress and promise ourselves a positive reward as we reach each objective. For instance, people on diets sometimes promise themselves new wardrobes when they attain a certain weight.

- *Countering* means replacing a negative behavior with a positive one. For instance, a person who is giving up smoking may substitute chewing gum for cigarettes.

- *Environmental control* means that we make sure we are spending our time in situations where our problem behaviors are not encouraged and our positive behaviors are valued. An alcoholic, for example, would avoid places where people are drinking.

- *Helping relationships.* This is asking for support from people who care, talking openly about feeling depressed, and discussing any negative routines we might have. It is asking people to help. Others tend to be very responsive to such requests.

An understanding of this stage also has implications in terms of helping others to enter the fundamental state of leadership. We might think about encouraging people to reward themselves for making the key decision. We might help them recognize that they are likely to miss some of the things they are giving up and may want to consciously substitute something to replace that which is lost. We may also encourage them to spend more time with people who will support and sustain them in their new efforts. Finally, we may want to create support groups to help people to share feelings and support as they move into the fundamental state of leadership.

Stage Five: Maintenance

Change does not stop just because we have taken action. Afterward comes the maintenance stage. This is when we consolidate the progress we have made in all the earlier stages. We put energy into guarding against relapses. As Joan moved forward, she began to consolidate and use her self-discoveries. Thus she remarks, "Based on my firsthand experience, I understand the importance of personal change as it relates to influencing organizational change. I am building new bridges at the same time I walk on them, and our corporation is adopting new ways of behavior and interaction, pathways that will support our continued success in the future."

Stage Six: Termination

In this stage, the old behavior is no longer a temptation, for we have lost all desire for the negative pattern. We have confidence that we will not relapse. We have achieved victory over self.

There seems to be great variation in the way different people handle this stage. One person may be able to completely conquer smoking and lose all desire for it. Others are still yearning for the old satisfactions even twenty years later. For such people, it is necessary to stay in the maintenance stage. The same appears to be true for alcoholics and even dieters.

In leadership, relapse is an even bigger problem. Joan did not mention this issue, but many of the people we met in Part One did. There is a constant pull back to the normal state. The power of entropy and the attraction of slow death are always working on us. This is why Jeremy Fish tells us that he sought out an executive coach. He needed help to continually examine his tendencies to get stuck in the comfort zone. He needed support in maintaining the vision and determination to keep growing and making a difference. We all do.

FURTHER INSIGHTS

There are some further insights of importance that come from the research on self-change. First, people do not tend to move through the self-change process in a straight line, from Stage One to Stage Two and so on to Stage Six. Prochaska, Norcross, and DiClemente (1994) and his associates found this happens in only about 20 percent of the cases. We might do well in some stages, poorly in others, and thus follow what might seem like a chaotic pattern through the different stages. Change often requires a great deal of energy, time, and money, and the truth is that most of us underestimate what is involved. We might have many starts and stops, with the average person going through the entire process as many as six times!

For this reason, the researchers came to call their model the spiral model of change. They see progress as a spiral on two axes, showing that people move forward and then backward on the horizontal axis (see Figure 16.1). The process seems discouraging, but there is a positive fact that we often do not realize. Progress is also moving on a vertical axis; that is, we are continuously moving upward toward success. Both the forward and backward movements are actually part of a larger learning process.

This point has implications for entering the fundamental state of leadership. Change is a messy process that includes failures. When faced with our failures, we feel frustration, shame, and other negative emotions. I have spoken to countless people who have attempted to take initiative in their organization, only to withdraw when they are sanctioned. Whenever challenged, they accurately point out, "This organization does not want change." Based on their experience, they choose to stay in the normal state. What they fail to understand is that punishment is

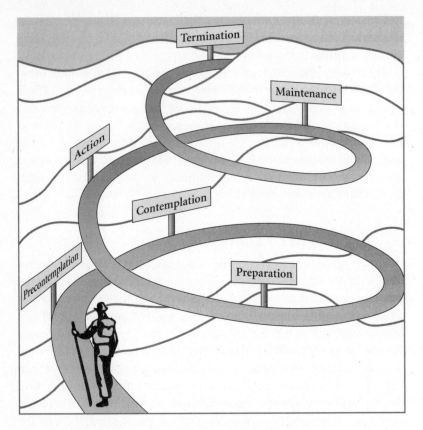

Figure 16.1. Spiral Model of Change

Source: Changing for Good by James O. Prochaska, John C. Norcross, and Carlo C. Di-Clemente. Copyright © 1994 by James O. Prochaska, John C. Norcross, and Carlo C. DiClemente. Reprinted with permission of HarperCollins Publishers Inc.

part of the process. To lead is to experience and transcend discouragement and despair. If we realize that punishment and failure are part of progress, we can engage them more positively. By continuously recycling ourselves, we are learning. We are developing an increased capacity for growth. Action followed by failure is far better than no action at all, because those who act and fail and keep on going are much more likely to succeed the next time. With each effort, we have increased probability of success. In helping others to change, this is a very valuable point to understand and communicate.

A second insight is that negative patterns tend to be related to each other. A person might quit smoking but replace that behavior with eating and then put on weight. Smokers who also drink are twice as likely to return to smoking, and so on. In other words, we might give up one negative pattern but then adopt another to replace it. If we want change to be permanent, we have to understand the underlying causes of our behavioral patterns. For example, the most frequent cause of relapse for smoking, drinking, and overeating is emotional distress. We need to get past our defenses, look deeply into ourselves, and monitor our hypocrisy.

In terms of leadership, this insight suggests a great need for choosing and pursuing purpose while examining our self-deceptions. To enter the fundamental state of leadership, we need to be committed to continuously monitoring and acting on our own hypocrisy. Our hypocrisy is a potential source of power if we monitor it and confront it, for in that process we change.

A third insight involves a misconception. Many people believe that the only reason we do not change is that we lack willpower or commitment. Commitment is one of the processes of change, but to rely only on commitment or willpower is to set ourselves up for failure. We need to draw on many other sources of preparation and support. We need to help others do the same.

We also make assumptions about the role of willpower in the exercise of good leadership. Here we might rethink leadership and leadership development in terms of the stages and strategies discussed here. I think they greatly alter what it means to develop leadership in an organization.

A fourth insight concerns the possible future. One of the change processes is called *self-reevaluation*. It actually takes two forms, one focusing on the present and the other on the future. The present form takes a negative view and primarily emphasizes our existing bad characteristics and emotions. The future form envisions a changed, happier, and healthier self. The most effective evaluations contain both. The negative pushes us out of the present, while the positive pulls us into the future.

In trying to develop leaders, we tend to give them 360-degree feedback with the intent that they identify and work on their weaknesses. Few people think about the possible future or invite feedback on their best self, their strengths. In developing leaders, we need to move away from problem solving toward purpose finding. We need to help people identify their strengths, and we need to help them hold a compelling picture of a better future. In Part Two of this book, I described several processes that can be helpful in creating a picture of our best present and future selves.

In developing leaders, we need to move away from problem solving toward purpose finding. We need to help people identify their strengths, and we need to help them hold a compelling picture of a better future.

A fifth insight is that we can take specific steps to facilitate the self-change process. Since change always involves uncertainty, it is natural to practice avoidance. We put off starting as a way to protect ourselves from failure. Committing to change is never easy, but the research into self-change shows there are five things that can help:

1. Plan to take small steps.
2. Set a specific starting date so that you neither act prematurely nor procrastinate.
3. Go public with your commitment so that you will be motivated by knowing that others are expecting you to succeed and are more likely to help you get back on track if you have a relapse.
4. Prepare as if you were going in for major surgery. Since change is often the psychological equivalent of major physical surgery, you and your support group should give this process a high priority.
5. Create your own action plans. In this way, you increase the likelihood that you will act.

All of these points can be useful to a person who seeks to help others enter the fundamental state of leadership. The fourth one is particularly noteworthy. When we want other people to change, we greatly underappreciate the magnitude of what we are asking. Thinking about it as the psychological equivalent of major surgery is a very useful concept.

A sixth insight is that we need to draw on the power of social networks. We live in groups that have norms, values, and roles. In any group we participate in, we are expected to be a certain way. Often when we are contemplating change, we worry about the resistance we will get from family members, peers, or others who are important to us. Fear of their reactions can keep us from taking action. If we do take action, we may relapse because of others' reactions and our desire to please them. It is important to consider this issue. It may even be necessary to choose to move into a new network of supporters that will support our success in whatever we choose to do with our lives. Similarly, in helping others, we would do well to pay great attention to their social networks as we help them think about the move from being reactors to becoming creators who redefine and transform the groups within which they live.

ENTERING THE FUNDAMENTAL STATE OF LEADERSHIP

We normally think of leadership as action in which a person is taking initiative and directing others. If this person is not doing this, he or she is not leading. Recall, however, that self-change involves stages that precede action and that 80 percent of the time people are not in the action stage. Entering the fundamental state of leadership also involves stages that precede action. Paying attention to this fact may greatly assist as we strive to enter the fundamental state of leadership and help others do the same.

PREPARATION FOR ENTERING THE FUNDAMENTAL STATE OF LEADERSHIP

Choose a quiet time when you can reflect on the meaning this chapter has for you. Begin by assessing where you are today, as honestly as you can.

Questions for Reflection

1. What implications do you see in Leo Tolstoy's remark, "Everyone thinks of changing the world, but no one thinks of changing himself"?

2. Give an example to illustrate or dispute the following: "Holding a position is not the same as leading. Most of the time, most top executives are simply administering. They are living in the normal state, doing what is normally expected."

3. Joan remarked, "The problems include everything from petty jealousy, to ego and personality clashes, to dishonesty, to withholding or distorting mission-critical information, and beyond. Such behaviors are natural to most top management teams. Such behavior tends to be normal, expected, hardly noticed." Is such behavior normal in your experience? If so, what implications does this have?

4. To what extent do you identify with the following statement from Joan? "For a long period of time, I sought to influence change, but gained only minor successes. I was very busy and delivering a significant quantity of valuable administrative work that certainly needed to be accomplished. But the real challenges of being an influential leader on the management team . . . were not being fully addressed."

5. Joan makes the following claim: "Based on my firsthand experience, I understand the importance of personal change as it relates to influencing organizational change. I am building new bridges at the same time I walk on them, and our corporation is adopting new ways of behavior and interaction, pathways that will support our continued success in the future." What does this statement mean to you? Have you experienced what Joan is describing? What would it take for you to have a similar experience?

6. Joan's story is a story of self-change. What does her story imply about the general development of leaders in a company?

7. Have you made a significant self-change—perhaps changing a habit like smoking or overeating or fundamentally changing the way you interact with others? If so, can you identify the six stages of self-change in your own experience? Which stage was hardest for you? To what extent did others support you?

8. If you have tried to make a significant self-change and not succeeded, what might you do differently the next time in the light of what you have read in this chapter?

Self-Improvement

1. Based on the discussion of self-change in this chapter, write a paragraph describing your own readiness to change. As you consider entering the fundamental state of leadership, where in the process do you think you are today?

2. Write a strategy for self-change in a specific area of your life. Try to be as concrete as possible in describing steps you are willing to take beginning today.

Helpful Hints for Self-Change

These hints are for getting yourself into the fundamental state of leadership:

Become more purpose-centered. Ask yourself, What result do I want to create? This will move you out of a reactive stance and into the creative state.

Become more internally directed. Ask yourself, What are my patterns of denial, and how can I decrease my hypocrisy? This will increase your self-trust.

Become more other-focused. Ask yourself, With whom am I joined, and how might I enrich our connectivity? This will help you increase your resources.

Become more externally open. Ask yourself, How can I move forward into uncertainty, trusting that I will adapt as I move and learn? Doing this will lead to exponential development.

In considering the above four issues, make specific commitments.

Develop your own specific change plans.

Prepare to take small steps forward.

Make your commitment public.

Treat the change process with the same priority as having surgery.

Align yourself with a supportive social network.

These hints are for attracting others to the fundamental state of leadership:

Clarify the shared purpose. Ask yourself, What is the collective future that we all want to create? This will increase the probability of moving the relationship or organization out of the reactive state.

Increase the sense of trust. Ask yourself, How can I model an orientation of genuine service, empathy, and concern? Modeling such an orientation will increase others' openness to possibility.

Stimulate mindfulness. Ask yourself, How can I disturb their current mind-set or paradigm by introducing variation into their experience? This will pull them out of their routine and cause them to engage in sense making.

Move them to feeling. Ask yourself, How do I move them from analysis to the exploration of their feelings? This will change the focus from what they know to what they are encountering.

Increase the challenge. Ask yourself, How can I put them in a situation that is more real and more challenging? This will increase their sense of risk and offer the reward of exponential growth.

Increase the support. Ask yourself, How can I maintain the unwavering challenge while helping them decrease self-doubt and increase confidence? This will assist them in exercising the courage to move forward.

Encourage commitment. Ask yourself, How can I help them understand that people do not get empowered; rather, they empower themselves? This will underline the necessity for freedom and independent choice.

Encourage helping relationships. Ask yourself, How can I help them to create support systems and learn how to ask for help that is needed? This will enrich their capacity to move forward.

Manage the endings. Ask yourself, How can I help them recognize the realities of what is being lost, accept them, and find positive substitutes? This will help others manage depression and move forward.

Clarify the gains. Ask yourself, How can I help them see the gains, celebrate progress, and reward milestones? This will provide learning, increase courage, and support progress.

Sharing Insights

If in responding to the questions above, you have an important insight or a meaningful story that you would like to share, visit www.deepchange.com and look for the links to submit stories for possible posting on the Deep Change Web site. You may thus help many people. If you would like to review such insights and stories, go to the same Web site.

CHAPTER SEVENTEEN

Inviting Others into the Fundamental State of Leadership

"*My teaching became much more personal. In each session, as I challenged participants to confront their integrity gaps, I challenged myself. And as I acted on those commitments, a new self emerged, a learner who now was a much better guide to others on journeys of discovery and transformation.*"
—DOUG ANDERSON

Throughout this book, we have seen that the concept of the fundamental state of leadership has some unusual and important implications. First, it redefines what leadership means. Leadership is not authority, and it is not merely a set of learnable skills. It is, at the most basic level, a state—a way of being. That is what the director of nursing told us in Chapter One. The ability to create productive community is not about behavior; it is about who we are. Productive community is a creative, collective state that is a reflection of someone having entered the creative individual state.

Second, an understanding of the fundamental state of leadership redefines what it means to develop leaders. We began to see what this means in the preceding chapter, where we learned that there is much that precedes and follows the decision to change ourselves. Accordingly, if we want to develop leaders, we need to understand the stages of self-change and support others as they go through them.

In this chapter, we consider how to invite others to embark on this process of deep change. By now, it should be clear that the first requirement for attracting others into the fundamental state of leadership is that we have entered that state ourselves. There is no way to "teach" what it means to be a leader except by being what we wish to invoke in others.

Here we encounter a difficulty. The fundamental state of leadership is somewhat fragile. Not only is it difficult to get ourselves into that state, but it is difficult to stay in it once we enter it. Let us consider this point before meeting three transformational teachers who exemplify leadership development at its best.

THE FUNDAMENTAL STATE OF LEADERSHIP IS EPISODIC

Many of the people we have met in this book have commented on the episodic nature of the fundamental state of leadership. Once we leave that state of being purpose-centered and internally directed, other-focused and externally open, it is difficult to reenter it. Yet having entered it previously becomes an asset because we understand that commitment and emergence are the keys to personal and collective revitalization. We know the path.

Jeremy Fish is particularly clear. He says:

> I have little doubt that I will face many more perspective changes in the time left to me in this life. Although I can't honestly say that I look forward to the paralysis and fear of walking naked into uncertainty that precedes my own shifts in paradigm, I have come to realize the great value of moving through the paralysis and fear of uncertainty in order to embrace my own emerging deep change reality. I recently found an executive coach skilled in appreciative inquiry to help me face my own moments of illusion, panic, exhaustion, and stagnation— moments of slow death and failure to stay in the transformative cycle.

Jeremy understands that we move into and out of the fundamental state of leadership. Yet he has come to value being in the fundamental state of leadership so much that he seeks help in facing his own fears. He finds an executive coach to work with him on a regular basis. This is most impressive.

Most people are not like Jeremy. When I ask others to tell me of the great moments in their life, they often respond in a recognizable pattern. First, they tell me they faced a very difficult challenge. Then they tell me a story of courage, persistence, and triumph. They describe how much they learned even if the experience was unwanted. They speak of the event as a peak experience. Then they say, "But I would never want to do that again." This is a telling statement. It illustrates the high cost of growth, and it illustrates why so few people remain in the fundamental state of leadership.

Other people turn such experiences into a great asset. Knowing that they have been in an extraordinary state before helps them move forward in the present. Such a man is Tom Glocer.

Tom was a young lawyer at Reuters, at the time a highly profitable operation making large profits in every country except in Brazil, where it had been losing money for a long time. Tom was offered the line management job of heading up the Brazilian operation.

In an attempt to reduce Tom's anxiety, the CEO told Tom that Brazil had been a problem for a long time and that it was unlikely that he would actually turn it around. Tom saw this as a challenge and prepared for his new assignment with the systematic orientation of the legal mind. He gathered information, analyzed trends, and made plans for improving the Brazilian operation. When he arrived in Brazil, it took only a half-day to discover how totally corrupt the operation was. Some managers were ripping off the company; some of the worst actually carried guns. Incompetence and cronyism were everywhere. Managers assigned from other countries were counting the days until they could leave. The operation was hopeless.

By noon of his first day, Tom made a fundamental decision. He threw out all of his analysis and plans. He instead decided to fire all but three people and rebuild the entire organization. Tom had no experience as an executive leading such a total change. He says, "I was not a surgeon, but the patient was going to die." Like a doctor in a crisis, he began to move forward, making profound decisions with insufficient information. He was truly building the bridge as he walked on it. He left behind the mind of the lawyer and walked naked into the land of uncertainty.

After an agonizing effort, the Brazilian operation eventually became profitable. Here is how Tom looks back on that experience:

There was so much urgency. I had no choice. I had to act. If something blew up, it did not matter. Things were so bad there was only one way to go. So I did what I had to do. It was terrifying, but we learned how to do what needed to be done. It was the best work I have ever done.

Once I was in London. My driver asked me why I was there. I told him I was in town to assist Reuters with an organizational change effort. He snorted and said, "Good luck."

His cynicism was widely held. Reuters had shared the fate of many information companies in the post–dot-com era, losing 90 percent of its share price. When that happens to a corporation, it becomes a place of extraordinary pain. The new CEO, the man responsible for the life or death of the company, was Tom Glocer.

As I write this chapter, Tom is building the most important bridge of his life. He is now trying to do to the entire corporation what he did in Brazil. He is in the midst of walking naked in the land of uncertainty. In doing this, he has had some interesting insights. He begins by reflecting on the cases of deep change he has read in the past:

> I am struck by stories of managers who, whatever their level, move themselves beyond fear or self-preservation to act with true and decisive freedom. Once so liberated, their power knows no limits, and with it, their value to their companies soars.
>
> Despite the heroism of so many of the personal and corporate stories of growth related in cases of deep change, the striking feature for me is that they are *told in retrospect.* I do not say this to demean the power or pathos of the personal journeys recounted, but rather to highlight my own discomfort at telling my story before I know the ending.
>
> Reuters is my company. It is a 152-year-old institution I deeply love and one that the world would be poorer without. I have launched it into a transformation that employees, investors, and customers find threatening. I am calmly confident; however, there is no other path.
>
> We at Reuters have been through a wretched time in the eyes of market analysts and the U.K. media. Out of their pessimism, however, has ironically grown a great freedom for me that I have known only once before in my career. I can do no wrong—and hence I can do great good—because I am free of the incrementalism born of mediocre success.
>
> I do not know how this story will end, but I could not care more, work harder, or fear less. To me these are the seeds of success.

"Out of their pessimism, however, has ironically grown a great freedom for me that I have known only once before in my career. I can do no wrong—and hence I can do great good—because I am free of the incrementalism born of mediocre success."

Note that in the middle of the chaos, Tom reports being calmly confident. He is calm because he knows that there is no other choice. He is doing what he must do in order to meet his greatest responsibility: to live with his conscience. Although Tom does not like the conflict and uncertainty of transformation, he is willing to live with it because he puts the corporate good ahead of his own good, something that is a little easier because of what he did in Brazil. Tom has been in the fundamental state of leadership before. Nevertheless, trying to transform the company is still terrifying. He has to exercise anew the courage to move forward.

There are important lessons here for those who would invite others into the fundamental state of leadership. First, we are not continuously in that extraordinary state, any more than a great artist is continuously in a state of peak inspiration and creativity. Second, each new episode is a new challenge. We must meet and conquer our fears again. Third, each time we enter the fundamental state of leadership, we acquire learning and confidence that make that state more accessible to us in the future. There never comes a time when we cease building the bridge as we walk on it. What is different is that we move forward into the unknown with greater confidence and faith because we have done it before. We have adaptive confidence as we practice responsible freedom.

People who have entered the fundamental state of leadership on multiple occasions become people of great wisdom. They may experience excruciating pain. Yet they all discover that the real source of power in life is not in external trappings but in the unfolding of human virtue. Collective transformation requires someone who exercises the courage to put the collective interest ahead of personal survival. When individuals exercise such virtue, it can spread to the collective level. Organizational transformation is all about increased collective virtue, about the ever-increasing integrity of both the individual and the organization.

TRANSFORMATIONAL TEACHING

The preceding reflections have important implications for how we go about educating and developing leaders. Many institutions are designed to facilitate leadership development. Most are less effective than they might be. Business schools and corporate universities, for example, claim to teach leadership. Such institutions are particularly prone to staying in their zone of comfort. They do not understand the fundamental state of leadership. They seek to develop leaders by altering how students think and behave. They tend to do this through pedagogies of analysis and imitation. They present academic analyses and case studies of the techniques and best practices of successful leaders and organizations, and they suggest that students imitate them.

The key to getting into the fundamental state of leadership is not the analysis of techniques and practices. Developing leaders is not about getting them to imitate the thinking and behavior of other people who have been successful. It is about attracting people to the decision to enter the unique state from which their own great thinking and great behaviors emanate. This is done only when an individual chooses to become more purpose-centered, internally directed, other-focused, and externally open. It is an act of courage toward which people must be attracted.

We attract others into the fundamental state of leadership not by imitation but by becoming unique. We increase our uniqueness by pursuing ever-increasing integrity. As we increase our integrity, we see and fit ourselves with the uniqueness of the emerging reality in which we live. Our courage invites others to do the same.

In Chapter Six, we learned that there are four general strategies of change: telling, forcing, participating, and transcending. Most people apply the first two, which are the easiest but also the least effective. Few ever apply the fourth strategy, which begins with self-change. In Part Two, we explored eight practices that we can use to stay on the path that leads to ever-increasing integrity. As we employ these practices, we can increase the frequency and duration of our experiences inside the fundamental state of leadership.

The objective of leadership development efforts should be the same: to attract people to increase the frequency and duration of the time they spend in the fundamental state of leadership. To achieve this, administrators would have to be willing to live with programs of greater authenticity and risk. Similarly, instructors would themselves have to be in the fundamental state of leadership.

Here we will meet three people who exemplify this truth. One teaches leadership in the M.B.A. classroom. Another teaches executive courses. The third serves as an executive coach and teaches in one-on-one relationships. Each has something uniquely valuable to convey.

Creating Sacred Space

Larry Peters is a professor at Texas Christian University with much experience in working with both executives and students. In the process, he has learned to help people enter the fundamental state of leadership. Here is what Larry has to say:

> I have spent considerable time consulting with senior executives and managers who seemed to view change as a detached, third-party management task, almost like delegation but with bigger aspirations. Their message seems to say that change was necessary for everyone but themselves—"Change you . . . but leave me unchanged!" I would confront them about the lack of commitment I saw and heard . . . in what they said, who they said it to, how they would spend their time, what they measured and rewarded . . . and, in particular, their personal stories of why their behavior did not reflect the action, passion, or commitment of a real leader.
>
> What I heard, in a number of different instances, was that it was too dangerous to really lead in the highly political world they lived in. In fact, every instance of failed leadership seemed to reflect a . . . concern for personal (that is, job and career) safety.
>
> How can one lead others to more effective solutions if one is not willing to challenge the foundations of the dysfunctional world that produced less than effective results?
>
> We can't unless we change . . . unless we experience profound change, transformational change . . . deep change. By any name, we need to care more about what is right, what is effective, what is moral, and what can't be denied any longer than we do about our personal well-being. We need to step out of the transactional reality we seemed trapped in to find something worth "dying for"—and worth living for!
>
> That is the essence of leadership. It's not simply processes as reflected in so many books; it's passion and commitment for a cause. It's caring more about one's mission or vision or people or justice more than about one's self. Process models of leadership can only produce

results if enacted by leaders. Detached, third-person leadership, no matter how well it follows the sage advice of those who teach "how to lead," do not produce the results we want and need. *It's not the mechanics, it's the person!*

Larry's insights suggested a way of teaching that would allow the people he was working with to connect with the message in a deep way. His method has much in common with the strategies for appreciative inquiry discussed in Chapter Ten:

> I recently shared this message in an Executive M.B.A. course on leadership. It resonated throughout the room. My students shared many examples of failed leadership . . . from those who settled for "peace and pay" to those who tried to "manage" people to a new future. I had my students think about deep change that they experienced in their lives (or that others close to them experienced) and had them share stories with class.
>
> We heard stories of a man who lost a child in a car accident (and who changed the seat belt law in Texas), another who had to sign papers authorizing surgery for newborn twins that were not yet named (wondering if he was signing a death or life certificate for them), a woman who was promoted to the toughest assignment in her company for which she had no prior skills and a visibly sexist employee group, and a man who was given the assignment of opening a market in China and found everything he knew about management didn't work. We heard stories of passion and focus and courage and commitment and perseverance and energy. We heard stories that produced results beyond anyone's expectations, and we saw the emotion and shared the feelings of pride these people had. We saw what was possible when people—our classmates—experienced deep change. It was a profound class for my students, those who spoke and those who just listened. Nobody in that room will ever mistake true leadership for management again; everybody in that room understood what was expected of them to really lead. They raised the bar on themselves that afternoon—and on everyone else who presumes to lead.
>
> People need help to see the truth about themselves and the choices they need to make to lead. I believe that we can help empower real leaders who face the integrity gap that's caused by slow death and choose a path that can change the world. Change me first! The message is so simple, so powerful.

"We heard stories of passion and focus and courage and commitment and perseverance and energy. We heard stories that produced results beyond anyone's expectations, and we saw the emotion and shared the feelings of pride these people had."

Larry is no ordinary teacher. Notice his wisdom with the executives. He recognizes the hypocrisy in their normal language, time allocations, measures, and personal stories. Not only does he recognize the hypocrisy, he challenges it. He understands that the many books that focus on the analysis and imitation of success and on the mechanics of processes and systems miss the point. He understands that we enter the fundamental state of leadership when we decide to do it. The responsibility is with us. The problem is that no one wants to hear such a message. Since people are in denial, it is almost impossible to teach these ideas. People have numerous defense mechanisms that automatically kick in when these challenging notions are taught. So how does Larry teach?

Larry does something brilliant. He gets out of the expert role. Instead of telling and forcing, Larry simply asks a question. He asks people to identify their own deep change experiences. He then asks them to share. This process transforms the classroom from a profane space to a sacred space. In sacred space, people establish richer, more trusting relationships. In such networks, learning and commitment are facilitated.

In the kind of sacred space that Larry creates, many of the principles of self-change articulated in Chapter Sixteen naturally emerge. People stop focusing on their differences and start to marvel at their commonalities. They begin to discover a common objective: continuous movement toward ever-increasing integrity. Trust skyrockets. They become more mindful, willingly exploring alternative paradigms. Instead of living in the realm of safe analysis, they start to become comfortable in sharing authentic feelings. The sense of living in truth expands. They feel both challenged and supported. Commitment to the collective and to their own future growth increases. They are more willing to ask for help and better able to see the need to manage endings for others. The gains and possible additional gains of moving forward in their own lives become clear to all.

All of these payoffs emerge in sacred space, created by helping people tell their own core stories. The stories in Larry's classroom are like the ones we have read in this book. They are stories of passionate focus and extraordinary results, of deep human connection and exponential learning. These are not the stories from some textbook. These are the stories of the person in the next seat. The stories are transformational. In the normal state, we are sure that what I have described as the fundamental state of leadership is a myth. Yet in our own personal histories and in the history of our peers, we find evidence to the contrary. Sharing such stories creates a new collective reality.

How did Larry get to become such a teacher? Since he does not share that background, we do not know for sure. Yet we can get a clue. Meet a man who shares his own story of becoming a more transformational teacher.

Braving the Hero's Journey

Doug Anderson is a founding partner of a major executive education firm. He was a Harvard professor who taught business strategy. In his years since leaving Harvard, he has helped to build a major business that has provided educational programs in many of the world's largest companies. Here he shares a story not unlike the ones that were shared in Larry's classroom:

> I have often heard it said that "you never really learn a thing until you teach it to someone else." And it is true—there is a powerful connection between teaching and learning. That's probably why I chose academic and business teaching as a profession. I have always been interested in learning, and teaching seemed like a great way to continue learning. But it is not the only way, and maybe not the most powerful way—there is also the learning that comes from applying or experiencing an idea.
>
> I was a member of a consulting team that was using the concepts of the book *Deep Change* to help a major utility transform itself from an engineering-driven company to one that was much more focused on market and competitive realities. I could readily see that the "deep change or slow death" concept was very powerful, and I was eager to learn how to use that and the related concepts to help business leaders transform themselves and their corporations.
>
> From the outset, I expected this to be a fascinating intellectual journey. It turned out to be far more than that. It became personal.

During much of the decade of the 1990s, my first marriage was slowly dying. The causes were complex, as they always are, and unique to our circumstances. Tolstoy recognized this in his opening line to *Anna Karenina*: "Happy families are all alike; every unhappy family is unhappy in its own way."

I knew my wife was not happy in our marriage, but I always believed we would get through it. Sometimes she'd try to talk to me about divorce, but I wouldn't consider it. When you are rafting down the Colorado River and encounter whitewater, I'd say that's not the time to jump out, or to push your partner out—that's the time to hold on for dear life. I was sure there would be calm water ahead.

She didn't believe it. In May 1998 the perfect storm hit. My younger brother had died one year earlier. I had planned a three-day business trip to Houston to coincide with the anniversary of his death so that I could be with and comfort his family. At noon on the day I was to leave, there came a knock on the door. I answered to find a marshal, an officer of the court, with divorce papers in hand. "Please sign here," he said. "I am sorry. Your court appearance is scheduled for day after tomorrow."

I was stunned. My wife hadn't come home. We hadn't quarreled; in fact we had spent what I thought was a pleasant weekend at her parents' house in a city 300 miles away. I had driven home with my son; she was to follow a day later by plane.

I couldn't see an option for canceling my client engagement. Sixty people were counting on me the next day for a course in strategic business concepts. They had traveled from around the world. Obviously, I would not be able to represent myself in court. I called the airline and arranged to take a later flight. Then I called an attorney friend and spent the afternoon with him. I arrived at the client's conference center well after midnight. The next morning at eight o'clock, I opened a three-day seminar. At the end of the three days, I visited my sister-in-law on the anniversary of my brother's death. Instead of comforting her, I collapsed.

The divorce took two years to become final. I was powerless to prevent it. As I spun through the grief cycle, I found myself returning again and again to the concepts in *Deep Change*. I had never experienced this kind of sorrow before. It made me desperate to find ideas that worked. *Deep Change* became a mirror for me. I was not always comfortable with what I saw there. I began to recognize integrity gaps that I had not previously acknowledged.

Although I cut back dramatically on my schedule of travel and work during these months, I continued to teach in the utility program. My teaching became much more personal. In each session, as I challenged participants to confront their integrity gaps, I challenged myself. And as I acted on those commitments, a new self emerged, a learner who now was a much better guide to others on journeys of discovery and transformation.

In the hero's journey, the hero sets out on a quest, and before returning to his home community as an "empowered and empowering" leader, he must slay the beast. The beast he slays is his old self. That's what deep change is all about: the renewal and the replenishment of self and the enlargement of others.

Here there are some important lessons about how one becomes a transformational teacher. Doug observes that the most powerful education comes from the experience of applying ideas and experiencing the consequences. This process is usually quite painful. I am very moved when Doug says, "I had never experienced this kind of sorrow." When we have such feelings, we are forced to work in a way we would never work when we are in the normal state.

As Doug moves into the fundamental state of leadership, he opens up and begins to redefine who he is. He begins to look at himself, and he sees what he would normally deny. He sees his hypocrisy. He acknowledges integrity gaps that he had not previously acknowledged.

As he seeks to move forward in his life, he spends much time teaching—not only business strategy but deep change. In the process, his teaching becomes more personal. He challenges his students to close their integrity gaps while he is striving to close his own. At that point, Doug is teaching with increased moral power. As he does such teaching, he continues to grow. He becomes more purpose-centered and other-focused, more internally directed and externally open. As he does so, he begins to attract others into the fundamental state of leadership.

From Larry, we learn that there is great potential to be tapped in the M.B.A. classroom, and from Doug, we learn that teaching in the executive classroom can also be transformational. Now let's turn to another kind of transformational teacher.

Continuous Learning

Stan Goss describes a childhood filled with tragedy. When he was eight years old, his grandfather, uncle, and father all died in the same month. Stan was alone with each one when they died. His mother became a severe alcoholic. When Stan was nineteen, his mother and sister were accidentally killed. He describes the impact:

I looked great on the outside, but needed tons of work on the inside. I always got things started well, but found ways to sabotage getting to the finish line. I started out in a fast-track corporate career and eventually transitioned to an entrepreneurial career, where I had a string of not-quite-successful experiences.

This pattern continued through most of Stan's adult life. Then at age fifty-two, he attended a weekend workshop on personal transformation. The focus was on embracing his shadow self, the self he was denying. He indicates that he made some fundamental decisions that resulted in deep change. He clarified his unique mission in life. He became a senior executive coach. The pattern of sabotaging his success disappeared:

That was thirteen years ago. My practice has grown and flourished during that time, and now, at the age of sixty-five, I am at the most productive and contributory time of my life. My clients include senior executives in a wide variety of industries, including health care, financial services, power production, energy, and professional sports. In each organization I have worked with, I can point to significant results.

Stan notes some of the issues that make his work challenging. The first is language. The second is having a process that facilitates transformation. From his process comes the dance of co-creation and the emergence of productive community:

The work of being a transformational change agent constantly requires finding language and concepts that enable one to "describe the indescribable" and to "explain the unexplainable" to a transactional world that demands tangibility for every argument and discussion. One can be "attractive" in the dialogue only if one is facile with language in that eternal dance in the space between the transactional and transformational.

With my clients, I use the eight seed thoughts from *Change the World* (envision the productive community; first look within; embrace the hypocritical self; transcend fear; embody a vision of the common good; disturb the system; surrender to the emergent process; entice through moral power) in a similar way that Alcoholics Anonymous uses the twelve steps.

Each one has an appropriate time and place. For example, "envision productive community" has become like an "entry-level test question." I ask the leaders how they view the group of people they lead. Answers vary from "This is a company" to "This is a business unit." But when

I ask the leader if he or she sees a "community" and this person's eyes light up and he or she leans into that, I know we are on our way. We start talking about, teaching about, and implementing productive community ideas. Maybe compensation plans need to be aligned. Maybe we hold an off-site meeting to explore how productive community can be created. Maybe the leader needs to do some personal work to move from "me-me" to "me-we."

The dialogue always starts with . . . "I know what I want to create but don't know exactly what to do." Then we begin the actions of co-creation with "unconditional confidence." It is a process of continuous learning, integration, and action with course correction as we go along. A little productive community here, a little disturbing the system there, several "epiphanies" along the way, sprinkled with some appreciative inquiry, and magic happens: positive energy is created, things get better, metrics improve.

"It is a process of continuous learning, integration, and action with course correction as we go along. A little productive community here, a little disturbing the system there, several "epiphanies" along the way, sprinkled with some appreciative inquiry, and magic happens: positive energy is created, things get better, metrics improve."

Some people argue they are too old to change. This really means, "I am too lazy to practice responsible freedom." At age fifty-two, Stan demonstrated that transformation is always an option. More accurately, it is always a requirement. We transform, or we move toward entropy and slow death. Because Stan spent much of his time in the fundamental state of leadership, he learned a language and developed processes that allow him to attract his clients into the fundamental state of leadership.

ATTRACTING OTHERS INTO THE FUNDAMENTAL STATE OF LEADERSHIP

In this chapter, we have observed that leadership development, like organizational transformation, begins with personal change. We learn from Tom the episodic nature of the fundamental state of leadership.

Each entry into the fundamental state of leadership is both terrifying and exhilarating, and while we are on the journey of deep change, there are no insurance policies that guarantee success. We do not know how the story will end. We learn from Larry's students that ordinary people—the people in the next seat—have a history of such experiences. We learn from Larry that it is possible to create sacred space and that in sacred space, all of the characteristics that invite people into the fundamental state of leadership naturally emerge. We learn from Doug that managers and teacher are human beings who themselves must face the challenge of deep change. The willingness to face deep change alters how we think about developing others. We begin to let go of telling and forcing. We begin to turn to transcending self and participating with others in the creation of sacred space. As we do so, we grow, and they grow. Finally, we learn from Stan that it is never too late to change. When we do, we gradually learn the language and processes necessary to attract others into the fundamental state of leadership.

In the end, Tom, Larry, Doug, and Stan teach us the very same things as the other magnificent people we have met in this book. We are all both ordinary and magnificent. We are all drawn to live in the normal state, and we all tend to move toward personal entropy and slow death. The challenge is to make deep change and enter the creative state. Our challenge is to live in ever-increasing integrity. When we choose deep change, we enter the fundamental state of leadership. In that state, we experience exponential growth, and we become living attractors, pulling some of those around us into the same state. With those people, we create sacred space, and we engage in a social movement. As a critical mass develops, we become a productive community continuously striving to adapt to emerging reality. Together we build the bridge as we walk on it.

PREPARATION FOR ATTRACTING OTHERS INTO THE FUNDAMENTAL STATE OF LEADERSHIP

Questions for Reflection

1. "It was terrifying, but we learned how to do what needed to be done. It was the best work I have ever done." What are the implications of this statement in your life?

2. "I can do no wrong—and hence I can do great good—because I am free of the incrementalism born of mediocre success." Who can achieve this kind of freedom? How?

3. Do you agree or disagree with the following statement? "I do not know how this story will end, but I could not care more, work harder, or fear less. To me these are the seeds of success." Explain your answer.

4. What meaning does the following statement have for you? "Organizational transformation is all about increased collective virtue, about the ever-increasing integrity of both the individual and the organization."

5. Do you agree with the picture presented in this chapter of the traditional approach taken by corporate training programs and business schools? For educational programs to effectively attract people into the fundamental state of leadership, what must administrators and teachers do differently?

6. What becomes possible in sacred space, like the space Larry created in his classroom, that is not possible in profane space? When have you experienced the creation of sacred space?

7. Doug indicates, "I had never experienced this kind of sorrow." There are productive and unproductive ways to respond to sorrow. Doug's response tells us much about how to attract others into the fundamental state of leadership. What did he do, and what can we learn from him?

8. Analyze the language and processes that Stan used to help executives change. How might you use what you learn from Stan?

Self-Improvement

1. Write a paragraph describing your own organization's approach to leadership development.

2. Write a memo capturing your insights about how you would improve leadership development in your organization.

Helpful Hints for Inviting Others into the Fundamental State of Leadership

Recognize that others seldom see anyone in the fundamental state of leadership.

Recognize that it is normal for others to deny the possibility of entering the fundamental state of leadership.

Recognize that most organizational cultures keep people in the normal state.

Recognize that most administrators and designers of leadership training are in the normal state, and they assume the telling and forcing strategies.

Recognize that most teachers are advocating analysis and imitation.

Recognize the need to model what it means to enter the fundamental state of leadership.

Recognize that others who deny it is possible to enter the fundamental state of leadership have actually been there in the past.

Recognize that the normal state is profane space.

Recognize the power of sacred space.

Recognize that sacred space can be created in any place and at any time.

Recognize that you can create sacred space by having the courage to move from analysis and imitation to the expression of your own unique and authentic feelings.

Recognize that in sacred space, we witness the emergence of productive community and the true creation of value.

Recognize that we do not stay continuously in the fundamental state of leadership, but that we can enter that state more and more frequently if we commit ourselves to practices that encourage us to be purpose-centered and internally driven, other-centered and externally open.

Sharing Insights

If in responding to the questions above, you have an important insight or a meaningful story that you would like to share, visit www.deepchange.com and look for the links to submit stories for possible posting on the Deep Change Web site. You may thus help many people. If you would like to review such insights and stories, go to the same Web site.

—ᴧᴧ— **References**

Bass, B. "Concepts of Leadership." In R. P. Vecchio (ed.), *Leadership: Understanding the Dynamics of Power and Influence in Organizations.* Notre Dame, Ind.: University of Notre Dame Press, 1997.

Blake, W. *The Poetry and Prose of William Blake* (D. V. Erdman, ed.). New York: Doubleday, 1965.

Byrd, A. D., and Chamberlain, M. D. *Willpower Is Not Enough: Why We Don't Succeed at Change.* Salt Lake City, Utah: Deseret Book Company, 1995.

Cameron, K. S., Dutton, J. E., and Quinn, R. E. (eds.). *Positive Organizational Scholarship: Foundations of a New Discipline.* San Francisco: Berrett-Koehler, 2003.

Campbell, J. *The Hero with a Thousand Faces.* New York: Bollinger Foundation, 1949.

Chatterjee, D. *Leading Consciously: A Pilgrimage Toward Self-Mastery.* Boston: Butterworth-Heinemann, 1998.

Chin, R., and Benne, K. D. "General Strategies for Effecting Changes in Human Systems." In W. G. Bennis, K. D. Benne, and R. Chin (eds.), *The Planning of Change: Readings in Applied Behavioral Sciences.* New York: Holt, 1969.

Creelman, D. "Interview: David Cooperrider and Appreciative Inquiry." [http://www4.hr.com]. July 9, 2001.

Csikszentmihalyi, M. *Finding Flow: The Psychology of Engagement with Everyday Life.* New York: Basic Books, 1997.

Frankl, V. E. *Man's Search for Meaning: An Introduction to Logotherapy.* New York: Washington Square Press, 1963.

Fritz, R. *The Path of Least Resistance: Learning to Become the Creative Force in Your Own Life.* New York: Fawcett, 1989.

Hanh, T. N. *Living Buddha, Living Christ.* New York: Riverhead Books, 1995.

Hart, S. L., and Quinn, R. E. "Roles Executives Play—CEOs, Behavioral Complexity, and Firm Performance." *Human Relations,* 1993, 46(5), 543–574.

Jackson, P., and Delehanty, H. *Sacred Hoops: Spiritual Lessons of a Hardwood Warrior.* New York: Hyperion, 1995.

Johnson, R. A. *We: Understanding the Psychology of Romantic Love.* San Francisco: HarperSanFrancisco, 1997.

Labarre, P. "Do You Have the Will to Lead?" *Fast Company,* Mar. 2000, no. 32, p. 222.

Merton, T. *Seven Storey Mountain.* Orlando, Fla.: Harcourt, 1948.

Merton, T. *Conjectures of a Guilty Bystander.* New York: Doubleday, 1966.

Palmer, P. *The Courage to Teach: Exploring the Inner Landscape of a Teacher's Life.* San Francisco: Jossey-Bass, 1998.

Prochaska, J. O., Norcross, J. C., and DiClemente, C. C. *Changing for Good.* New York: Avon Books, 1994.

Quinn, R. E., and Quinn, S. E. "Becoming a Transformational Change Agent." In L. Greiner and F. Ponfett (eds.), *Handbook of Management Consulting: The Contemporary Consultant.* Cincinnati, Ohio: South-Western, forthcoming.

Riley, P. *The Winner Within: A Life Plan for Team Players.* New York: Putnam, 1993.

Schriesheim, C. A., House, R. J., and Kerr, S. "Leader Initiating Structure—Reconciliation of Discrepant Research Results and Some Empirical Tests." *Organizational Behavior and Human Performance,* 1976, *15*(2), 297–321.

Thoreau, H. D. *Civil Disobedience and Other Essays.* New York: Dover, 1993.

Torbert, W. R. *Managing the Corporate Dream: Restructuring for Long Term Success.* Homewood, Ill.: Dow Jones Irwin, 1987.

Warner, C. T. *Bonds That Make Us Free.* Shawnee Mission, Kansas: Shadow Mountain, 2001.

Welch, J., and Byrne, J. A. *Jack: Straight from the Gut.* New York: Warner Books, 2001.

Wheatley, M. J., and Kellner-Rogers, M. *A Simpler Way.* San Francisco: Berrett-Koehler, 1996.

Wright, K. *Breaking the Rules: Removing the Obstacles to Effortless High Performance.* Boise, Idaho: CPM Publishing, 1998.

Youngblood, M. D. *Life at the Edge of Chaos: Creating the Quantum Organization.* Flower Mound, Tex.: Perceval Publishing, 1997.

—∿— The Author

Robert E. Quinn holds the Margaret Elliot Tracy Collegiate Professorship of Business Administration at the University of Michigan and serves on the faculty of Organizational Behavior at the University of Michigan Business School. He is one of the cofounders of the Center for Positive Organizational Scholarship. Quinn's research and teaching interests focus on organizational change and effectiveness. He is known for his work on the competing values model, which has been recognized as one of the forty most important models in the history of business. He has published over fourteen books. This book completes his trilogy on change. The first two books of the trilogy are *Deep Change: Discovering the Leader Within* (1996) and *Change the World: How Ordinary People Can Accomplish Extraordinary Results* (2000). Quinn has over twenty-five years of experience in working with organizations on issues of leadership and change.

⟞⟋⟍⟞ Index

A

Abusive relationship: adaptive confidence in leaving, 149–151; impact of self-change on, 29–31, 32, 37; sharing story of, 33–35

Action: from principle, change due to, 32–33; as stage in self-change, 205–206. *See also* Reflective action

Action learning, 148

Adaptive confidence, 90, 148–158; description of state of, 151–152; examples of individuals practicing, 56, 148–151, 153–155; relationship between integrity and, 155; tips for practicing, 157–158; as unconditional confidence, 152; unrecognized experiences of, 153

Alvis, M., 8, 9–10, 21, 23, 63

Anderson, D., 216, 225–227, 230

Appreciative inquiry, 90, 122–135; "best self" exercise for, 129–132; Cooperrider's organizational development method of, 122, 127; description of state of, 125–126; humility and, 131–132; personal application of, 127–129; tips for practicing, 134–135; transformational questions in, 123–125, 126–127

Army, story of transformation in, 8–10

Authentic engagement, 90, 110–121; description of state of, 113–115; executive's turnaround experience transformed by, 115–117; fundamental choice as entry into, 117–118; mother-daughter relationship transformed by, 111–113; tips for practicing, 120–121

Authenticity: developed with personal transformation, 51–55, 56; relationships with others affected by, 59–60; writing to reflect on, 106

Awareness: expanded with personal transformation, 55–60; relationships with others affected by, 59–60

B

Bass, B., 91

Benne, K. D., 70

Bennis, W., 153–154

"Best self" exercise, 129–132

Blake, W., 35, 36–37, 60

"Building the bridge as you walk on it," defined, 5

Byrd, A. D., 110, 114–115

Byrne, J. A., 188, 189

C

Caesar, J., 91

Cameron, K. S., 62, 127

Campbell, J., 60, 177

Catalyst for change: becoming, with personal transformation, 58; as leadership role, 57; seeing oneself as, 53

Chamberlain, M. D., 110, 114–115

Change: action from principle causing, 32–33; catalyst for, 53, 57, 58; failure to, 19; strategies for creating, 70–75; in world around us as result of self-change, 23–25, 37, 43. *See also* Organizational change; Resistance to change; Self-change

Change the World (Quinn), x, xii

Changing for Good (Prochaska, Norcross, and DiClemente), 173, 201